LEADERSHIP
THROUGH
COLLABORATION

LEADERSHIP THROUGH COLLABORATION

The Role of the Chief Academic Officer

Ann S. Ferren and Wilbur W. Stanton

AMERICAN COUNCIL ON EDUCATION
PRAEGER
Series on Higher Education

Library of Congress Cataloging-in-Publication Data

Ferren, Ann S.
  Leadership through collaboration : the role of the chief academic officer / Ann S.
Ferren and Wilbur W. Stanton.
      p.   cm. — (ACE/Praeger series on higher education)
  Includes bibliographical references and index.
  ISBN 1–57356–574–1 (alk. paper)
    1. College administrators—United States.   2. Education, Higher—United
States—Administration.   3. Educational leadership—United States.   I. Stanton,
Wilbur W.   II. Title.   III. American Council on Education/Praeger series on higher
education.
  LB2341.F42   2004
  378.1'01—dc21   2003058160

British Library Cataloguing in Publication Data is available.

Library of Congress Catalog Card Number: 2003058160
ISBN: 1–57356–574–1

First published in 2004

Praeger Publishers, 88 Post Road West, Westport, CT 06881
An imprint of Greenwood Publishing Group, Inc.
www.praeger.com

Printed in the United States of America

The paper used in this book complies with the
Permanent Paper Standard issued by the National
Information Standards Organization (Z39.48–1984).

10 9 8 7 6 5 4 3 2 1

Copyright Acknowledgments
The authors and publisher gratefully acknowledge permission for use of the following
    material:
Chapters 7, 9, 10, and 11 are adapted from "Using Qualitative and Quantitative
    Information in Academic Decision Making," *Balancing Qualitative and Quantitative
    Information for Effective Decision Support.* New Directions for Institutional Research,
    No. 112. Published by Jossey-Bass. (www.josseybass.com), 2001.

Contents

Preface

*L*eadership through Collaboration: The Role of the Chief Academic Officer* was inspired by many conversations with administrative colleagues about the challenges of our jobs and our shared need to know more about how to handle the increasingly complex and varied issues that academic leaders face. In these conversations, it appeared that each individual knew something that could be of value to another and, together, we could generate a kind of collective wisdom. The lively exchanges were often punctuated with comments such as "How did you know how to do that?" and answers such as "I just had to figure it out."

Over the course of our collective 40 years as academic administrators, we have had ample experience with just having to figure it out and sometimes, in hindsight, the awareness that if we had known more, had better information, or understood all of the alternatives and their consequences, we might have made different decisions or taken different actions. Although we have consoled ourselves with the notion that every problem is an opportunity to learn, we also know that higher education deserves more than trial-and-error academic administration and leaders that learn on the job. Indeed, critics of leadership in higher education claim it is the "last bastion of amateur management" and suggest a need for greater knowledge and forceful decision making (Munitz 1995, 10).

We began this project by asking ourselves, "Which issues seem to be most difficult for chief academic officers?" Clearly, personnel matters such as dismissal of a faculty member or denial of tenure are extremely stressful; however, there are policies to follow, precedents to adhere to, and legal guidance at hand. The next most difficult areas were financial matters and the business side of the institution where decisions are increasingly challenging because of severe budget constraints. In that arena, academic administrators find limited guidance.

As participants in the recent initiative to bring together academic affairs and business affairs, sponsored by the Association of American Colleges and Universities and the National Association of College and University Business Officers, we understand firsthand how differences in the goals, language, expertise, and roles of chief academic officers (CAOs) and chief financial officers (CFOs) inhibit collaboration. CAOs find it difficult to explain the costs of academic activities, which are based on an elaborate system of cross-subsidization. CFOs, focused on technical matters and balancing the budget, are unsure how to make meaningful recommendations about how to maintain academic quality with limited resources. Thus we set out to help academic administrators learn more about how to understand the "business" of academic affairs in order to collaborate more effectively with their colleagues.

Assuming chief academic officers have a level of confidence and competence in dealing with typical academic issues, this book addresses several key administrative areas that are not under their direct or sole authority yet significantly impact academic effectiveness and efficiency. It is, in fact, a book with an "attitude" as it argues strongly for a collaborative perspective on academic leadership and management, urges chief academic officers to provide institutional not just divisional leadership, and encourages CAOs to ask questions and seek information in order to plan, develop alternatives, and analyze the implications of choices. It makes no attempt to offer so-called "best practice" nor easy answers. Instead, it aims to help academic leaders think well, be perceptive, and trust their intuition but also to seek hard data and be willing to say "I don't understand," "We need more information," or "We are making the best decision we can at this time" when dealing with complicated problems.

The selected issues are framed by analysis, guiding questions, and the use of data in decision making. Our experience in many administrative roles, ranging from department chair to provost, has given us the opportunity to conduct and use numerous studies, including budget adequacy modeling and salary equity studies. Equally important, we have had the responsibility for implementing the decisions based on those analyses, and that has helped us to understand that collaborative processes are as important as informed decision making. When academic administrators have both broad perspective and expertise, a partnership among those providing leadership to a campus can develop—whether it is chairs with the deans, deans with the vice president, faculty leaders with administrators, or the chief academic officer with members of the president's cabinet.

There is no shortage of books, journal articles, dissertations, and higher education association publications to provide research findings, ideas, and innovative approaches to academic leadership and management. In addition, one can read case studies from institutions about "what we did" as well as reflective pieces summarizing the best thinking on what should be done if only campuses would "be bold" or "take risks." Much can be learned from these writings, but it is not always clear how to import an idea to a different campus environment and what information would be needed to support a decision in a different institutional context. Because chief academic officers are less likely to read what business officers and vice presidents for administration read, they cannot take full advantage of their colleagues' expertise. This book aims to integrate differing institutional perspectives and explain rationales, processes, and criteria so that CAOs can tailor their decisions to institutional circumstances and solve difficult problems with greater insight, creativity, and accountability.

In the course of our administrative work, one of our biggest challenges has been gathering the data we needed to analyze issues and support decisions. More often than not, we had to build the data sets needed to address issues such as program review and faculty workload. Colleagues on other campuses face the same challenge. The list serves we participate in are filled with requests for information on everything from how to determine compensation for student teaching supervision to what factors an institution should use to identify its peer group. Offices of institutional research are becoming increasingly sophisticated in their support of academic affairs, and CAOs can improve that support by knowing what questions to ask.

An initial step in explaining the relationship between data and decision making and calling for a stronger relationship between institutional research and academic affairs was worked out in the article *Using Qualitative and Quantitative Information in Academic Decision Making* (Ferren and Aylesworth 2001). The response to that piece made us think more deeply about the need for a more fully developed reference to help academic administrators. With permission, the chapters on program review, faculty workload, compensation, and institutional research draw upon that earlier work.

METHODOLOGY

Leadership through Collaboration relies on extensive reading, careful consideration of published case studies, and our experience as administrators in various roles on several campuses, both public and private. Perspectives, ideas, and tools were also gathered in the course of a decade of accreditation visits and consulting on numerous campuses and to numerous businesses. Direct access to campus processes, policies, and problems has been a rich resource. We have served on boards of national higher education associations, attended national meetings, and carefully monitored and participated in the national conversation about higher education, tracking the changing environment and new challenges for over twenty years. This book is our effort to distill what we have learned from what campuses and chief academic officers are doing, tease out the practical implications, and convey that collective wisdom in a succinct and readable manner.

In past years, to do this kind of work one conducted interviews and made campus visits to seek out the "fugitive" literature—the documents, memos, and task force reports from campuses that reveal the thinking that supports activities and decisions. That task is easier now with e-mail, list serves, and the Internet. Most campuses post much of that "fugitive" material on the Web for easy access by members of the campus community, and search engines make that material available to anyone who wants to read strategic plans, program review guidelines, or workload studies. State policies, procedures, and accountability reports also are accessible on the Web. The research task is not to track down information, but rather to make sense of it, seeking out those trends and patterns that are really significant in revealing how campuses function.

In that spirit, each chapter addresses a specific issue, provides a context for understanding, explains basic principles, describes the range of campus practices, and makes recommendations on points to consider and useful data analyses. More important than our suggestions, however, are the lists of questions the CAO might ask. We hope these many prompts will encourage the mind-set that there is "no such thing as a dumb question"—even when you are the chief academic officer.

ORGANIZATION OF THE BOOK

Leadership through Collaboration is organized around 11 topics. Chapter 1, "Academic Leadership," establishes the foundation for the other chapters by providing the rationale for the collaborative role of the chief academic officer in meeting institutional challenges, identifying the values implicit in this role, and describing the personal qualities and skills essential to provide effective leadership within the institutional context of competing interests.

The following three chapters focus on strengthening the infrastructure that supports academic affairs. Chapter 2, "Strategic Planning," focuses on the chief academic officer's role in eliciting and maintaining faculty support for change whether the campus is beginning strategic planning, implementing a plan, or reviewing the current effectiveness of the campus plan. It analyzes the context for planning, the planning process, the elements of the strategic plan, the importance of linking funding with planning, and the role of accountability in sustaining a change effort. Chapter 3, "Facilities Planning," offers a variety of perspectives and guiding questions that connect academic planning and facilities planning, and it encourages chief academic officers and business affairs administrators to be positive partners for change as they care for and invest in the campus learning environment. Chapter 4, "Technology Integration," provides the chief academic officer with the perspective and questions necessary to participate in addressing specific technology challenges, including planning, financing, organization, and training. In addition, it describes the accumulating wisdom about faculty involvement, improved learning, student technology competencies, and academic management applications.

The next two chapters focus on the importance of developing new resources and linking resources to academic priorities. Chapter 5, "Financial Resources," focuses on the specific role of the chief academic officer in budget planning and management at both the institutional and divisional levels. The chapter highlights the purpose of the institutional budget, sources of revenues, the academic affairs budget planning process, sources of flexibility necessary for effective management, strategies for cost containment, and the challenge of reallocations and reductions. Chapter 6, "Academic Entrepreneurship," suggests processes for developing new academic products, examples of outreach offerings and potential partnerships, and guidelines for evaluating the budgetary implications for these new academic activities. The ways in which campuses fund research and development activities through grants and contracts, market their intellectual capital, and extend their impact through activities such as community service relationships and corporate parks are also analyzed.

The next two chapters emphasize the strategies and processes for assessing academic quality and improving programs and services. Chapter 7, "Program Review," provides advice on how to make program review more effective and suggests opportunities to link program review with other decision-making processes, including planning and budgeting. In addition, the chapter establishes the role of the chief academic officer in communicating results and helping faculty act upon the findings. In this way, program review serves as a basic tool of good resource management.

Chapter 8, "Continuous Improvement," provides an overview of the rationale for continuous improvement and describes some of the analytic tools used for identifying areas for enhancement. It calls for a shift in thinking from merely "what we do" to include "how we do it" and "how we need to change in order to do better." Particular attention is paid to the way in which time and cost savings can be achieved.

The two following chapters emphasize the central importance of investing in an institution's most valuable resource—the faculty. Chapter 9, "Faculty Workload," addresses how the chief academic officer can analyze the two intertwined issues of workload (what faculty do) and productivity (what faculty achieve) to respond to concerns of external stakeholders, the needs of the institution, and the interests of the faculty. The tools and data described can support academic planning, guide allocations of resources, and support decisions about how to align faculty activities with the mission and the strategic priorities of the institution. Chapter 10, "Faculty Compensation," discusses factors that affect compensation, the importance of both good policies and good procedures, methods for ensuring equity and responding to market competition, the role of merit in determining individual salary increments, and the importance of conducting systematic salary reviews.

The final chapter, Chapter 11, "Improving Academic Decisions," brings closure to the book by discussing the essential role of data in decision making—the necessary partnership with institutional research—and analyzes several of the critical questions facing today's chief academic officers that go well beyond day-to-day management of academic affairs as they strive to provide institutional leadership to align higher education with the realities of the twenty-first century.

AUDIENCE FOR THE BOOK

The intended audience is chief academic officers and their administrative colleagues in academic affairs, including assistant and associate vice presidents, deans, and department chairs, who are striving for academic quality at a time of both great challenge and opportunity. Indeed, as we write this book the nation's economy is struggling, there is worldwide instability, and the prospects for additional support for higher education appear limited. Yet at the same time, we are encouraged by the positive impact of technology, renewed commitment to high standards, and greater access to higher education. In this environment, all academic administrators can benefit from broader knowledge and the expertise necessary for prudent and strategic leadership at all levels of the organization.

The perspective and ideas can also be useful to nonacademic administrators who want to collaborate more fully with the chief academic officer in guiding higher education as it adapts for the future. *Leadership through Collaboration* should also be revealing to the many graduate students in higher education administration programs whose idealism and aspirations need to be tempered with a practical approach to academic leadership. This overview should encourage them to develop specific expertise to complement the interpersonal and management skills necessary for a successful career in academic administration.

ACKNOWLEDGMENTS

Our thinking has been shaped by many colleagues too numerous to mention, although Milton Greenberg, former Provost and interim President of American University, and Harlan A. Philippi (1926–1995), former interim President of the University of Southern Maine and former interim Chancellor of the University of Maine System, were particularly important to our development as academics and administrators. The manuscript has benefited both from the opportunity to test ideas in public forums and from consultation with many academic administrators around the country. Early drafts were given a close reading by several of our colleagues, and the final text benefited from their observations and criticisms.

We especially would like to thank Kay Mussell, Dean, College of Arts and Sciences, American University; William W. Geller, Vice President for Student and Community Services, University of Maine at Farmington; Ivan Liss, Dean, College of Arts and Sciences, Radford University; Martin Aylesworth, Professor of Educational Studies, Radford University; Bert C. Bach, Vice President for Academic Affairs and Provost, East Tennessee State University; Carol Geary Schneider, President, Association of American Colleges and Universities; Jerry Gaff, Senior Scholar, Association of American Colleges and Universities; Angela D'Auria Stanton, College of Business and Economics, Radford University; and Jonathan D. Fife, Visiting Professor, Virginia Polytechnic Institute and State University and former Professor of Higher Education Administration and Director of the ERIC Clearinghouse on Higher Education, The George Washington University.

CHAPTER 1

Academic Leadership: Collaborating for Institutional Effectiveness

Although charged with running a multimillion-dollar operation, few who aspire to or hold the position of chief academic officer (CAO) have had any formal business training. Most academic leaders emerge through campus experience focused on teaching, learning, and research and add to their management expertise on a "need to know" basis in their service role. Academic administrators may first venture into leadership roles as department chairs, faculty senate leaders, program directors, or associate deans. In those roles they rely on the strengths honed as a faculty member—analytic thinking, organization, the ability to make persuasive presentations, a sense of the institutional culture, and a commitment to collegial decision making. If they stay at the level of a mid-level administrator, these are sufficient skills. The step to chief academic officer, however, requires broader expertise, collaboration across multiple constituencies, an institutional perspective, and the courage to act as an agent of change.

Job descriptions in the *Chronicle of Higher Education* for the positions of academic dean, dean of faculty, vice president for academic affairs, and provost list a daunting range of academic responsibilities, for example, strengthen curriculum quality and assessment; enhance faculty leadership and development; increase student satisfaction and retention; improve cost-effectiveness of academic programs; streamline the operations of academic affairs; promote diversity; and support an atmosphere of collegiality, trust, and open communication. Such challenges are usually followed by a litany of personal attributes, ranging from a sense of humor to stamina to good listening skills. Seldom included is the critical role the CAO plays in the collaborative leadership of the institution, essential to strengthening the conditions for academic quality.

The importance of "fit" with both the campus community and the president causes search firms to advise campuses that chief academic officer positions are among the most difficult to fill. CAOs who move up to the position on their own campuses may feel comfortable and supported, yet they often find it challenging to bring fresh thinking to issues, create a new persona that emphasizes collaborative leadership over colleagueship, and shift from advocacy based on local interests to the institutional agenda. When academic administrators move to another campus, not only must they learn a new culture; they will no longer be able to rely on the history of success and trust with faculty built up over time. They will not know which allegiances to honor, whose information to rely on, nor where the informal boundaries of authority lie. Success in either case depends upon the ability to read and shape the environment.

Most aspiring CAOs have significant political savvy and are able to create confidence in others. What they often lack is an appreciation of the scale of the job of the chief academic officer and experience with the nonacademic areas of the campus. Their new portfolio and collaborative role requires, for example, managing a very large budget, allocating resources, institutional planning, and accessing relevant data to analyze complex issues. As one new CAO put it, "I had to put away my library card and pick up my calculator!" Previous experience is necessary but not sufficient. Until one is in the central administration and viewing the institution as a whole, it is hard to have perspective on how important cross-divisional collaboration is to ensure that the parts of the system work together to accomplish the academic vision. It is even more difficult to appreciate the challenge of focusing the individual self-interest of faculty, staff, and administrators from all divisions into a coherent, collective institutional effort.

To do so, chief academic officers need to balance their academic expertise with a solid understanding of how to do the kinds of planning, data gathering, and analyses required to address what is often referred to as the business side of the academic enterprise. Academics long have been criticized for making decisions based solely on "academic criteria" with little regard for "financial realities," while at the same time those making financial decisions have been charged with doing so "separate from considerations about the academic program" (Schuster, Smith, Corak, and Yamada 1994, 18). That gap can and must be closed. CAOs need to be prepared to take the first step.

Fundamentally, this book is designed to give the chief academic officer both the critical questions and the analytic tools to provide data-informed institutional leadership and to deal comfortably with business officers and administrative vice presidents who carry much of the responsibility for managing the infrastructure of the campus. Each chapter addresses the role of the CAO in institutional matters, for example, finances, technology, facilities, and entrepreneurship. The more standard academic responsibilities, such as faculty development, faculty evaluation, curriculum, and student learning, are addressed only tangentially, assuming academic administrators have significant expertise in those areas. Since all members of colleges and universities play a part in achieving academic excellence, this book can also be useful to deans, department chairs, and nonacademic administrators who need to understand how their actions affect the overall academic enterprise and who want insight into the role and perspective of the chief academic officer as a collaborative leader.

THE UNIQUE ROLE OF THE CHIEF ACADEMIC OFFICER

Chief academic officers recognize that, other than the football or basketball coach, theirs is the most difficult position on a campus because of the high expectations of diverse constituencies and the number of persons affected by their actions. They know they have to have the right personal chemistry with their president, build strong alliances among the cabinet members and other administrators, and work well within the faculty culture of the campus. Using both their knowledge and their interpersonal skills, they must be effective both vertically, within academic affairs to develop the faculty and departmental support essential to the teaching/learning/research mission, and horizontally, with the other vice presidents or deans who provide essential support services to accomplish the academic mission. In managing both dimensions, they quickly learn that there are conflicting expectations and roles for the chief academic officer.

Previous research on managerial roles suggests that ten roles ("monitor," "entrepreneur," "resource allocator," "leader," "disseminator," "disturbance handler," "figurehead," "liaison," "negotiator," and "spokesperson") are applicable to managers in every organization (Mintzberg 1980, 54–99). The emphases among these roles are defined to some degree by the type of organization as well as the level of the position in the organization. Applying that role analysis to higher education reveals that CAOs are least involved in the strategic decision-making aspects

of the campus (monitor, resource allocator, entrepreneur) and more involved in trying to run a smooth operation (leader, disseminator, disturbance handler) by coordinating the work of the faculty and
maintaining a cooperative environment through personal influence
(Mech 1997, 289–91). To provide leadership in the changing environment of higher education, however, demands that CAOs learn to give
equal attention to strategic roles and provide clear direction on how to
enhance academic quality.

Given the various constituencies to be served, it is not surprising that
the CAO position is fraught with role conflict. Faculty and staff in academic
affairs look to the chief academic officer for inspiration and appreciation. They expect the CAO to function in a collegial environment—
building consensus, motivating, and seldom exercising position authority.
Even as chief academic officers are recognized for their administrative
abilities in negotiating difference, communicating effectively, and getting
things done, they must retain the respect of their academic colleagues
with their intellectual leadership. On some campuses that means also
finding time to maintain a distinguished record as a teacher and scholar.
On all campuses it means participating in the intellectual life of the
campus and articulating the values, purposes, and standards of academic
activities.

In contrast, the president expects support in adapting to external demands and providing practical leadership to move the institutional
agenda forward. Increasingly, the president, board, and legislators look to
the CAO for ideas on how to do more, better, and with less. Because
resources are limited and not all programs and ideas are equally valuable
to the organization, the CAO can easily feel caught in the middle between protecting faculty interests and managing for institutional viability.
Conveying the hard realities facing higher education has a dampening
effect on faculty morale, unless they have confidence in the academic
leadership and the CAO's commitments. Even then, faculty are quick to
criticize if they detect a business mentality that gives attention to the
bottom line over faculty values such as tenure and time for scholarship.

Clearly, the passion and perspective required to inspire faculty to academic excellence are far different from the skills required for responsible
management of resources or effective institutional decision making. The
CAO who tries to remain primarily an academic colleague and leave the
tough decisions about budget, technology, or facilities to the business
officer or administrative vice president risks the academic agenda. At the
same time, if the chief academic officer leans too far in the other direction
and spends too much time engaged with these infrastructure issues, the

CAO loses intellectual standing with the faculty and has little credibility for setting the course for academic quality. The challenge is to balance these many roles, maintain the confidence of both the faculty and administrative colleagues, and be a strong advocate for the academic agenda.

LEADING FOR RESULTS

Because the other divisions of a campus have very different cultures of consultation, decision making, and communication, administrative colleagues often do not understand the complexity of the leadership role of the chief academic officer. Nonacademic administrators have difficulty understanding the CAO's conscientious attention to faculty concerns and faculty opinion. Adding to the complexity are some special characteristics of colleges and universities, including the degree to which decisions must be made with imperfect information, the way in which the system of shared governance appears to contradict administrative authority, and the extent to which options are limited when aspirations outstrip resources. Faced with hundreds of decisions, both large and small and affecting both individuals and the institution, the chief academic officer needs both natural instincts about when to be decisive as well as the capacity to hold back when circumstances are not clear.

The chief academic officer must be the voice for academic purposes for the campus and a source of energy supporting the activities of others. Fundamental to effective academic leadership is communication with all members of the organization about the needs, options, and actions necessary for academic excellence. Not all academic leaders will use the same leadership approach nor do all organizations need the same approach. Classic studies identified the need for "situational leadership" in an effort to help leaders become flexible and match their approach to the organizational culture, needs of the institution, and complexity of the issue (Blake and Mouton 1978). Both research and experience suggest that successful leaders have a portfolio of approaches and can call upon several leadership styles, as appropriate, without appearing to be chameleons or untrustworthy. To manage both vertical and side-to-side relationships requires a deep understanding of oneself and the institution.

Chief academic officers must maintain a scholar's curiosity and always be systematically learning more about the issues facing the institution and higher education. Informed leadership requires that CAOs ask the right questions, learn from colleagues, and take a long-term perspective on what it takes to transform colleges and universities for the future. In business lingo, it is the difference between "doing things right" and "doing the right things." For example, finding a way to cut budgets has a short-term effect, but restructuring the academic organization to be more productive pays off over time. Similarly, conducting regular program review can help a unit improve its current performance, whereas connecting program evaluation to institutional priorities can ensure collective improvements that continuously realign the academic enterprise with emerging circumstances in order to accomplish higher standards of performance.

Given competing demands on time and a heavy workload, the chief academic administrator must be selective and set a proactive agenda of those key matters that will sustain momentum for institutional improvement and, potentially, institutional redesign. Day-to-day operations are delegated to college deans and department chairs. Confidence is expressed in the faculty's commitment and capacity. That empowering stance requires an optimistic CAO who has a "can-do" attitude, provides energy without asserting control, and creates an environment for shared responsibility and collaborative problem solving. Because colleges and universities rely on collegiality for making and effecting many decisions, academic leaders need to maintain the right balance between concern for tasks and concern for feelings of members of the campus community. Every campus has a comfort zone; thus managing both aspects well is essential to overcome inertia, reduce stress, and get results.

Although this book emphasizes the rational and data-informed side of institutional and academic planning and decision making, it does not ignore the psychological and political dimensions that affect administrative success. To overcome "turf protection" and encourage cooperation, chief academic officers must know the capacities of their colleagues, understand their motivations, encourage the discourse of conflicting perspectives, provide incentives and appreciation, share information widely, and set high standards. Although committed to responding to faculty interests, CAOs must also be able to withstand pressure when they make hard decisions. To engender confidence in those with whom they collaborate, CAOs must be perceived as competent, disciplined, fair, and decisive. The chief academic officer who wallows, appears puzzled by the challenges, makes tentative recommendations, retracts decisions, is inconsistent, or avoids risk out of fear of making someone unhappy or doing the wrong thing cannot generate the support necessary to produce a coordinated effort that gets results. Even under the best of circumstances, sustaining campuswide collaboration is difficult because it depends more on how people work together than on the formal organization, more on trust than on position authority.

INSTITUTIONAL DECISION MAKING

The old joke about a university being "nothing more than a group of individuals linked together by a central heating system and a common concern about parking" captures one of the most challenging aspects of campuses as organizations. Colleges and universities are "loosely coupled systems" with academic units and individuals valuing autonomy and independent decision making (Weick 1983). Many faculty, when they see formal lines of authority, call it bureaucracy. Others take a political view based on negotiating everything and assume there has to be an adversarial relationship between faculty and administrators. They claim any management is micromanagement and argue that administrative responsibility is antithetical to shared governance.

Despite efforts on many campuses to modify administrative structures, reduce hierarchy, and strengthen the voice of faculty in campus affairs, chief academic officers find authority is still suspect and timely decision making is difficult. Higher education has been widely criticized for its "inertia" and "inherent inefficiency" (Gumport 2001, 14). Indeed, in the "face of adverse conditions," there is evidence that administrators lose confidence in shared governance and move toward more centralized power (Schuster et al. 1994, 4). No matter what the external circumstances, campuses will always need clear formal ways to make informed decisions. At times, there will be conflict between the assumption that decisions should be made through democratic processes and the need for administrators to retain their authority for many decisions. One commentator on governance notes that "the challenge for campus leaders is to reconcile the need to act decisively with the need to do so wisely" (Gumport 2001, 15). Consequently, the chief academic officer must create effective organizational structures, clarify the scope of authority of units, establish dependable relationships and linkages, strengthen lines of communication, facilitate informed participation, and encourage respect for colleagues. In that environment, faculty can recognize appropriate distinctions among being informed, consulted, or involved in decisions.

Typically, the president is responsible for establishing organizational structures, setting the tone of the campus, facilitating communication, and creating the administrative team. Despite evidence from the business environment that teamwork leads to creative solutions and high levels of commitment, colleges and universities lag behind in using a team approach to institutional administration (Frost and Gillespie 1998, 10). One of the most extensive studies of administrative teams reveals that even when campuses believe they have a team, in many cases the team is "illusory" rather than "real" as evidenced by presidents being most comfortable working one-on-one with administrators (Bensimon and Neumann 1993, 45).

Not only is teamwork often weak at the leadership level but also in the other academic decision-making bodies. Despite widespread experience with committees, task forces, and cross-functional work groups, members of these bodies do not always achieve the level of reciprocity necessary to function as a true team. Too many committees are hampered by individual members trying to protect their own interests. Teamwork can only develop when individuals understand the goals of their work, play effective roles in the group, are able to see multiple perspectives, do not care who gets credit for ideas and accomplishments, and link their efforts to institutional goals. These attitudes and behaviors require a significant reorientation in thinking from individual interests to institutional needs.

COLLABORATION ACROSS DIVISIONS

If not full teamwork, what chief academic officers can encourage is greater collaboration through sharing information, expertise, ideas, and responsibility in order to solve problems more effectively. No matter what style of presidential leadership or historic degree of bureaucracy on the campus, chief academic officers can promote better communication and cooperation by helping others think about the institution as a whole and understand how the actions of one division directly affect the success of another. Many campuses are examining the norms and traditions of the academic community and are working toward new forms of leadership, changes in the culture, and clarification of roles in order to overcome the fragmentation and limited perspective that negatively affect decision making. The analyses in this book aim to help chief academic officers know how and when to get involved in institutional issues, and how best to influence and support their colleagues in other divisions as they make decisions that affect academic affairs. Much of that involvement will be in the form of asking the right questions of the right people.

In order to accomplish the academic work of the campus, it is critical that the vice presidents have a positive working relationship in addition to that defined by the president for interactions of the cabinet members in their advisory role to the president. The relationship must make it possible for vice presidents and their staffs to collaborate directly on issues where the support of others is crucial to their success. For example, decisions about classroom renovations, while the responsibility of facilities management under the direction of the vice president for finance and administration, should be made in consultation with faculty and students. The public relations staff who must manage the image of the university under the direction of the vice president for university relations and development should produce brochures and marketing materials after consultation with academic affairs and student affairs. The vice president for student affairs may want to change admissions criteria but should do so in consultation with those who will provide the student support services. Similarly, the vice president for academic affairs must review ideas for new programs with administrative colleagues.

These cross-divisional interactions must go beyond merely informing to true consultation in order to make the best decisions. On too many campuses, a divisive tone permeates everyday operations. Time is spent on criticizing the intentions of others as well as the results of many small decisions, rather than on working together on the big issues that really matter to the future of the institution. For the sake of harmony, efficiency, and better decisions, rather than consult on every minor matter, vice presidents can serve their campus well by agreeing on guiding principles, sharing information freely, and making sure the members of their staff are informally communicating with others around campus on a regular basis. They must also model cooperation and trust in their own interactions.

On most campuses, there are few formal ways for those in other units and divisions to regularly meet, exchange ideas, and develop a shared vision at the operational level. Strategies that strengthen working relationships include monthly cross-divisional meetings focused not on "show and tell" but on issues that need group problem solving, regular communication on major projects through e-mail status reports, and involvement of resource persons from other divisions in staff meetings where important decisions are being made. Many campuses conduct midlevel manager-development programs not only to provide essential skills on supervision or how to run a meeting but also to develop a culture of "our work" rather than "my work." These efforts go well beyond building community and sharing information and also aim to encourage commitment to high levels of institutional excellence.

OVERCOMING THE BARRIERS TO COLLABORATION

The barriers to administrative collaboration are political, cultural, and practical. Whether conscious or not, some campus administrators instinctively view issues in terms of their power, influence, and position. Cooperation is seen as giving up something rather than getting something;

thus competitiveness overcomes reciprocity. When chief academic officers seek advice and help from others outside of academic affairs, they may be unaware of how uncomfortable that makes the other administrators who have little experience being recognized for their information, ideas, and perspectives that come from different responsibilities. Even when administrators are comfortable working together, they will not achieve the sense of mutual obligation necessary for collaboration if they do not believe the work of the institution belongs to all of them.

Resource allocation processes on many campuses are also a barrier to cooperation, especially when campus needs significantly outstrip current resources. If financial decisions are made by the business officer on behalf of the campus, rather than through a formal collaborative process, there is less trust that the allocations to divisions are appropriate to the priorities. If incremental budgeting is used year after year, yet priorities or needs change, administrators lose confidence that they will have the resources necessary to do what is expected of them. If business officers cautiously hold back funds to prepare for unexpected events, yet distribute largesse at the end of the budget year, it gives many on campus the idea that there are always special pots of money that they just need to figure out how to claim. Those campuses that use an open operating budget allocation process, collaboratively define the priorities and resource needs, and allow funds to be reallocated at the unit level find that this shared responsibility for sound financial management reduces adversarial feelings.

The culture of many campuses betrays an inherent mistrust between divisions, with CAOs noting that their most difficult relationship is with the business officer who exerts strict control and questions the legitimacy of an academic's involvement in institutional budget matters. Chief academic officers who believe open information and collaboration could help them do a better job and make academic affairs more efficient experience resistance from chief financial officers who believe too much budget information leads to meddling and misunderstandings. Some business officers claim it takes away their degrees of freedom, especially for the use of end-of-the-year funds, which are needed to cover unexpected expenses, overspending, or new activities. At the other extreme from this expectation of control are institutional advancement officers who often are reported to sit silently in many meetings, not only failing to contribute but failing to attend at all, declaring that the campus issues under discussion are not their concern.

Chief academic officers are not blameless in matters of limited collaboration. Student affairs staffs have long advocated stronger relationships with academic affairs, yet they have noted the lack of respect they receive for their contributions. Several campuses have appointed faculty to key positions in student affairs hoping to overcome this dilemma, yet those individuals report that they immediately feel demoted in the eyes of their faculty colleagues. One cause of this tension among divisions is the considerable disparity between staffing size, budget, and centrality of activities with academic affairs being preeminent. Campuses that have overcome these cultural norms and attitudes have done so by establishing new expectations for behavior through shared problem solving and significant collaborative work. When presidential leadership requires that the annual institutional agenda be set through active participation of all divisions, cooperation and commitment are increased (Bensimon and Neumann 1993, 36).

Because of the historical fragmentation of campuses, the leadership must find ways to help the parts of the institution understand not just their unit but the entire institution. Strategic planning, for example, aims not only to identify goals for the future but also to change attitudes, values, and expectations by involving the campus community in the planning process and recognizing shared success. Campus administrators can also be helped to see the big picture by reading widely and attending national meetings to learn how other campuses are addressing similar issues. Bringing consultants to the campus to help with issues that cut across divisions, such as technology, can facilitate a broader perspective as well. Repeated positive experiences and shared success are necessary to redress some of the contentious experiences on campuses that lead to a divisive culture.

At a practical level, there are many central administrators who see their calendar filled with meeting after meeting and simply do not feel they have the time to help anyone else. They do not like meetings, do not feel informed on the issues, and do not want to take the time gearing up for one more problem in a busy schedule. To overcome that pressure, administrators need to experience how investing time up front saves time as it empowers others to do their work with confidence that their efforts will be congruent with overall institutional needs. So too, they need experience getting real help from their colleagues. Many CAOs turn to colleagues off campus for support, failing to recognize the value of meaningful peer support from the other administrators on campus. The downside of developing too close a relationship with administrative colleagues, however, is becoming isolated from the rest of the campus and succumbing to "groupthink" (Bensimon and Neumann 1993, 9–10).

Oddly enough, many central administrators believe their president would not like them to be more cooperative with each other, fearing it will appear to undermine executive authority. Similarly, there are CAOs who are uncomfortable with the deans working closely together and meeting without him or her. There are deans who are uneasy when the department chairs meet alone. One campus invested in a department chair development program in order to create more cooperative leadership at the unit level only to have the deans protest because they feared the chairs might gang up or attempt to usurp authority. Fortunately, the CAO could assure the deans that they were in no danger of being overthrown, and in time the campus benefited from a more committed and professional approach to chairing the department. Some analyses of administrative roles advocate careful monitoring of relationships developed outside of direct reporting lines noting the "potential for conscious or unconscious mischief" (Wolverton 1984, 11–12). All of these perceptions confirm how important trust is to collaboration.

COLLABORATION WITHIN ACADEMIC AFFAIRS

To create a collaborative environment, there are boundaries within the academic affairs division that are just as challenging to cross as those between divisions. Departments, colleges, and programs all have specialized interests that push to take precedence over larger institutional issues. Typically, the chief academic officer relies on a deans' council, an academic program directors' council, department chair meetings, and similar structures for communication and coordination of efforts. The skilled academic leader easily develops a sense of shared purpose in these groups through open information, well-structured meetings, and a focus on real problem solving. Reports from many chairs and deans suggest, however, that these groups too often suffer from one-way communication, limited discussion, a norm of not challenging authority, and underlying tension based on competition for attention and resources.

The CAO who emphasizes the roles related to running a smooth operation and maintaining a cooperative environment uses these formal meetings as opportunities to disseminate information, celebrate successes, and establish expectations for linking activities to institutional plans. In this role as coordinator of the efforts of many subunits, the focus is on demonstrating how the activities of many are joined together into a coherent divisional effort. Any differences or problems are handled privately behind closed doors. As a result, participants feel informed about what their colleagues are doing, are able to share information with their faculty and staff, and maintain a sense of predictability. Unfortunately, because open communication is limited, this approach is not dynamic enough to handle

a changing environment such as midyear budget reversions, shifts in enrollments, or external requirements for accountability. Nor is there much
group energy to tap for new ideas and new programs. Indeed, if there is
a pattern of adversarial relations with the central administration, participants may "go along to get along" in public and express doubts and
criticism in the parking lot.

Alternatively, the chief academic officer can establish the norm that
these groups are not merely part of a communication network aimed at
keeping everyone focused but are also working groups charged with strategic thinking about the future of the institution. In this model, difficult
problems are set before the group, data is gathered to help analyze the
situation, all information about all units is public, diverse viewpoints are
given equal consideration, and difficult choices are made. In setting the
agenda, the chief academic officer needs to be honest about the challenges
facing the institution and not shrink from sharing negative information
such as a decline in the retention rate. Participants are expected to accept
shared responsibility for the difficulties and successes of their colleagues
and bring their informed and critical perspectives to the table. In this
proactive and collaborative model, there is little place for turf protection,
competition for resources, or elbowing others out of the way as change is
expected and the need to realign resources to match priorities is accepted.
Principled decisions are made with the expectation that they will be
consistently supported.

Deans and department chairs charged with "bringing home the bacon"
by their faculty are vulnerable in this collaborative model unless the CAO
is able to also communicate the larger academic vision to the whole
division and persuade faculty that their individual well-being is linked to
the well-being of their department, college, and institution. To do so, the
CAO can hold open meetings with faculty in colleges and departments,
report regularly to the faculty senate, and consult broadly to gather firsthand information to complement the work of these strategic groups. The
two-way communications must be based on honest assessments of real
issues facing the campus and consideration for how decisions will be
made. As trust is the cornerstone of academic leadership, the CAO must
be vigilant about not letting faculty go around their department chairs or
deans, must avoid sharing information with just one dean or having a
backdoor for negotiations, and must be consistently evenhanded in all
matters. The CAO cannot undercut the authority of deans and department chairs by publicly second-guessing them or getting involved in matters for which the deans and chairs are responsible. At times, this means

supporting those to whom one delegates daily responsibility for academic affairs even when the CAO disagrees with their actions.

CAOs must be able to rely on a strong team of deans, and deans must be able to rely on the department chairs. This requires constant attention to promoting a collegial and positive environment based on appreciation and valuing the members of the community. Part of leadership is building the capacity of individuals and the organization. In this role the CAO has considerable responsibility for helping the other academic administrators develop the skills and perspective necessary to function proactively. The CAO acts as both a teacher and a researcher—bringing new information, asking questions, being reflective, defining problems, and encouraging others to have an inquisitive mind about how higher education can be not merely managed, but improved. In this way, individuals at all levels of academic affairs are empowered to participate in the hard work of seeking academic excellence and promoting an environment open to challenging past ways of functioning.

MODELS OF DECISION MAKING

Decision making is an imperfect art. It is especially difficult to make decisions that stay made when changing circumstances require constant adjustment. Yet, colleges and universities necessarily advance through an iterative process of successive decisions based on the best information they have at the time. Further, while chief academic officers must generate support for institutional decisions, they must also recognize that it is not possible to achieve full group agreement because the many constituencies in higher education have conflicting interests that are not easily reconciled. To seek full consensus on important institutional issues could mean doing nothing.

Theoretical discussions of decision making appear far more tidy than the reality of decision making. Indeed, academic administrators are not always sure of the process they use in making decisions. When asked, one CAO described how he decides what he wants to do and then lines up the committee members and the data that will produce that decision. Another CAO described a fluid process of informal consultation to sense where there would be the most agreement and the least resistance. Another claimed guidance by principle, stating that "There is always a right thing to do and you have to do it." Another looked for the decision rule, such as "You can't get tenure without a book." Yet another described the value screen he uses for every decision: "How will this be good for students?" Still another described getting the best minds in the same room, brainstorming creative approaches to the issue, picking one based on intuition, and then going out to sell the decision on campus, claiming both expertise and fresh thinking went into it. Yet another described a highly analytic, systematic process in which options are generated, the pros and cons of each are discussed, and the implications modeled based on data. It is the latter model that is assumed in this book. However, the complexity of the matter, time available before an action is required, and degree to which there are standard operating procedures as well as personal values, previous experience, and political pressures can lead chief academic officers to choose several of the other approaches described.

Chief academic officers who want to broaden their perspective on organizational decision making can consult the literature that documents a variety of models, among them the bureaucratic, political, collegial, and rational choice models (Chaffee 1983; March 1994). The rational choice model is relevant because its processes provide guidance but not boundaries for handling complex matters. The processes include defining the issue carefully, determining the goals or purposes to be achieved, identifying the criteria that must be met, determining what information is needed and how it is to be interpreted, generating the options or alternative solutions, deliberating, consulting as appropriate, making the choice, and then acting on the decision and monitoring the results. Each chapter in this book is structured with these elements in mind and provides questions to guide analysis, suggests relevant data, describes practices on other campuses, and includes special considerations as the chief academic officer works in the institutional context.

How CAOs believe they make decisions and how they are actually made reveals some of the limitations of the rational choice model. The limitation is not with systematic thinking but rather with the fact that too often administrators find themselves muddling through because they lack expertise or experience in an area that causes them to not ask the right questions or seek appropriate data. When faculty ask, "What were you thinking of when you made that decision?" the administrator may hear, "That was not the decision I expected," when what is really being said is, "The information and analysis were not persuasive." Equally detrimental to good decision making is letting practiced solutions or unchecked expectations constrain thinking in new ways. CAOs must be able to rely on their capacity to think their way through the challenges facing higher education; thus it is imperative that they become more conscious of their thinking processes.

Because faculty are trained to do research, they often demand a level of problem definition and data analysis that would meet standards for journal publication. They are not comfortable when administrators use intuition, anecdotes, and perceptions to point the way to problems, nor do they recognize that because of cost and time imperfect information must often be used to make many decisions. In response, administrators will claim that "you need to act your way toward change" rather than succumb to paralysis by analysis. The chief academic officer can walk this fine line of the rational versus the pragmatic by staying well informed on faculty views, having sufficient information to mitigate negative impacts of decisions, and investing in relationships with faculty to increase their level of trust and understanding of difficult choices. Equally important is building coalitions with other divisions on the campus so that they do not make precipitous decisions without regard for academic consequences.

A fundamental assumption in this book is that genuine participation in decision making leads to better decisions, broader agreement, and fuller commitment. Cross-divisional collaboration creates continuity in perceptions about what needs to be done to strengthen the campus. Ultimately, a decision is worthless until acted upon. Implementing decisions requires the commitment and support of others to stay the course and achieve the strategic vision for the campus. Neither the position authority nor specialized expertise of the CAO can overcome foot dragging if productive relationships among the many different constituencies on a campus have not been established. Thus the CAO must be prepared to enlist others in providing the consistent support necessary as individuals and the institution adapt and change.

ROLE OF FACULTY IN DECISION MAKING

The mainstay of colleges and universities is the concept of shared governance with a clear role for faculty in academic decisions. Growing out of the original concept of a self-governing faculty gathered together as equals to educate students, faculty have always had the responsibility for determining the courses of study, curriculum offerings, and standards for grading and granting of degrees as well as the right to select, evaluate, and retain faculty colleagues. That authority has been codified by the American Association of University Professors (American Association of University Professors 2001, 221) and few question the role of faculty in academic matters. However, as pressures on campuses have increased, faculty have asked to add their voice to critical matters beyond this core of functions. Faculty expect to participate in an ever-wider variety of institutional decisions that affect their welfare and ability to deliver the kind of education they want, for example, planning, budget, enrollment management, and hiring and evaluating administrators. As a result, there is increasing confusion about the authority of faculty opinion and the meaning of "shared governance."

For faculty on campuses with collective-bargaining agreements, participation in administrative decisions may be limited (Kezar 2001, 5). Even without that formal limitation, most faculty are content to make teaching and research their primary focus. They may take their turn participating in the decision-making processes of their unit or on the faculty senate, but basically they expect the institution to run well. They do not want to administer the institution and are often charged with intentional ignorance of critical issues. From time to time, when they do not feel there is effective leadership, they seek greater involvement and claim a stronger role in governance, but they do not expect to maintain that vigilance forever. Thoughtful chief academic officers take note of such shifts in involvement as a barometer for faculty morale.

At the same time most faculty defer to the administration, many are also willing to defer to other faculty. On many campuses, a core of faculty make a career of governance and expect to play a significant and continuous role through the faculty senate or bargaining unit. These faculty members proudly report the number of years of such service on their curriculum vitae and sometimes explain that limited productivity in other areas, especially research, is the result of their extensive commitment to serving the institution. Faculty can be reelected year after year to the senate if there are no term limits. Although this continuity of experience can strengthen faculty leadership, it can also preclude new perspectives and reduce open communication with the campus. From time to time, an accrediting body flags the ineffectiveness of the governance system on a campus, sometimes charging the faculty with undermining the authority of the administration or, conversely, charging the administration with failing to sufficiently involve faculty in important decisions.

REASSESSING SHARED GOVERNANCE

As the pressures and challenges for higher education have increased, the tension between responsive decision making and faculty involvement has caused many campuses to review their internal governance processes. As proposals for revision are made, several common themes emerge.

First, given the demands on faculty time, real efforts are being made to reduce the burden on faculty of committee work and to increase efficiency. One campus questioned whether it was really necessary to have a

22-member parking committee when there were only three decisions to be made—cost of a parking permit, number of spaces available, and the process for appealing a ticket—and even those did not require constant attention. Streamlining is not easy, however. Another campus reduced the total number of governance committees, yet the CAO admitted that within a short time informal committees were "popping up" everywhere. As campuses reduce the size and number of formal committees and replace many of them with work groups and task forces, however, some progress is made in that the groups are temporary and can be disbanded when the task is done.

A second theme is the role of administrators and the nature of faculty representation. Many campuses are unresolved about whether administrators should be members of the senate or even in attendance, yet on some campuses the president convenes the senate. In addition, campuses debate various membership questions. How big should a representative body be to be representative? How small should it be to function well? Does reliance on an executive committee effectively exclude the larger body? At what level should representatives be elected to increase legitimacy and accountability? How empowered can sub-units and committees be? What voice should students have on institutional issues? (Baldwin and Leslie 2001) The key issue is how best to facilitate communication and participation so that the work gets done in a timely way and the decisions are credible.

A third theme emerging from reviews of internal governance is how to reduce the adversarial and watchdog nature of the processes. To some degree, the tensions between units of a campus and between administration and faculty are natural extensions of differences in points of view and standing. When carried to an extreme, the environment becomes political, fragmented, and contentious with administrators reviewing the work of other administrators and committees reviewing the work of other committees. Some campuses have turned to a strengthened administrative council that is more representative of all campus views in an effort to balance faculty opinion with staff and student opinion and ensure broader community participation (Kezar 2001, 8). However, good decisions rather than harmony in governance should be the goal. If conflict is understood as positive, CAOs can learn from the differences of opinion rather than become defensive.

A fourth theme in the review of governance is the scope of authority for faculty senates and committees. Faculty recognize that policies and recommendations are submitted for final approval to the administration and the board, and they accept this limit on their authority. Critics of campus decision making believe that faculty demand "excessive consultation" resulting in weakened presidential leadership (Association of Governing Boards 1996). Trustees accuse campuses of "failing to respond to emergencies or to take advantage of opportunities," and in the name of being more nimble, boards urge presidents and administrators to make decisions with input from faculty, only as necessary (Kezar 2001, 6). Even faculty question whether collegial processes are designed to make difficult decisions such as cutting programs or eliminating positions. A limited advisory role, however, is not satisfactory to many faculty, although they would concede that there is a difference between academic decisions and administrative decisions that might appropriately lead to a distinction between being involved and being consulted. On some institutional issues, faculty need only be informed, though timing can make a difference.

Too many quick and decisive administrative actions that have a direct impact on faculty inevitably test faculty confidence. The CAO has an especially critical role as advocate for faculty interests and liaison between the faculty and administration when there is no structured process for faculty input in an institutional decision. At a minimum, faculty should expect an explanation on important matters even as they may need to be reminded of the limits on their input and that having input does not mean getting your own way. The chief academic officer must make good relations with the faculty a high priority because the legitimacy of shared governance is based on mutual trust and relies on openness—"open plans, open policy statements, open rules, open findings, open reasons, open precedents, and fair informal and formal procedures" (Mortimer and Caruso 1984, 45–46).

SUCCESSFUL ACADEMIC ADMINISTRATION

Despite the challenges and role conflict, chief academic officers find their jobs rewarding because the issues are intellectually challenging and their faculty colleagues are smart and innovative. Those that thrive do not accept the current state of their campus nor the notion of impossibility in addressing needs for the future. They ignore low expectations and are determined to put energy and ideas into improving the quality of the curriculum, the faculty, and the institution. Much of their enthusiasm and confidence comes from years of positive experience working with faculty as they experiment, create, and innovate. Even when faculty complain about the state of the budget or claim morale is slipping, CAOs note that they continue to pursue high standards.

Although the rewards are many, on a day-to-day basis the CAO's job is stressful and draining. To handle the workload, successful CAOs set a manageable agenda that balances improvement of ongoing activities with selected new goals. To handle the responsibility for the many decisions that must be made, successful CAOs learn which matters they can delegate and which matters are ultimately theirs to shoulder alone. To reduce the stress of confrontation and conflict with faculty, successful CAOs legitimize differences in perspective, share responsibility for the future of the institution by disseminating information widely, and create a participatory environment for decision making. Understanding that no decision will have universal support, they do not fall victim to the inevitable call to revisit issues once decisions are made. They are courageous and keep their focus on outcomes.

Increasingly, CAOs feel the stress of limited resources that appear to many to reduce opportunities for institutional improvement. Among the options institutions have is the possibility of new revenues, and CAOs are active participants in actions ranging from increasing enrollments and retention to pursuing grants. At the same time, CAOs also collaborate in seeking greater efficiency and reallocating resources to higher priorities. Some institutional changes will take money; however, most progress takes ideas. Thus, the more critical role for the chief academic officer is empowering faculty and administrative colleagues to think about new ways of doing things. Academic leaders who create this sense of empowerment and confidence in the future, even in the face of difficulty, enjoy broad support and are energized by their colleagues. They become adept at creating the coalitions necessary for collaborative progress in many areas and at aligning the activities to ensure sustainable change. They help others understand that actions have impacts throughout the institution. CAOs must have the ability to see the complexity of the organization and the environment and not be overwhelmed.

Noting that change and adaptation are constants, successful chief academic officers work hard to develop the technical expertise and knowledge necessary to ask the right questions, generate alternatives, and base decisions on solid principles and information. In this way, their leadership is grounded and sensible, and they model for others appropriate ways to handle difficult challenges. The chapters that follow focus on strengthening the institutional infrastructure for academic activities, generating and allocating resources to be effective, pursuing quality in academic programs and support systems, and investing in the most valuable resource on the campus—the faculty. Threaded through the discussion are the critical themes of leadership, change, collaboration, and rational decision making.

Higher education has been adjusting and changing for two decades, yet both academic leaders and external critics predict that increasingly dire circumstances will demand more fundamental changes if institutions are to survive. Although readers may be disappointed that a wholly new approach to higher education for the twenty-first century is not sketched out here, we believe a first step for chief academic officers, their colleagues, and faculty is to fully understand current practices and processes. Collaborative efforts to improve and strengthen an institution will reveal both limitations in current approaches and opportunities for innovation and redesign. The ideas and recommendations that follow are informed by the experience and practices of many effective chief academic officers who on their own campuses are providing strong leadership for change while also mentoring the next generation of academic administrators.

CHAPTER

Strategic Planning: Designing Institutional and Academic Change

M any an alumnus back for a twenty-fifth reunion will observe, "I hardly recognize this campus." Although higher education has been accused of changing at a glacial pace, that alum will see new buildings, new curricula, new activities, new standards, and new types of students. To put those changes in perspective, some were shaped by institutional aspirations whereas others were responses to the external environment. For two decades, campuses have used strategic planning adapted from the business world in order to respond to environmental changes and intentionally guide their institutions into the future (Rowley, Lujan, and Dolence 1997). Despite widespread use of planning, however, many critics argue that higher education has not changed enough.

A review of college and university strategic plans, case studies, and internal campus documents reveals both varied purposes and good intentions. Campus presidents use strategic planning as a framework for their leadership and often initiate a widespread institutional change process as the first step in their tenure. Governing boards use strategic plans as the basis for evaluation of presidential and institutional performance. Regional accrediting bodies endorse planning as evidence that a campus has a systematic way of pursuing the mission of the institution and addressing changing circumstances. State agencies require strategic plans from public institutions as a measure of accountability. To some degree, these applications are not proactive enough to handle the challenges and criticisms facing higher education.

In some cases, the strategic plan itself appears to be the goal rather than serving as the vehicle for engaging faculty and staff in bringing about necessary changes. The introductory statements to plans, letters of transmittal to governing boards, and letters to faculty imply that strategic planning is a task to be performed and, when finished, one to be claimed as an accomplishment. The product, often a glossy-covered bound report, may even be distributed widely as proof that skilled leaders with vision and purpose guide the institution. Clearly, if the process is truncated after the plan is written, the plan is likely to end up on a shelf rather than be used to guide everyday activities.

College and university administrators who have experienced the power of a continuous planning process, however, describe the plan as a "living document," the change process as "unfolding," and the value measured by the "thinking that goes into the plan." Noting how many faculty are involved and praising their participation as a development opportunity, chief academic officers are confident that strategic planning results in a greater sense of community and shared purpose for the campus. They know that faculty will gladly attend day-long retreats to envision the future of the campus but understandably become critical if they then have little to do with later administrative decisions to forge that future. If cynical, faculty will not be enthusiastic about implementing the plan.

Many campuses are well into their third or fourth round of strategic planning and are learning from previous strengths and weaknesses in their efforts. They now know that successful strategic planning requires attention to the political and cultural context of the campus, to specific action steps with appropriate funding, to clear time lines and accountability, and to processes for modifying the plan as circumstances change. Strategic planning also benefits from continuous acknowledgement and reaffirmation of what is working well. Planning based only on a premise of institutional deficits creates resistance as faculty infer that their dedication and standards are not valued. When significant institutional change is at stake, the chief academic officer plays a critical role in helping faculty understand how new internal and external circumstances as well as aspirations for the future are positive reasons for change.

As presidents must spend more and more time off campus, it falls to the chief academic officer and administrative colleagues to maintain the forward momentum of a campus. This chapter focuses on the chief academic officer's role in eliciting and maintaining faculty support for change whether the campus is beginning strategic planning, implementing a plan, or reviewing the current effectiveness of the campus plan. It analyzes the context for planning, the planning process, the elements of the strategic plan, the importance of linking funding with planning, and the role of accountability in sustaining a change effort. In addition, the chapter emphasizes the importance of campus-wide collaboration in thinking about the future of the institution, considering alternatives, making decisions, and then carrying out the plan. When done well, strategic planning can be a dynamic and continuous process for guiding colleges and universities through difficult times and bringing about the changes necessary, not merely to survive but to prosper (Cope 1987, 3; Rowley, Lujan, and Dolence 1997).

MAKING PLANNING STRATEGIC

Strategic planning in academia began in the early 1980s when higher education underwent a fundamental shift in the way it viewed itself and the way it responded to external conditions and future prospects (Morrison, Renfro, and Boucher 1984). Part of the shift was the result of the work of academic management visionaries like George Keller (1983), while other motivators included shrinking state appropriations, a changing demographic profile of students, and an increased emphasis on outcome assessment by accreditors (Rowley, Lujan, and Dolence 1997, 16–29). Campus administrators responded to the changing circumstances with a new emphasis on academic strategy when they realized that campuses could have a good product with well-documented results but still be vulnerable to competition, unstable financial circumstances, and shifts in student interests.

Campuses had long been encouraged to undertake planned change rather than merely react to a changing environment (Lindquist 1978). Although campuses believed they were responding, by the 1990s it was clear that long-range planning with its internal focus and only periodic evaluation was not adaptable enough to manage in a turbulent environment that called for greater institutional agility (Leslie and Fretwell Jr. 1996). No longer able to consider negative economic conditions temporary, nor willing to feel powerless to respond to increased competition, campus leadership had to envision new ways of performing. After years of emulating others—for example, comprehensive institutions seeking doctoral programs and liberal arts colleges adding graduate programs to become like small universities—colleges and universities recognized the need to refocus their energy from expansion to quality (Hawkins 1998, 12). Many campuses began to think in terms of positioning, competing, market niche, and differentiation—all organizational strategies adapted from business.

Despite becoming more proactive, many campus planning efforts are still not strategic enough. Long-range planning assumes a future based on forecasting trends in current resources, markets, and personnel rather than seeking new opportunities. Thus the future of the campus is shaped by planning, but within defined limits. Strategic planning is externally focused, attends to environmental changes, and assumes that the institution can and should be redesigned to exploit emerging opportunities and create an "interesting future" (Morrison, Renfro, and Boucher 1984, 5–13). The chief academic officer (CAO) plays an essential role in helping faculty face the reality of changed circumstances and blending these two planning perspectives in order to link internal capacities with external opportunities.

A comparison of several successive plans for a campus may well show the first plan is an enthusiastic list of goals and activities for the next decade, whereas each plan that follows is more strategic, more sharply focused, has a shorter time frame, and is closely linked to resources. Chief academic officers reviewing the academic components of their current plan should see a greater emphasis on environmental challenges, stakeholder expectations, and core competencies of the campus as well as a clearer delineation of specific roles and expectations for faculty. The implementation processes of the strategic plan should also show increasing sophistication about what it takes to initiate and sustain institutional change.

Unfortunately, many planning processes produce few innovative ideas that break new ground. Taking a hard look at both the planning assumptions and leadership can reveal where the problem lies. Merely trying to extrapolate from the past or improve what an institution already does, rather than consider doing things differently, is constraining. Administrators must know when a bold new direction is called for and provide strategic leadership. To manage the clash of cultures between their urgency and the more reflective stance of faculty requires that CAOs connect faculty interests and aspirations to economic and environmental realities. Perhaps the most important planning lesson that higher education can learn from business is that success in a changing environment has less to do with finding "the right strategy" than with "the ability to transform itself, continuously" (Gouillart 1995, 15). By that measure, higher education needs to be bolder.

Planning for Institutional Change

- How will the environment in which the institution operates affect it in the future?

- What are the strengths and weaknesses of the institution?
- What are the internal and external opportunities and threats to the institution?
- Who are the stakeholders and what are their expectations of the institution?
- What does the institution aspire to be in five years? ten years?
- What data is available to encourage new views, evaluate choices, and support decisions?
- What strategies and actions will help achieve those goals?
- Who will be responsible and accountable for accomplishing each strategy and action?
- What measures of performance will be used to determine progress in achieving the plan?
- How will the information on performance be fed back into the institution so that it can respond to and adapt to changes?

INCREASING THE IMPACT OF STRATEGIC PLANNING

Campuses that evaluate their planning process in order to improve it invariably recognize that the perspectives of administrators and of faculty are very different. Despite skepticism about faculty willingness to change, on most campuses the strategic rethinking of purposes and processes has caused faculty to make significant changes in teaching and curriculum in the last decade. For example, interest in new pedagogies, an emphasis on active learning, the application of academic theories to real-world problems, a shift from faculty-centered to student-centered programs, a shift from process-oriented to outcome-oriented teaching, and a broadened global perspective in the curriculum are evident. Major redesign such as giving up credit hours, semesters, or degree requirements has not been embraced.

When administrators talk of "transforming" the campus and "restructuring," they feel the faculty resistance. Efforts to change the structures and habits of the academy that could mean crossing the organizational boundaries of divisions, colleges, and departments; reducing the intellectual barriers separating disciplines; redesigning the delivery of instruction; and increasing the integration of individual self-interest with institutional interests have not gained enough support to transform campuses. Even in the face of dramatically declining resources, few faculty voluntarily support realigning units or reducing program offerings. Indeed, they use delaying tactics, such as calling for more information, to prevent the administration from making essential structural changes. In those cases, campus planning leads only to incremental changes rather than the transforming changes that many believe higher education must make to thrive.

This limited success is not due to the inappropriateness of strategic planning to higher education. Nor is it due to lack of effort. Rather, the traditional autonomy of units, decentralized nature of decision making, inconsistency of involvement of members of the community, and difficulty linking actions and outcomes make change efforts in higher education complex (Eckel, Green, Hill, and Mallon 1999, 3–5). As a result, many campuses with high hopes for their planning efforts find that these characteristics of academic communities result in avoiding difficult choices or dissolving into controversy (Keller 1997, ix). For faculty to accept their central and collaborative role in helping the campus adapt through new thinking, they must see direct positive benefits from functioning in a different way.

Fundamentally, strategic planning is about leading a significant collaborative change effort. When it works well, as one college president noted, "Strategic planning is a collegial process for the design of an imaginable future—one harmonizing diverse activities while providing a good fit between opportunities and strengths" (Cope 1987, 6). Leading this collegial effort requires skill in managing the emotional and creative aspects of the process so that participants with diverse perspectives can be productively engaged in what is, to only a limited degree, a practical and rational process. Campus leaders who assume others see things as they do and fail to take time to educate, to listen, and to negotiate difference will not generate a following. The chief academic officer plays a key role in ensuring that faculty perspectives are heard, that academic choices are evaluated based on data not perceptions, and that finding better ways to serve students and achieve the goals of the university are the focus of the plan.

Engaging Faculty in the Process of Change

- Which techniques are most appropriate to involve faculty in thinking about the future of the campus as opposed to focusing on routine activities?
- What kinds of reassurance can help faculty believe the planning activity is meaningful and worth their time to be involved?
- How might individuals and units begin to reconcile their conflicting interests and seek compromise and collaboration, if not full consensus, on needed changes?

- What strategies will reduce resistance and help faculty take risks? What strategies help faculty overcome habits and become more intentional?

- What is the CAO's role in managing the destabilization that comes with change?

- How might collaborative leadership for strategic planning be developed at many levels to include administrators, faculty, and staff and to promote shared responsibility for success?

UNDERSTANDING THE CAMPUS ENVIRONMENT

Successful strategic planning requires inspired leadership with an appreciation of the complexities of the campus political environment and the psychological aspects of change. Most often, the president takes the primary leadership role with guidance from others who have insight into the decision-making culture of the campus at all levels and are savvy about how best to time a planning initiative among the variety of competing campus initiatives. When a campus does not have an ongoing planning process, to gauge the readiness of a campus for potential change the president may host a variety of forums, town meetings, and small group discussions to share critical data and suggest ways in which change is both necessary and beneficial. Through this process a collective sense of need is developed, complacency is reduced, and the campus community commits to planning the future. This same approach can also renew strategic plans on an annual basis.

Perceptions about what should change will vary at the outset yet intersect around academic matters. Despite an agreed upon mission of quality education, faculty inevitably have different perspectives about how best to contribute. Intellectual and social alignments fragment even a small campus. Institutional political forces related to resources, power, authority, and communication are also divisive. Often faculty "focus on perpetuating familiar and comfortable practices" rather than accepting the challenge to be better (Rowley, Lujan, and Dolence 1997, 27). As the strategic planning process will challenge faculty comfort as well as the status quo of these communities of interest, many faculty members can be expected to take a defensive posture as they wait to see how their programs will be affected rather than how the institution as a whole can be enhanced. More than any other leader on the campus, the chief academic officer has direct knowledge of these alliances and factions and must find appropriate strategies and faculty leaders to engage faculty in seeing the campus in a new way and choosing change.

Although many assume that resistance to change is caused by anxiety about the unknown, an equally powerful motivation for maintaining the status quo is that those who benefit, through prestige or resources, are unwilling to give up what they have (Eckel et al. 1999, 5). As any CAO knows, competition for resources inhibits cooperation and collaboration. This is especially relevant because strategic planning in an environment of no new resources will certainly call for reallocation. The chief academic officer must first anticipate areas of resistance by taking a mental inventory of haves and have-nots, that is, departments, programs, and individuals who are likely to be impacted either negatively or positively by a change in priorities and resources. The next step is to seek ways to productively involve these units in the planning process through incentives rather than coercion. Perhaps the strongest incentive is the realization that many alternatives will be evaluated in the planning process, and participating in the decisions can help shape the agenda for the future.

Whether working in a contentious or cooperative environment, the chief academic officer and president must use their authority carefully and recognize that a change in strategic direction can create resistance if it comes as an administrative directive rather than also emerging from the community. These leaders must decide how much change is called for, how fast change can reasonably be accomplished, and, more important, how to create support to sustain change. Past experience with planning can be a guide; however, if it was a negative experience, the leadership must be able to explain how the current planning effort will be different. Even under pressure from external forces for rapid change, the chief academic officer must take time to involve, not merely consult, faculty. For the CAO, the specific challenges are how to engage faculty to provide leadership; how to reach decisions, if not through consensus, at least by working collaboratively within a shared governance structure; and how to fashion compromises that do not undermine academic integrity or administrative authority.

Shared authority and shared decision making are distinguishing features of academic institutions. Consequently, "If institutional leaders want to achieve comprehensive, widespread change, they must create strategies to compensate for this decentralization" (Eckel et al. 1999, 4). On many campuses, those who do not have position power but do hold informal influence as power brokers and opinion leaders are enlisted in the hope of co-opting them. Most campuses find that the more effective strategy is to invest in leadership throughout the campus, create multiple conversations through interlocking discussion groups to maintain commitment, and reinforce the ideas and activities that contribute to the forward movement of the campus.

It is not unusual for presidents to expect position power to be influential in the change process and then run into difficulty when they fail to create the broad participatory process required to overcome vested interests and promote common goals. Faculty resist being told what to do and may not fully trust the motives of the administration (Opatz and Hutchinson 1999, 23). In an effort to learn from previous efforts, administrators seek practical strategies to link top-down and bottom-up planning processes and perspectives. As the strategic priorities must come from the collective vision of many, most campuses rely on an iterative process and two-way communication carefully linked to both informal processes and campus governance.

The challenge facing the chief academic officer and president in strategically redirecting the university is often less about what to do than it is about how to get it done, especially if momentum from the last plan has been lost. Faculty are notorious for their slow deliberative pace, demands for incontrovertible evidence, and local perspective. Moreover, they already have enough on their plates with teaching and research so that any discretionary time for a major institution-wide endeavor is weighed against the expected payoff. To overcome the barriers to faculty involvement in planning, many CAOs call upon the trust previously built through other initiatives, emphasize open communication, and regularly interpret to the faculty the benefits of direct involvement in planning (Opatz and Hutchinson 1999). They also forge alliances with the leadership of the other divisions in support of the academic vision. Most important, to overcome institutional inertia they create a sense of urgency with timely and consistent messages.

An analysis of case studies detailing various ways campuses have tried to balance the need for "no-nonsense" planning with the "sluggish" campus governance process revealed the need for a new concept called "strategic governance," that is, an approach that "successfully blends the requirements of intelligent strategic planning with those of legitimate, participative governance" (Schuster et al. 1994, 7–12). The premise of *Strategic Governance: How to Make Big Decisions Better* is that strategic planning and traditional governance processes are incompatible and threaten an institution's ability to make strategic decisions that are transformational and timely.

Based on a careful analysis of the efforts of eight campuses to link governance, planning, communication, and leadership, the researchers concluded: "We had anticipated that a strategic planning council [SPC] would be a catalyst for boldly shaping an institution's future and would undertake the necessary reprioritizing of commitments. And we anticipated further that these SPCs would be able to act expeditiously (at least compared to the slowly paced norms of academic organizations). But we were disappointed" (Schuster et al. 1994, 180). Readers of these case studies will surely find similarities to their own campus and gain an understanding of how to integrate these two functions despite the natural tensions between them.

As these case studies reveal, simply establishing a representative group to guide the campus is not enough to make strategic thinking, planning, and budgeting successful. The involvement of the campus leadership, with its symbolic and functional influence and authority, is essential if planning is to be engaging and continuous. A planning council cannot be charged and then ignored. Although there are differences of opinion about the role of the president as opposed to the chief academic officer in providing continuing leadership (Keller 1983, 61; Schuster et al. 1994, 186–87), the connection with the administration must be clear.

To maintain momentum, strategic planning committees rely on regular and open communication with the campus to overcome misunderstanding and rumors and to vet their recommendations with campus constituencies. The factors limiting the success of these councils are many, including appointing such a committee primarily for symbolic purposes, changes in administrative leadership, lack of clarity in purpose, focusing attention on small issues rather than the big issues shaping the future of the campus, and rapidly changing economic conditions calling for hard decisions (Schuster et al. 1994, 179–92). To guard against being derailed, the strategic planning committee and leadership must attend to the unique political, cultural, and practical realities of the campus.

Assessing the Context for Planning

- What are the component parts of the institution and what is the degree of authority with regard to decision making?

- Which leadership roles have the greatest credibility with members of the campus community?

- What are the customs of consultation, information sharing, and management of differences of opinion?

- What attitudes, norms, and beliefs of the campus affect affiliation and trust?

- What is the level of tolerance for ambiguity and expectation for evidence?

- What voices expect to be heard and in what forums?
- How might the intellectual politics of the campus (e.g., disciplines and perspectives) affect participation, sense of authority, or expression of controlling values?
- What processes will productively engage members of the community in taking responsibility for the future of the campus?
- What strategies and incentives will strengthen buy-in to the final plan?

GUIDING THE PLANNING PROCESS

The most important lesson learned during the last two decades is that strategic planning is as much about the journey as about the destination. To have an impact, it must be a process of continuous self-analysis; a process of coming together and committing to a shared vision; and a process of collectively developing strategies for making the vision a reality (Rowley, Lujan, and Dolence 1997, 37). Campuses can learn from the experience of others, but both the planning process and the plan must be tailored to the campus.

The success of a planning effort depends upon the skill of those who guide the process and the campus community's perceptions about their credibility. Before undertaking strategic planning, those providing the leadership, including the CAO, will want to learn as much as they can about planning: the general framework, sequence of steps, useful tools, thoughtful questions, and how to avoid dead ends. If the campus has had experience with strategic planning, the leadership will also want to learn from these previous efforts. Most campuses use a steering committee to guide the planning process, with membership on the committee based on the member's broad understanding of the university and ability to set aside special interests in order to see the bigger picture. The ability to learn from others and understand varying perspectives helps the steering committee evaluate the consequences of priorities and choices.

The steering committee members should not do the strategic planning, but rather should serve as "catalysts, inquirers, educators, and synthesizers to shape the planning process effectively" (Hax and Majluf 1996, 34). In most cases, the committee members write much of the plan, regularly pulling together the work of many others and sending it out for review by the larger community. Whether through campus forums, study groups, on-line discussions, or other techniques, the committee encourages the active participation of as many people as possible, including faculty, administrators, staff, students, alumni, and members of the board and the community (Andrade 1999). Ownership of the plan and commitment to effecting it can only develop through active involvement in the debate, negotiation, and compromise that create the plan. Since strategic planning aims to affect the operations of the entire institution, everyone, at least through representation, needs to be involved in the development of the plan.

Many campuses do an excellent job at this stage of engaging the campus community in lively dialogue yet fail to have good processes for taking notes, recording ideas, writing progress reports, and making sure the conversation does not die. One campus took such elaborate notes at every meeting that the institutional research staff, charged with coding and linking all the ideas to an overarching framework, took almost six months to complete the task. By that time, momentum was lost and the plan became only a white paper to the community with limited impact. Another campus held engaging campus conversations for most of a year, then the president, working with a small task force, issued a draft campus plan that appeared to be more the agenda of the president than a true reflection of the thinking of the campus community. It took some tactful work on the part of faculty leaders to reorient the draft and gain faculty support for the final version of the plan. As campuses gain experience with planning, they anticipate such problems and create a workable process suited to the institution.

To get more than incremental change, discussions must go well beyond sharing perspectives to include real learning about new possibilities. To open up thinking requires risk takers and futurists. Some campuses engage process consultants to stimulate creativity. Some study innovations on other campuses. The more effective the process, the more it frees individuals from preconceptions about their institution and encourages fresh ideas. Campuses can use specific strategies such as consensus groups to help focus campus responses to key questions: How might the institution be improved? What change is necessary to position the campus in the twenty-first century? What current achievements will provide the foundation for change? When significant changes are sought, extensive discussion and scenario testing are crucial to create the understanding and confidence necessary to implement the plan.

When strategic planning is first initiated on a campus, the steering committee functions as a task force of consultants. After several years, as campuses integrate the planning effort into campus life, it is natural to seek a more dependable structure so that planning and accountability are a continuous process. Many institutions have integrated the planning committee into the internal governance system, which can have the effect of limiting community participation if the standing committee takes full responsibility for evaluating and updating the plan on behalf of the campus. As a consequence, although a standing committee can ensure legitimacy and continuity in strategic planning, campuses must be vigilant to ensure planning does not lose the freshness and intellectual vitality that comes from an open process.

Once part of the governance structure, the rules for assigning committee members can also make it more difficult to appoint key members who have creative or unconventional ideas. An overemphasis on representative membership often leads to compromises that in turn can limit the results. Studies of change processes note: "Negotiations and political tradeoffs may give everyone a little but not add up to much. However, setting a limit on participation has real costs and risks; it may cause the change effort to be embraced only by a minority, which, in turn, may cause its demise." (Eckel et al. 1999, 8). Observers of participatory decision making also recognize that if planning efforts are too time consuming, few faculty will want to be elected to a multiyear term. Clearly, if planning is to be continuous, the campus needs to establish a credible and renewable participatory process.

In the final analysis, planning for and implementing change is a persuasive process and, whether guided by a standing committee or a special taskforce, requires moving the conversation out from the initial committee in ever-widening circles of communication that also bring feedback to the committee and campus leadership. As faculty are the most outspoken constituency on the campus and academic matters are at the heart of the plan, the CAO must conscientiously be a link between faculty sentiment and institutional views. In doing so, the CAO walks a fine line between honoring the past while also making a realistic assessment of the institution's potential and encouraging innovation and new directions. When strategic planning is a mature process on a campus, it becomes interwoven into the entire fabric of the institution. As one campus entering its third phase of planning noted, it was time to move "from strategic planning as a separate activity to strategic decision-making as an integral part of all levels of the University." They expect strategic thinking to be a pervasive institutional attitude.

Focusing the Work of the Steering Committee

- Who is commissioning the strategic plan? Why is the campus planning?

- What is the level of support from the administration and the board?
- What conditions make this the right time to plan? When should it be completed?
- What is the history of previous planning activities? What can be learned from those experiences?
- How will involvement of the campus community at various stages throughout the process be facilitated?
- How can the committee identify and respond to skeptics, critics, and resistors?
- How often and how much reality testing is necessary to ensure congruence between the plan and the environment?
- How can the committee keep a sense of urgency and move the process forward while also allowing time for reflection and participation?
- Which resource persons and information are needed to energize the process?
- What kinds of communication will ensure regular interaction with all of the campus?
- How will alternatives be evaluated and decisions made to ensure legitimacy and support?
- How will strategic thinking be integrated into the daily operations of the institution?

STRENGTHENING STRATEGIC PLANNING

Many of the steps in strategic planning seem formulaic and convoluted to faculty who may simply want to know, "What are we going to do? When are we going to do it? and Where will the resources come from?" Nonetheless, whether designing a planning protocol or evaluating the current plan, the CAO needs a systematic approach to planning and a perspective on where problems might emerge that could hinder the forward movement of the campus. Some of the typical steps that campuses use as a guide may be found in Robert A. Sevier, *Strategic Planning in Higher Education: Theory and Practice* (2000), as well as an analysis of the experience of many campuses.

Mission and Vision

Strategic planning starts with reaffirming the institution's mission and vision. Typically, the university's mission statement describes the type of institution and its purpose, such as "a public comprehensive institution serving the needs of the region," and how the institution aims to achieve that purpose, such as "by providing a wide array of degree programs, a balanced program of applied and basic research, and a faculty who is active in public service." Many campuses do not regularly revisit the mission statement and, when they do as part of a planning process, find it no longer reflects the emerging nature of the campus. A mission statement that is precise and up to date will reflect new responsibilities and new approaches to learning, for example: "The University facilitates student and faculty participation in the community through internships, community service, and applied research." A generic or bland mission statement provides little focus for the change agenda.

The vision statement provides the context for the institution's mission and should define a strong sense of identity and aspirations for the coming decade. Vision statements should motivate the entire university community and move it to action to achieve the desired level of performance. Often the president takes the lead in expressing the vision in powerful language, such as "excel at its task of transforming human potential." Establishing a strong vision in measurable terms, such as "manifest a level of excellence and innovation that leads to recognition as a leader within the ranks of the nation's major research universities," can energize the planning process.

Congruence between Core Values and Core Competencies

More recent planning efforts reaffirm the institution's guiding principles or core values in order to make clear what is important to the university and what gives it a distinctive identity. For example, the campus may assert its commitment to "a community that promotes free and open inquiry and treats each person with respect, tolerance, dignity and civility." It should be evident in the plan how this shared value guides thinking about matters such as diversity and access.

Affirming core competencies also helps an institution preserve what is important even as it undertakes change. Deciding to offer on-line professional courses for adults could be seen as a departure from both the values and the core competencies of a residential liberal arts college. Focusing greater attention on research and publication, however, may be a change but not a deviation from endorsed values and competencies. For a plan to bring the university community together, it must embrace long-standing values and strengths of an institution or show how new values and directions can build on the past and create a stronger future. The chief academic officer must be able to assess faculty confidence and, when necessary to overcome inertia, move the campus forward in incremental steps, rather than take on an aggressive plan that challenges the governing values of the institution. If too bold, the plan will be resisted.

Establishing the Scope and Premises of the Plan

The strategic plan clearly states what is to be accomplished in a specific time frame. Most campuses take a comprehensive approach so that all university constituencies can see their programs and their needs reflected in the plan and know they have a stake in the outcomes. When a new planning process is initiated, the chief academic officer works with the president and the president's cabinet to determine the primary justification and the issues driving the planning effort such as enrollment or improved undergraduate education. Failure to understand the premises of the plan may begin a process that is more detrimental than helpful. For example, campuses updating their plan and setting priorities for the coming year need to take a focused approach. If they begin with an unstructured brainstorming and issues clarification session, they are likely to be surprised by critical community reactions when the many issues raised do not reappear later in the plan.

Conducting the Environmental Scan

To be strategic, the university must continuously analyze its external and internal environment, noting not just local but also national trends. The environmental scan identifies the institution's strengths, weaknesses, opportunities, and threats in terms of each of its markets and each of its competitors. Data on the many factors affecting the institution, including economic, social, demographic, political, and technological changes, are analyzed (Rowley, Lujan, and Dolence 1997, 101–34). A responsive plan usually has alternative scenarios to allow for adapting the plan should there be a change in the environment.

As part of this environmental scan, the chief academic officer must direct faculty attention to a similar analysis of academic programs focused on national trends in the discipline, core competencies, distinguishing characteristics, faculty strengths and weaknesses, employer demand for graduates, and centrality of the program to the mission and vision of the university. If the university already engages in program review, the connection between the strategic plan and program review should be evident.

The CAO can help faculty make program review more strategic by tracking national trends, student demand, and program competitors and then taking a holistic look at the entire portfolio of academic offerings to determine strategic priorities.

Because the environmental scan requires a thorough analysis of higher education issues and trends, it must be a collaborative effort. For instance, the business affairs officer should monitor the trends dealing with fiscal matters, physical plant, and the local economy. The development officer should monitor trends in fundraising and endowment investment. The governmental affairs officer should monitor trends in state appropriations for higher education and legal and legislative issues. The student affairs officer should monitor demographic trends that impact admissions, financial aid, and student services. The chief academic officer should monitor trends in accreditation, salary levels, and instructional technologies. The institutional research staff must keep information current and guide course corrections based on the collective data of the entire administrative team.

Identifying Assumptions

Every strategic plan is based on assumptions. They should be clearly identified, for example: "The successful revitalization of College Town will result in an improved environment for students attending this college," and "The percentage of the overall budget from state resources will continue to decline." The validity of the assumptions is essential to the plan's stability. If the assumptions are false or if conditions change, the strategic plan must be revised. Failing to understand or monitor assumptions can lead to unrealistic expectations and wasted effort.

Stating the Priorities

Strategic priorities are the fundamental issues the organization has to address to move toward its desired future. These priorities are identified by various stakeholders, for example, the students' program needs, the faculty's commitment to quality, the administration's expectations for learning outcomes, or the board's interest in enrollment. Priorities should be limited in number, otherwise the plan will be beyond the management capabilities of the campus. They also must be instantly recognizable in reading the plan. Most campuses format the written plan so that the priorities stand out, for example, in bold print stating "Stabilize Enrollments" or "Expand Technology." Some campuses group several priorities together under key strategic themes such as "engagement" or "discovery" to reinforce the language of the vision for the institution.

Reality Testing through Gap Analysis

Two kinds of gap analyses inform the planning process. The first analysis determines how well the institution is meeting the needs and expectations of its students and other stakeholders and serves as the basis for setting strategic goals (Sevier 2000, 87). The second analysis determines what it will take to close the gap between current performance and future goals. The strategic plan aims to answer the question "How far do we have to go to accomplish our mission and achieve our vision?" If the "vision" for the university and the "real" position of the university are so far apart that existing and expected resources would be inadequate to close the gap, the situation needs to be addressed. If the strategic priorities are not perceived as realistic, the plan will have little or no positive impact on the future of the institution. At the same time, if the plan has no "stretch goals," the institution may be too conservative and unnecessarily limit its potential.

Determining how much change is realistic is a challenge for campuses. For example, the faculty may share the same academic vision for the university as the president, but be less sure that closing the gap is achievable within the time frame of the plan. To maintain momentum, the chief academic officer can suggest staged goals or different time frames contingent upon the necessary supporting factors such as the success of the fund-raising plan or an increase in enrollments. Similarly, a campus may identify a precondition for success in achieving the priorities and, rather than lower expectations, build that gap into the plan. One campus noted such a challenge by stating as their first priority: "Foster risk taking inherent in realizing strategic planning goals."

Strategic Goals and Objectives

Specific goals and objectives must be developed and aligned with the strategic priorities. In the early stages of strategic planning, the goals and objectives will be evolving; thus a process of testing and redesign should be encouraged. As the institution plans, participants should be encouraged to assess not only what they do but also how they do it. To facilitate new thinking, it is particularly important to engage faculty and staff in discussions of areas outside their daily activities. For example, faculty should weigh in on operational goals such as facilities and endowment, and staff should be encouraged to comment on programmatic goals such as academic initiatives or workforce development.

A review of campus strategic plans reveals many formats and varied terminology, but all share a common focus on setting clear goals and anticipated levels of achievement. Some campuses prefer their own terms such as "envisioning statement" instead of priority, "outcomes" instead of goals, "initiatives" instead of strategies, "tasks" instead of tactics, "metrics" instead of measures. The terminology is not as important as stating clearly what is to be achieved (excellence in learning), how it will be achieved (through introduction of innovative instructional methodologies), and how the institution will know (number of classes demonstrating technology integration). Agreeing on terminology at the outset facilitates discussion; providing the glossary as part of the plan increases understanding.

Strategies and Time Frames

Stating strategies and time lines for actions clarifies how the plan will come together, how responsibility is shared, and how progress is to be monitored. Strategies should be short statements that capture the purpose with as few words as possible such as "increasing access (the goal) through the application of distance learning initiatives" (the strategy). Usually goals, objectives, strategies, and time-to-assessment are included in a single statement. For instance: "Increase the number of credit hours produced (the goal) by 5 percent (the objective) each year for the next five years (the time-to-assessment) through enhancing programs offered to nontraditional students (the strategy)." Obviously, there can be more than one strategy associated with each goal and objective, and the time to assessment may vary. The choice of a strategy or a combination of strategies will be influenced by resources.

Some campuses make the distinction between goals, objectives, strategies, and actions based on when the activity will be accomplished. For example, goals have a five-year time frame and objectives have a two-year time frame. Because strategies are a "means to an end," they are assessed annually with modifications made as needed. Action plans and tasks represent the shortest duration events and are the immediate "to-do list." The weakness in many strategic plans is that they do not include a timetable for accomplishing actions, leaving that detail to the annual operational plans of units. If the details are not written out, it is very difficult to review progress, ensure activities are coordinated, and sustain momentum within the division. The CAO may want to consult a comprehensive list of key performance indicators to provide guidance in developing the actions and measures (Bottrill and Borden 1994). Regardless of the steps followed, the format applied, or the terminology used, the best written plan is the one the campus understands and is committed to making real in a timely way.

Evaluating the Presentation of the Strategic Plan

- Is the plan responsive to the hard questions facing the campus?
- Is it clear how this plan is related to previous plans (e.g., revision, extension, or departure)?
- Does the plan use active language and portray a campus on the move?
- Is the plan both comprehensive and concise?
- Does the order of presentation reflect the priorities of the campus?
- Does the format facilitate understanding and ease of reporting on progress?
- Is it clear how the plan will be revised and updated?
- Have the purposes, procedures, and primary participants in the preparation of the plan been included as reference points for those who come to the campus in later years?
- Is the plan accessible to the campus community utilizing multiple media?

LINKING PLANNING AND BUDGET

Regardless of how one measures success, an organization is more likely to succeed if there is alignment between strategic goals and resource allocation "in order to assure strategic consistency" (Hax and Majluf 1996, 3). Whether just beginning a planning process or evaluating the traction of a current plan, the CAO will want to understand how planning and budget will be linked. Because resource allocations reflect priorities, it is essential that the entire university be aware of the resource implications as the strategic plan unfolds, especially if change is taking place in the face of resource constraints. Strategic planning has no meaning if the institution is not prepared to align existing and planned resources with strategic intent.

During the planning process, the campus leadership should evaluate the degree to which various funding sources, including special state initiative funding, fees and tuition, grants, private giving, and revenue from auxiliary enterprises could contribute to the priorities. Phases of a strategic plan often coincide with initiation of a capital campaign. Presidential leadership is particularly crucial at this time to reassure the campus that a substantial effort will be made to increase the resources of the campus and that each dollar will be viewed as an investment in the future. Realistically, most campuses must be prepared to reallocate resources rather than rely fully on new funding. As the current allocation of resources will match historical patterns rather than the strategic initiatives of the new plan, to try to implement a strategic plan while assuming business as usual would be myopic. Worse yet would be to decide not to plan for change because of limited resources.

As units develop rough cost estimates for each goal and accompanying strategies and identify potential sources of funding, they will be faced with questions about which strategies require additional resources and what will be given up in order to reallocate resources to the new priorities. Both monetary and human resources must be accounted for. There are no easy answers for the CAO since each division, college, department, and unit will usually expect more, not fewer, resources to support their action plans and tasks. However, few campuses are in a growth mode enabling them to continuously add new activities; thus planned change will come through elimination, substitution, or redesign. The CAO may be able to demonstrate that not all aspects of the plan require dollars. Many strategies require a mental adjustment to change the ways in which things have been done in order to improve quality or be more productive.

Linking planning and budgeting calls for a significant change in typical annual budget processes in which, after advocacy-based budget hearings within the division, the vice presidents merely present a list of initiatives to the president and request funding in the next year's budget. Based on an incremental and line-item approach, individuals see themselves as openly bidding for unclaimed excess resources. If funds are forthcoming the project is undertaken. If not the idea might be put forward another year or be forgotten. Under that model, budget requests are hardly strategic as there is no expectation that the initiatives are connected to systemic change. Other budget processes that rely on equity, and either distribute or take back a set percentage from every unit, also eliminate the opportunity to judiciously invest for future return. Clearly, if campus budget processes are not redesigned to support planning, the whole concept of strategic management is undermined (Anderes 1996).

Investments in the strategic plan need to be identified as one-time or as continuing base budget adjustments. Some campuses use one-time competitive incentive grants to implement strategic priorities, resulting in support at the unit level where the project is based but not much impact on the campus as a whole (Powers 2000, 292). When the plan requires a redistribution of base budget operating funds, the president, the president's cabinet, and the planning and budget committee need to do so in such a way that the ongoing operation of the institution is not jeopardized. To fully implement a plan, redistribution of operating funds may require a multiyear process. Campuses use a variety of approaches, for example, setting an annual reallocation target from all resources to be redeployed to the priorities of the strategic plan or requiring each unit to submit a three-year budget showing how its initiatives that support the plan will be self-funded (Newton 2000).

All actions and all costs must be accounted for because facilities plans, technology plans, hiring plans, and curricular initiatives developed at all levels must be aligned with each other and with the university strategic plan. Most campuses hope that by strategically redirecting existing resources to fund key initiatives revenues will increase and sustain support for the plan. Further, they count on leveraging current resources for future return from a stronger institution with greater impact. Indeed, few campuses would change if they did not believe that a careful investment of time, creativity, and money would bring both educational and financial returns.

Funding the Strategic Plan

- Which of the strategies and actions require new resources? Which of the strategies require new thinking?

- How are additional costs accounted for as units align their plans with the university plan?

- What resources can be generated from new sources such as grants? increased enrollments? state initiative funding?

- How will funds be reallocated within divisions? How will funds be reallocated across divisions?

- What activities should be eliminated as new strategic directions are pursued? Over what time frame will the reallocation of time and staff take place?

- What role will the strategic planning steering committee play in determining resource allocations to the plan?

- What techniques will keep the planning and budget processes integrated into a comprehensive process?

IMPLEMENTING THE STRATEGIC PLAN

Once the institutional plan is approved by the governing board, each division, college, department, and other academic and nonacademic unit develops its strategic plan with the same time frame. Many campuses keep the steering committee in place to continue to focus campus attention on implementation through unit plans. They may also be responsible for overseeing the reporting systems that both recognize accomplishments and identify problems in implementation. To reinforce the importance of unit plans, some campuses have them formally approved by the planning committee, others by the appropriate administrator, and a few at the presidential level. The chief academic officer can strengthen the alignment of efforts within the academic affairs division by sharing all of the unit plans within the division. Better yet, the steering committee can facilitate implementation and alignment by posting all unit plans electronically for the entire campus community. The committee's most important role is to make sure the strategic plan maintains its central place on the crowded institutional agenda.

Developing Unit Plans

All units' strategic plans and their supporting action plans are designed to support the vision, priorities, and goals of the university plan in distinct but connected ways. For example, for the institutional objective: "Create a campus culture in which excellence in teaching is recognized as a high priority," the implementation at the college level might be: "Provide ongoing teaching effectiveness seminars" or "Establish a reward system for improvement in teaching." It is essential that all university divisions understand that their annual operational plans must reflect and support the institutional plan and budget priorities. To reinforce the linkage, some campuses require that each unit develop a three-year plan that rolls forward each year accompanied by a budget plan based on the prior year, the current year, and the subsequent year.

Developing Action Plans

When institutions plan down through the organization, individuals are both empowered and accountable for their part in creating the institution for the future. Detailing how the various activities will be accomplished, who will be responsible, and when outcomes can be expected is a particularly taxing part of strategic planning. Nonetheless, the action plans should clearly delineate what activities or tasks will be performed in direct support of a specific goal, objective, or strategy. Action plans state who will make the actions happen, what resources will be needed, when the actions will be taken, and how success of the actions will be measured. It is particularly important for faculty to be involved in identifying measures that are meaningful to them and link with what they want to achieve. Without action plans, a strategic plan has no life and no staying power.

Strengthening Accountability

Stating the anticipated outcomes of a plan is far easier than identifying the specific measures of those outcomes that will show that the plan is having the desired effect. One weakness experienced by many campuses is the assumption that completing the action step is the measure and can be checked off as a sign of success. Accompanying the action "establish interdisciplinary centers" with the measure "dollar amount of sponsored funding per center" is a clear demonstration of how progress toward the goal of "increased recognition for interdisciplinary research" will be effected. Measures of accountability can be a one-time measure, such as "increase enrollments to 15,000," or a continuing measure, such as "annually increase the proportion of course enrollments as a result of articulation agreements with each of the community colleges." When outcomes and measures are directly associated with actions taken, if an outcome is not met the effectiveness of the action can be evaluated and corrective action recommended.

Monitoring Progress

A review of strategic planning efforts that have accomplished less than was hoped for reveals that the failure to assign accountability allows the change effort to get lost in the day-to-day operations of the institution. The chief academic officer can help deans, department chairs, and program directors keep focused on their responsibility for fulfilling the goals of the plan. Typical strategies include using the goals of the plan as the basis for administrator evaluation, developing annual reports from units aligned with the strategic plan, and calling for monthly progress reports on contributions to accomplishing the strategic plan. To ensure cross-division integration, the steering committee might meet with the vice presidents at regular intervals to review action plans, monitor progress, and reinforce accountability. When campuses keep the process simple and direct, it facilitates action rather than deflecting energy to documentation.

To effectively sustain a change process, straightforward reports on progress must be shared regularly throughout the campus and not be merely part of the annual report from the president to the board. Some campuses use an electronic newsletter to track progress. Many campuses continue to hold regular open meetings as the forum for reporting on and reshaping the plan, believing that members of the campus community can help identify any barriers to success. Celebrating success is motivating; however, it is just as important to be honest about areas where there is limited progress rather than to carry an issue silently forward year after year.

Adapting the Plan

During early stages of implementation, an assessment must be made of the congruence between what everyone thought the plan would be and how the plan, in operation, is now perceived. Sometimes a disconnect develops between the approved plan and the operational reality, calling for course corrections. In one university, after working collaboratively to develop objectives, timelines, strategies, and action plans, when the strategic plan was implemented, faculty became concerned that the administration's emphasis on facilities, finances, and enrollment were overshadowing the academic program and student support priorities. Recognizing that the foundation of planning is adaptability and working collaboratively to find common ground, the planning committee worked with the administration to respond to faculty concerns and refocus the plan to counter the growing disaffection.

One challenge facing the chief academic officer is maintaining connection between the very publicly approved strategic plan and a changing presidential agenda. After so much hard work and consultation, the written plan may appear fixed and deterministic of all campus activities, when, in fact, the administration must remain responsive to new opportunities. If the president announces an initiative based on a donor's gift or a partnership with a local business, members of the community may expect to test it against the strategic plan in the same way they tested all other ideas during the planning process. Consequently, the CAO and the president must work together to help the campus understand that the plan can accommodate and should accommodate unforeseen opportunities without creating friction, appearing to disregard campus community views, or threatening shared governance.

Adapting to Unexpected Circumstances

In increasing numbers, CAOs are having to respond to unexpected situations, such as a reduction in state appropriations or an enrollment shortfall, that may seem to jeopardize the strategic plan. Needing to work quickly to adjust to reduced resources, the administration may not have time to enlist the campus again in data gathering and brainstorming alternative responses. Adjustments in strategies need to be made based on the best available information with the administration taking significant responsibility for the revisions. Explaining what was done and why will ease the situation but may not keep some from second-guessing the actions. Timely communication is especially important in times of crisis to prevent rumors from derailing the campus from its strategic priorities.

Faculty will support a crisis-planning effort if they can see that the process is rational, objective, and principled. They will trust the administration if they believe their perspective is recognized. One campus faced with a reduction in state appropriations used the press effectively to explain, to both the campus community and the legislature, that they had no choice but to cut faculty, which, in turn, might well prevent them from achieving their strategic goal of increasing their research capacity and recognition for excellence. Although no one expected the public disclosures to lead to an exemption, the campus community felt reassured that the administration understood the consequence of the budget reduction to them individually and collectively. The good will developed through a well-designed strategic planning process carries over when unexpected events impact the campus.

Testing the Power of the Plan

- To what extent are the strategic directions for the campus reflected in everyday activities?
- Do all units of the campus have strategic plans and action plans aligned with the institutional plans?
- How is progress monitored and corrective actions taken, if needed?
- How are divisions and units of the campus accountable to each other for progress?
- What stake do the various constituencies have in the activities that will change the campus?
- How is campus confidence in the change effort monitored and supported?
- Are the processes through which the plan can be modified understood and supported?

- If unexpected events impact the plan, is there a reservoir of good will to build on?

SUCCESSFUL STRATEGIC PLANNING

Even if the planning process is flawless and the timing perfect, the strategic plan is still vulnerable as participants change and circumstances shift. At the same time the CAO helps to maintain focus and accountability in concert with the rest of the central administration, the CAO also is a source of energy and encouragement for those within the division of academic affairs who are making the plan a reality. To keep things on track, the chief academic officer needs to make the strategic plan the framework for assessing institutional and individual success and regularly recognize and celebrate progress. This commitment is essential if faculty and staff are to feel their involvement counts, that they will benefit, and that the reward structure of the campus recognizes their contributions.

Strategic planning requires a high level of imagination, analytic ability, and energy to design, commit to, and carry out a course of action. Because academic programs must be dynamic and responsive to change, it is important for the CAO to continue to encourage the forward looking and creative thought process that is part of strategic planning. Finding opportunities to reinforce the change agenda must be a high priority. Simultaneously, the CAO must be sure that the daily business of the institution is attended to. Thus the CAO must artfully keep running on two tracks at the same time, that is, keeping academic affairs going while also making changes. To do so requires regularly making the mental shift from proactive and creative work to the focused follow through required for standard operations.

Because strategic planning is so engaging, it is often difficult for participants to make the mental shift from the role of exploration, discovery, and participatory decision making to accept other types of decision making. For many who have been deeply involved, there is a let down because they found the process energizing and they miss being "in the know." For others, there will be a sense of relief and a tendency to get back to the way things were. Understanding these psychological forces helps the CAO understand some of the assumptions and misperceptions that emerge around change efforts. It is not unusual, for example, for some faculty to claim in the end, "We had nothing to do with this plan," others to claim that all the meetings were "a waste of time," whereas others are confident that overnight everything will be accomplished. In short, as engaging, collaborative, and well paced as the process may be, it will not be enough to overcome some of the personal dispositions of members of the community. The best the CAO can do is support faculty leadership, reinforce the continuous hard work of faculty, and conscientiously socialize newcomers to the campus into the ongoing work of change.

Ultimately, the purpose of strategic planning is to help a university identify and maintain an optimal alignment with the most important elements of the environment within which the university resides (Rowley, Lujan, and Dolence 1997, 14–15). Environments change, administrations change, and members of governing boards change. If the plan is robust and the process is responsive to both internal and external conditions, appropriate adaptations can be made as circumstances change. Administrators, faculty, and staff must believe strategic planning is worth doing and do it as well as they can. In the end, the real success of strategic planning emerges when strategic thinking is institutionalized in the collective consciousness of the campus as a way of maintaining the vitality of the campus.

CHAPTER

Facilities Planning: Linking Campus Environment and Academic Purpose

I magine that you are touring your campus for the first time and seeing it from the vantage point of a new student or new faculty member. Do imposing stone buildings suggest dignity and authority? Do buildings facing a green space encourage connection and community? Does the campus pick up energy and pace from its location in the heart of a city? Do glass multi-story buildings surrounded by lighted parking lots reflect efficiency, access, and career-related learning? Clearly, every campus, both its environment and its buildings, has a distinctive character that influences both students and faculty as they look for the right fit. Moreover, the campus establishes expectations for academic life more directly than the faculty or the classroom, including the extent to which one is connected to the community, the amount of time spent on campus, and the degree to which social and personal development are linked with learning. Experts note, "A campus' physical character—its forms, spaces, styles, and visual messages—provides the most tangible, direct, visceral, and insuppressible expression of what an institution is all about" (Brase 1990, 1).

Despite conscientious attention to facilities and capital planning, campuses do not always reflect what is known about engaging and supportive learning environments. Space constraints, surging enrollments, and budget limitations have forced campuses to make hard choices about maintaining facilities while also trying to adapt to new needs. The campus layout, internal design of buildings, and aesthetics are both created and compromised over time. Since the publication of the national report, *The*

Decaying American Campus: A Ticking Time Bomb (Rush and Johnson 1989), higher education has been on alert about the multibillion dollar renewal, replacement, and deferred maintenance needs nationwide.

Observers note that the "condition of institutional facilities reflects the vitality, leadership, and interest of the academic community in providing quality education" (Kaiser and Klein 2000, 13–17). Too many campuses have let facilities languish and accepted a "make-do" mentality. Faced with scarce resources, the physical plant has been a lower priority than academic programs and student services. Only the rare campus escapes the problems of deferred maintenance and poor use of space because it has been either recently built or relocated to build anew and intentionally link facilities to academic purposes. Ideally, all campuses would recognize the impact of facilities on academic activities and develop a proactive approach to regularly rethinking the learning environment to support strategic priorities and evolving modes of faculty and student interaction.

Given the challenges, chief academic officers (CAOs) can be helpful by suggesting ways in which facilities can be adapted, encouraging the reallocation of space for greater efficiency, and making recommendations about new facilities necessary to advance the academic priorities. To do so, they must be included in deliberations about facilities and able to communicate effectively with those responsible for the physical environment whether they be architects, engineers, physical plant managers, or business officers. More important, CAOs must be persuasive in arguing for the value—indeed necessity—of collaborative cross-institutional campus planning.

It is this last goal, collaboration, that challenges most directly some of the prevailing practices by which space is allocated, master plans are developed, and facilities are designed, built, and renovated. Typically, campus master planning, capital budgeting, facilities management, and space allocations are key responsibilities of the chief administrative and financial officers and special interests of presidents and boards. Even the most conscientious business officers and the most respected facilities planning consulting firms admit that at times they are caught between strategic long-range academic interests and the more immediate expectations of a board or a president who wants to leave a lasting footprint on the campus through building projects. Nonetheless, as planners recognize that buildings are the physical manifestation of campus values, they are in the best position to advocate for broader participation in setting priorities for the physical plant that reflect academic purposes.

If chief academic officers want to have an effective role in such planning and bring academic needs to the table, they must have a realistic understanding of the process for replacement and renewal of facilities, the myriad decisions to be made in designing facilities, and the financial considerations. This chapter offers a variety of perspectives and guiding questions that connect academic planning and facilities planning and encourages academic affairs administrators and business affairs administrators to be positive partners for change as they care for and invest in the infrastructure of the campus.

HISTORICAL PERSPECTIVES ON THE CAMPUS

All facilities planning must begin from an appreciation of a campus' rich history to be sure that changes embody both the original and the emerging character of the institution. Serving purposes unlike those of any other institution in society, the college or university campus is a constructed environment. Each campus' design demonstrates purposeful and, often, innovative approaches to supporting the human relationships that lead to learning. Whether based on the "collegiate ideal rooted in the medieval English universities, where students and teachers lived and studied together in small, tightly regulated colleges" or on modern conceptions of functionality and integration with the larger community, planners and architects have always worked together to create an environment that expresses academic values including openness, connection, and hard work (Turner 1984, 3).

Both the layout and the architecture of a campus are at once functional and symbolic. For example, many campuses site the library as the centerpiece or place the administration building at the gateway. Classical columns suggesting a temple for learning or Gothic structures suggesting permanence are important design elements on 200-year-old campuses as well as more recent ones (Turner 1984, 116). College location is also intentional. Many older campuses were located in rural areas based on the idea that a college should provide privacy and protection from distractions. Newer campuses may be in the heart of the city or at an exchange off a major highway to facilitate access by commuting students. Adding to the symbolism drawn from the founding values, sometimes church related, are dramatic architectural features such as spires, bell towers, and domes. It is particularly challenging for century-old campuses to add buildings that are consistent with the historic ones. Ideas about the degree to which unity is important may well be called into question when there is a donor who wants control over the design as a condition of the gift.

Whether serving a residential private college, an urban university, a suburban community college, or a large land grant university, the chief academic officer must be sensitive to the academic ideals and design elements that create the environment. Each campus expresses a moment in the long history of higher education in the United States, ranging from emulation of the formality of European institutions to the creation of more flexible American environments, accommodating the dramatic expansion in access to higher education (Turner 1984). Fortunately, no matter when founded, campuses have attracted outstanding architects to create just the right environment for the institution's purposes. As a result, some of the finest buildings and landscape designs in America are on college campuses.

Administrators, faculty, students, alumni, and community members have a stake in keeping campuses both beautiful and functional. The guidance of professional planners who recognize that, despite constant change, each campus is a product of its history and its purpose can ensure consistency and adaptability. Planners may tactfully explain how demolishing a building or two can create a more integrated design as the campus expands or how an above-ground parking garage would scar a campus. Thoughtless departures from founding principles can result in mistakes that a campus lives with for a long time.

Some observers of higher education believe the emerging features of a campus, even if unintentional, reveal institutional politics and priorities (Minnich 1995, 2). An aerial view of a typical campus would show the administrative offices prominently located in the best facilities and traditional programs such as history and biology housed in permanent buildings, whereas newer academic programs such as ethnic studies or peace studies are given space in old homes on the fringe of campus. Whether or not the implication that campuses enthrone the past and relegate emerging ideas to the margins is really true, the observation does suggest the importance of not merely finding space for new needs but also of trying to regularly reconceptualize the physical whole of a campus as intellectual and social relationships evolve and change over time.

To strengthen their ability to contribute to the planning effort, chief academic officers would do well to walk both their own and other campuses in order to understand the campus historically, functionally, and aesthetically. In that way, they can harmonize their views of changing needs of the academy with the historical institutional values and not risk contributing to the claim of "catastrophic disruption that the last two generations of building have wrought on every campus in the country" (Kaiser 1998, 46).

Understanding the Campus

- What is the predominant architectural style of the campus? Is consistency a goal?
- How do elements such as plantings, walkways, gates, sculpture, and signage contribute to the overall "feel" of the campus?
- How do the axes and paths of the campus direct activities and interactions?
- How do the boundaries of the campus separate or connect it to the community?
- How do the traditional, historical elements of the campus shape future opportunities?
- To what degree have space constraints altered the original conception of the campus?
- How does the allocation of space and juxtaposition of facilities reflect the priorities of the campus?

ANTICIPATING THE FUTURE

While campuses strive to preserve their heritage, academic life continues to change. The most prominent changes are in the relationship of teachers to learners, the use of technology, the boundaries of the classroom, and access to the campus. Faculty want more flexible classrooms to accommodate group learning and more "wired" to enrich content via the Web. Students expect to learn outside the classroom in their home, at their work site, and in the community. Changing views of how leadership should be dispersed throughout a campus make large administration buildings obsolete. Campuses expect to share facilities with the community and with other institutions in a consortia. Twenty-four/seven now describes the learning day as well as access needs to academic support services such as libraries. The CAO plays a critical role, working with the chief administrative officer, in assessing the degree to which these changes can be accommodated in current facilities.

Campuses increasingly need facilities where activity and flexibility are fundamental to design. Multiuse facilities, landscape furnishings, and more open space to support new ideas about community and collaboration may run counter to the traditional single-purpose facilities and fixed boundaries that were once designed to support needs for privacy and territoriality. Yet even as faculty protect their space, they adapt to new technologies and want more productive environments. Librarians worry about preserving collections and quiet, yet support adding soft seating, cyber cafés, and group meeting areas to make the library more inviting. Commuting students expect ease of parking and comfortable lounges. Clearly, there is tension between the old and the new. The chief academic officer can mediate these tensions by remaining open to new ideas and helping those who lead facilities-planning processes recognize that resistance to change is as inevitable as creativity and innovation.

Architects and planners can suggest new ways of looking at the campus for the future, but educators are responsible for maintaining the fit between academic goals and facilities. In doing so, both faculty and administrators are broadening their definition of academic space. Campuses include quasi-academic facilities such as museums as well as nonacademic facilities such as fitness centers. The addition of such facilities to the traditional office/classroom base recognizes that learning takes place well beyond the classroom and that higher education has a responsibility for more than intellectual development. Whether a residential or commuter campus, the data on undergraduate student learning demonstrate that a well-rounded life and engagement with the campus are as important as teaching quality to student success (Kuh et al. 1991). Consequently, when funding is limited, chief academic officers often find that if they align their interests with student affairs, they can make a persuasive case for mixed-use facilities that intentionally link academic and cocurricular activities.

As campuses shift their focus to be more student centered, they are adopting ideas from other social institutions. Embracing service improvement principles from the business world has led many campuses to rethink how students use space and to create one-stop enrollment services centers that co-locate admissions, advising, registration, financial aid, and billing. New housing is built with both more privacy and more homelike features. Food courts replace cafeterias and are integrated into classroom buildings. One business practice that has not caught on, however, would have parking by the front door for student customers with administrators, faculty, and staff relegated to distant employee parking lots. Although some ideas are clearly more acceptable than others, these applications of principles from other industries such as hotels, shopping malls, and airports demonstrate how different campuses might be if different assumptions about facilities and human interactions were applied.

Accommodating Future Academic Needs

- What new understanding of student learning will require changes in classrooms?
- How will technology impact learning, the conduct of campus operations, facilities management, campus communications, and more?
- What emerging nonacademic needs of students must be planned for?
- What new office arrangements are called for to serve an increasingly mobile and temporary faculty?
- What new specialized facilities are called for to support research, changing pedagogies, and new academic offerings?

STRATEGIC PLANNING AS THE FRAMEWORK FOR FACILITIES PLANNING

Faculty often wonder how they can get their needs for office or program space taken seriously. Because strategic planning takes into account both current capacities and future aspirations and is fundamentally about the academic vision for an institution, planning provides the ideal framework for coordinating diverse ideas about facilities. When campus strategic planning is an inclusive process, faculty and academic administrators have the opportunity to project new facilities needs to support anticipated programmatic changes. Academic participants in strategic planning can extend general goal statements such as "undertake a renovation program to increase the utilization of existing buildings" into academically focused goals. For example, plans for new research and instructional programs would be supported by explicit statements about the type and quality of facilities required. Academic priorities will not necessarily take precedence over those of other divisions, but should not be left as only an implicit commitment within a general strategy.

A review of strategic plans from many different campuses reveals that facilities needs are often identified as priorities, but are not always specific enough to guarantee that academic needs will be met. The chief academic officer, as well as other academic administrators and faculty, must take responsibility for encouraging more detailed attention to facilities that will reflect changes in pedagogy, interdisciplinary research, student/faculty interaction, and campus culture. On some campuses, the CAO takes responsibility for helping faculty develop a separate detailed academic facilities plan through broad collaboration with the facilities planning staff. The strategies in such a plan might include "renovate the science building to provide flexible space to support undergraduate research," "refurnish lecture halls with seating that can be turned to facilitate student interaction," and "design classrooms with a compact teaching podium to house and control teaching technologies."

Facilities priorities in strategic plans must reflect changing views of education practices as well as relationships within the learning community. For example, one university's strategic plan calls for an increase in "facilities that foster student, faculty, and staff interactions and relationships." Such statements depart from the teacher-centered campus of the past and endorse a philosophy of active learning and increased interaction between faculty and students. Similarly, a plan for multiple "smart classrooms" reveals the way technology is changing instruction so that students may not even be on campus. To link the campus environment to academic values requires congruence among strategic planning, facilities planning, and academic planning. Well-thought-out changes in the physical environment not only reflect academic values but can also help shape a new academic culture.

Linking Strategic Planning and Facilities Planning

- What is the academic vision of the institution throughout the next decade?

- To what extent are the facilities goals congruent with these academic program goals?

- What are the specific strategies to accomplish the facilities goals that reflect both the current and future philosophy of teaching and learning on the campus?

- What specific activities to accomplish the goals are included in the annual operating plans?

- What are the specific measures that enable campus facilities planners and academic leaders to track progress toward strategic goals?

- How do the proposed projects fit logically into an overall space management plan for the institution?

- How do assumptions about revenues, enrollments, and programs impact the facilities goals of the strategic plan?

DEVELOPING THE CAMPUS MASTER PLAN

The campus master plan, an outgrowth of the strategic plan, is the key tool for anticipating the future of the physical plant and environment of the campus. The plan describes how the physical plant will change over a fixed period of time based on assumptions, including projected enrollments, new academic programs, current space use, condition of facilities, and community considerations. Despite efforts to develop accurate master plans, changes in academic organization, funding, programs, or enrollments often mean that the plan no longer fits the institution and needs to be updated. Just as the tool of long-range planning has been replaced by the more responsive approach of strategic planning, which takes into account a changing environment and internal conditions, campus master planning has changed to be more strategic, realistic, and subject to the same requirements of accountability, annual review, and revision.

Campus master plans are by their nature more guides than promises. They essentially state the highest aspirations for the campus and establish the right to develop facilities. When that is not understood, faculty critics with institutional memory report they no longer take the master plan seriously as they see plans for structures that have never materialized in their many years on campus while land and other buildings are added opportunistically. Experts provide this cautionary note: "Although campus master planning is a creative exercise and should push the envelope, unrealistic expectations can quickly doom a plan" (Caruthers and Layzell 1999, 76). Plans are equally vulnerable when they are prescriptive, rather than responsive, to student and faculty needs. To guard against such failures in confidence, the master plan must be logically connected to the strategic plan and financial realities without dampening the opportunity to dream or to take advantage of changing circumstances.

Broad communication beyond the campus is also critical to successful campus development. Board and legislator support is necessary whether the campus is responding to the positive impact of donor dreams or the negative impact of fiscal uncertainty. Neighbors in the community can effectively delay or even block plans for a new building if they have not been involved in analyzing how best to manage the impact of the new facility on neighborhood traffic patterns and parking. Academic leadership can be critical in the persuasive process to keep the focus on the purpose, not just the building—for example, how the community can benefit from a new fine arts facility or an addition to the library.

To help ensure realistic and supported plans, colleges and universities have found it useful to have a representative committee involved in the planning process from the outset, both to set priorities and to communicate regularly with their constituencies. Depending upon the complexity of the master plan, special studies may be called for or consultants used. The best planning processes are somewhat messy as they allow for differing perspectives, encourage openness, and call for creativity. One planning expert notes, "If your institution has a physical planning process that appears orderly, involves few participants, generates few contradictions, surfaces few controversial issues and responds neatly to administrative authority, your institution is either standing still and has no need for an effective physical planning process, or it is very small, or it is heading for trouble" (Brase 1990, 2–3).

Although an open planning process has many supporters, there are many presidents who control facilities planning because they "see erecting new buildings as a part of their job, and as a concrete way for others to measure their success" (Williams 2002, A28). Given the time it takes from fundraising through planning to finished building, many presidents would rather face down critics than take additional time to create support. Noting how many building projects are controversial, one observer wryly commented, "A ground breaking on a college campus sometimes stirs up more than just dirt" (Williams 2002, A29). The main sources of opposition coalesce around designs that do not blend with the rest of the campus, projects that do not seem necessary, and high costs.

The least-understood aspect of capital planning is capital budgeting. Unfamiliar with the difference between the operating budget and the capital budget, faculty inevitably demand the rationale behind a new facility when they believe the higher priority is more full-time faculty as they "think it's money being taken from their academic budgets" (Rosenberg and Adelman 2002, 22). A bond issue that brings a multimillion-dollar windfall to a campus for buildings at the same time the operating budget is being cut is particularly hard to understand. As with all planning and decision making, open information, careful explanations, and effective communication coupled with representative campus involvement increase the credibility of decisions. Campuses also find that consultants build confidence in the planning process if they provide a neutral perspective, consult widely, synthesize disparate views, establish realistic project management timelines, and explain cost estimates and required funding. To facilitate faculty understanding of the relationships between facilities plans, academic plans, and budgets, the chief academic officer must be involved and keep faculty informed.

Typical Questions from Master Planning Consultants

- What new courses or programs are being contemplated, and what are the facility, enrollment, and staffing implications of these potential offerings?
- How are instructional delivery methods likely to change during the next five or ten years?
- What types of existing spaces are most in need of renovation?
- What types of fused-use facilities (e.g., classroom/library and office/lab) could meet campus needs?
- Where do students, faculty, and staff go to socialize and interact?
- Where do students go to study individually or in groups?
- Would some programs function better if they were physically located adjacent to other programs?
- How might the unit function better if moved to a new location?
- Which programs or services could be relocated on the campus perimeter or off campus entirely and not affect delivery of services?

USING A SPACE-ADVISORY COMMITTEE

While the campus master plan shapes the desired future of the campus, space allocation and facilities management must be addressed on a continuous basis. These are the issues that most often end up on the CAO's desk. Typically, the chief financial officer (CFO) and the facilities staff bear the burden for sorting among the never-ending mundane needs, such as fixing a roof, while also managing the more compelling projects, such as designing distance-learning classrooms. Unaware of the challenges facilities staff face, many across campus may question everything from the priorities to the results of facilities-maintenance and space-management activities. The chief academic officer who establishes a process for setting priorities within academic affairs can reduce the number of random requests from faculty and department chairs directly to the facilities staff and maintain a consistent overall plan for assignment and maintenance of academic space to meet the needs of the campus community.

If left without guidance, the facilities staff, committed to being responsive, may try too hard to respond to every "squeaky wheel" and make short-term decisions that blur the overall conception of the campus and its future. When space for a new project is demanded, the facilities staff often capture and reassign space opportunistically with the goal of minimal disruption of others. As a result, it is not uncommon to find offices from several unrelated units on a single hall, faculty offices tucked into the basements of residence halls, or programs located off the main campus. Such random arrangements have the unintended consequence of isolating individuals from their colleagues, which reduces productivity and community.

To facilitate collaboration and coherence and reduce conflict, many campuses have long used a standing committee within the internal governance process charged with the responsibility for establishing principles by which the facilities staff can do their work, whether it be renovation, maintenance, or space allocation. Ideally, the committee has broad representation from all divisions; includes faculty, staff, and students; tolerates intense deliberations and diverse viewpoints; and serves as a buffer between individual demands and the facilities staff. With clear but limited authority, described by one planner as "controlled participatory involvement" (Bruegman 1989), and access to necessary information such as space inventories, space guidelines, and space needs, the committee can provide systematic guidance and help set priorities. Their advisory role reduces fragmentation in decision making and reassures others across campus that there is a rational basis for reallocations of space or renovation priorities. Such committees become less effective when they try to micromanage or bend to special interests or when the facilities staff ignores the recommendations.

The work of space and facilities committees on many campuses is being professionalized and making greater use of technology applications for room scheduling, classroom occupancy studies, on-line building blueprints, physical facilities inventories, institutional data on space utilization, and building condition audits (Kaiser and Klein 2000). The chief academic officer may ask that some of this information be reviewed at the unit level to increase awareness as well as to check the accuracy of space assignments. Because of the complexity of work on many large campuses, central administration oversight is necessary to integrate the work of the unit-level committees working on multiple projects as well as to keep academic planning and facilities planning separate but coordinated (Brase 1990, 11).

From time to time, the CAO and other academic administrators must do a walk-through of all academic facilities to understand their use and suitability. It is particularly important to identify unused space, poorly used space, and space no longer suitable for how it is assigned—all qualitative matters that may not show up in the quantitative data. When linked with periodic academic program review and accreditation, this assessment of academic facilities is very productive, especially if the CAO has funds to address immediate needs of a unit such as furniture and equipment replacement. When large-scale needs emerge from program review such as for a new recital hall, the needs and rationales must be handed on to the capital planning task force.

Perhaps more than any other issue on campus, space has symbolic value, creates turf battles, and leads to misunderstandings about who controls space. Deans and department chairs believe they "own" the space they occupy and can make office moves and classroom changes without notifying facilities management staff. The chief financial officer can eliminate some headaches by strengthening the role of the chief academic officer in overseeing academic needs in the institutional context. The CAO can reduce tension by making academic space as important a resource as the operating budget or faculty positions and subjecting it to the same kind of analysis and allocation criteria as any other resource. Once deans and department chairs understand the principles behind managing space, the chief academic officer can then advocate on behalf of the division through an annual memo that sets strategic priorities, integrates needs with institutional goals, and recommends specific projects. The business affairs staff can then be confident that their work is responsive to student, faculty, and program needs.

Planning Academic Space

- What variety of types of classrooms including those appropriate for lectures, active learning, and seminars are needed?

- To what extent are specialized facilities such as sound studios, science labs, television studios, and music practice rooms developed based on enrollment demand, program needs, and accreditation requirements?

- What priority is given to single faculty offices with appropriate technology?

- Should faculty be co-located with department or unit staff and administrators to support ease of administration and collegiality or dispersed to promote interdisciplinary work?

- How can colleges, departments, and other academic units be housed so that they have an identity?

- How much common space for informal faculty-student contact is appropriate in each building?
- How can storage space and behind-the-scenes space help make facilities more functional?
- How should space assigned to academic affairs be controlled and managed?

CREATING A POSITIVE LEARNING ENVIRONMENT

Because of budget pressures, higher education has for too long put basic refurbishment of faculty offices and classrooms in the category of "nice, but not necessary." As a result, on many campuses faculty share small offices with battered metal desks, mismatched side chairs, and limited storage. With little privacy or comfort, faculty and students avoid office hours and communicate by e-mail. Many faculty prefer to work at home where it is clean, quiet, and their materials are close at hand. In some cases, new faculty cannot expect to get an office co-located with other members of the department because there is no contiguous space. The cumulative effect of neglect and poor management is that both faculty and students choose not to be on campus and then lament that there is little intellectual community.

Classrooms on many campuses are also dismal. Faculty expect a positive learning environment but, too often, are faced with fixed seating or tablet armchairs, inadequate lighting and air circulation, and limited technology support. Facilities designers as well as research on the relationship between learning and such elements as color, light, acoustics, windows, personal space, and room arrangement can provide guidelines for designing optimal classroom conditions. Even without access to the research literature, both faculty and students know intuitively which rooms are better than others for learning.

Given the varied approaches to teaching, it is not always easy to outfit classrooms. Most classrooms are fitted with one size chair and, perhaps, a few left-handed desks, though many faculty would prefer tables and chairs to make the room arrangement flexible enough for small-group work or a seminar. As the standard class meeting time has shifted from the 50 minute lecture to longer sessions, students want comfortable chairs and a place to put their belongings. Rather than let the facilities staff continue the practice of replacing broken tablet armchairs in each room, which reinforced teacher-centered instruction, faculty on one campus advocated moving the needed desks from other classrooms so that one room at a time could be redesigned and refurnished to match needs for flexible seating. Even when it comes to installing audio-visual equipment, faculty have views that differ from the "all eyes front" model that is perpetuated by the facilities staff. When faculty design a classroom, they may reorient rooms so that students enter the back and screens are mounted so that they do not cover the whiteboard.

Inevitably, without adequate attention, what may initially have been functional deteriorates over time. Dirty overhead projectors, torn window shades, out-of-order signs on computers, and broken chairs in the corner all signal an indifferent attitude and create a psychologically negative response. To fight the effect of simple daily wear and tear, which can go unrecognized by those who do not regularly use the room, one campus attached classroom evaluation forms to the semester grade sheets asking faculty to describe any problems with the room and to rate its effectiveness. A campus walk-through based on that feedback led to numbers of overhead projectors cleaned, loose floor tiles fixed, old furniture removed, wall switches replaced, banging radiators repaired, and more. Some classrooms had such glaring deficiencies that they needed to be taken off-line and reallocated to other use. The information was also used to make better matches of faculty pedagogy with classrooms.

The chief academic officer must help promote strategies that involve many in the care of the campus as all campuses have added space without being able to add the required maintenance funding. This is particularly important as a well-kept campus not only increases pride in the institution and a sense of shared responsibility but also reduces graffiti and wear and tear. When the CAO provides systematic oversight for academic facilities, faculty gain confidence that their needs are being attended to within the resources of the campus.

Maintaining Academic Space

- How might faculty share responsibility for maintaining their office space?
- How can classrooms be made more comfortable without adding to maintenance costs?
- Should there be limits on food and drink in the building or in the classrooms?
- What role could building liaisons with facilities management play in bringing small maintenance needs to their attention before they become serious problems?

- Can limited funds be used more effectively, if instead of doing a little in every room, a few spaces at a time are fully brought up to standards?

- How might efficiency increase if the registrar had responsibility for the classrooms and their furnishings and worked directly with the faculty users?

PRESERVING HISTORIC BUILDINGS

One of the most difficult decisions a campus faces is whether to retain an historic building by spending the large sums necessary to upgrade it or to tear it down. In recent years, there appears to be a shift in thinking toward saving interesting old buildings through renovation (Rosenberg and Adelman 2002, 20). The decision may be a practical choice or it may be motivated by the desire to preserve a campus landmark. Indeed, when one college lost its domed administration building in a fire, they argued persuasively for state support for full replacement to restore their identity even though it would be costly. The decision to pursue renovation for historical and emotional reasons is understandable; when a building is not a landmark, the decision is more difficult.

Architectural firms that specialize in the restoration, not just renovation, of old buildings recommend a systematic process to determine how realistic it is to consider adaptive use that preserves the original design. They note, "Many persons are easily misled by the visual quality or emotional appeal of older buildings. A good feasibility study can avoid costly mistakes" (McKinney, Missell, and Fisher 1994, 17). They identify two kinds of buildings that are likely candidates for restoration and renovation. Those built between 1800 and 1930 usually have solid construction with strong exterior walls, substantial load-bearing floors, and generous internal space. In addition, they are usually architecturally interesting and an historic feature of the campus. The second type of building, built during the rapid expansion of higher education between 1945 and 1975, is often less interesting in design and constructed with inexpensive materials.

It takes experts to evaluate whether a building can be renovated cost-effectively or should be replaced. Many public campuses find that renovation is their only choice due to limits on new construction funds. Certainly, the CAO should ensure that if renovation is the choice, it is a remodeling and not a "remuddling" effort. If faculty do not participate, they may find pillars in the middle of a classroom making the space structurally sound, but unsuitable for instruction.

Campuses with buildings on the National Register of Historic Places have particular obligations for preservation. Several campuses have been happily surprised to find stained-glass windows, beautiful arched ceilings, fine wood paneling, and original ceramic floor tiles underneath some of the carpet, wallboard, and dropped ceilings installed during previous renovations. Restoring a building to its original form is not just aesthetically pleasing but also re-establishes the heritage and founding academic values of the campus.

The community as well as the campus may be a candidate for historic preservation or rehabilitation. Several campuses, faced with student concerns about the lack of amenities and activities in the locality, have welcomed efforts of alumni and the community to invest in the town. Town residents more interested in recapturing historic significance than meeting student needs may be split on the importance of a local history museum versus a bagel shop. Even while resisting change, however, few want a town criticized for having no character. In some major cities, colleges and universities have been forceful partners in urban renewal rather than become islands in blighted neighborhoods.

Evaluating Renovation Projects

- What factors should determine whether a building is worth keeping?

- How are historical and architectural significance weighted against sentimental value?

- What criteria help decide on a major renovation for new use as opposed to merely making the building more attractive and usable?

- How will new use affect revenues? If it is a residence hall, will it be self-supporting?

- How much of the work can be done within the improvement budget? If additional funds are needed, is the project interesting enough to attract funds?

- What are some of the alternative design concepts that support the program/building fit?

- What is the expected outcome of the project? What is the new life of the building?

- Is the building suited for the institution's current goals as well as for future goals?

UPGRADING FACILITIES

Deciding between a major renovation that moves walls, changes the flow of students and faculty, and reconfigures space versus simply upgrading a building with floor coverings, paint, and improved utilities is not just a matter of cost. The untrained eye of the chief academic officer or faculty member may dream of opportunities that are not possible when engineers examine which walls are load bearing, the condition of the foundation, or any one of a number of aspects that may block a renovation. In that case, settling for new carpet, furnishings, or other cosmetic upgrades can make a welcome difference in atmosphere.

When renovation is possible and cost-effective, broad consultation with users is essential, especially if the building is to be reallocated to new users. Faced with limited funds or unable to reach consensus, some campuses have taken shortcuts and renovated parts of a building. When one floor is renovated for new use or a section redesigned, it is even more difficult in future years to create a unified concept for the building. One campus redesigned a single floor by taking out the central hall of the "egg-crate" design, placing service desks and lounges in a comfortable open space and locating the faculty offices on the outside walls. This design structurally blocked redesign of the floor below. Another campus, with the aim of preserving beautiful arched windows renovated only the central core and then found that planning for the entire building a few years later would require destroying what had just been renovated. Chief financial officers are often tempted to do piecemeal work because they can undertake small projects using maintenance reserve funds rather than seek approval for a capital project. If not linked to the overall plan for the campus and for academic affairs, the result of many such projects adds to the incoherent feeling of the campus environment.

Small projects do work well when they are self-contained single-purpose projects such as creating a coffee shop in the library, designing a technology lab in the psychology department, or developing an advising center for the business school. An efficient way for the users to be involved in the planning is to tour similar facilities on other campuses, discuss the strengths and weaknesses of various plans, and learn from others how best to match academic goals and facilities and integrate the new facility into the rest of the building. The facilities staff can then use its expertise in costing out the options and executing the selected plan.

Technology facilities are particularly challenging to design because they require special furniture and utilities while meeting the needs for group instruction as well as individual student use. A variety of furniture options and room arrangements can provide instructional flexibility and meet guidelines on lighting, sight lines, and ergonomics. One ingenious technology support manager, tasked with developing a new lab, designed several different room layouts, e-mailed them to potential users as well as administrators, and asked them to rank them and respond by e-mail. Within a week he had a good plan to be carefully reviewed in a face-to-face meeting. He saved hours of unnecessary discussion yet maximized input.

Although chief academic officers are not directly concerned with such issues as utilities capabilities or asbestos, they are concerned about disruption to programs if there is no swing space available during a renovation. It is particularly challenging to relocate programs with specialized facilities such as dance floors and chemistry labs. Disruption of a program for too long can have a depressing effect on both enrollments and faculty hiring. A few campuses have solved this problem by having one building designed simply as swing space to be used again and again as they renovate and redesign the campus continuously. Most campuses use a migration plan and do successive renovations.

One area where academic expertise should be tapped is in addressing Americans with Disabilities Act (ADA) compliance. While not particularly interested in the technical details of changing out doors, putting in ramps, creating fireproof safety rooms, and reworking bathrooms, faculty are interested in disabilities modifications as a clear statement about inclusiveness on a campus. Faculty especially need to be consulted for ideas on how to adapt labs, studios, residence hall rooms, and other specialized facilities, not just for the campus but to serve also as models for homes and businesses. Involving health and human services students and interior design students can help them appreciate the value of these modifications as well as bring their creativity to the problems.

Planning Special Projects

- What can be learned from other campuses with similar facilities?
- To what extent have all users been involved in the planning?

- What impact will the special project have on contiguous space?
- How might the facility be designed to accommodate future changes in equipment or increases in student use?
- What types of projects can attract a donor or be sustained through user fees?
- Does the facility require any special supervision or support from other divisions of the campus (e.g., food service or technology)?

PLANNING A NEW BUILDING

Nothing is more exciting, or more frustrating, than having the opportunity to design a building for a specific purpose such as a new science building or a cultural arts center. Whether funded by a private donor, a state initiative, or bonds, there will never be enough money to meet the dreams of all those who will plan the building. As one CAO wryly noted when conducting a tour of the new library that had been scaled back to be affordable, "This building has something to make everyone mad!" Nonetheless, the first step in planning is to begin with the dreams, visions, and goals of all who will use and benefit from the building before setting practical limits.

Designing a building is much like designing a new general education curriculum—goals will be set, alternatives will be proposed, choices will be made, and compromise will be necessary. Some choices are easier to make than others. Faculty can see the wisdom of foregoing special design features such as clock towers and glass bricks in order to have funds for multimedia rooms. What is different about designing and building a facility is the sheer number of choices to be made, the dizzying array of possibilities, and the wide varieties in taste.

One strategy for getting the dreams on the table is to have all who have a stake in the building prepare written "wish lists." Business faculty may request tiered classrooms, U-shaped seminar rooms, alumni lounges, and technology in offices, labs, and classrooms. Arts faculty will want high ceilings for dance studios, special acoustics, varied performance spaces, and special lighting labs. Science faculty will require water and gas hookups, safety showers, dedicated faculty research lab space, and low-static-electricity facilities for special equipment. No matter how accomplished the planners, architects, and facilities managers are, they simply do not have the expertise to make the decisions without the input from faculty and students. The selection of architects should be based on their experience with academic facilities and their willingness to make available research on how space impacts interaction. For example, studies show a relationship among building configuration, circulation patterns, informal communication, idea generation, and faculty productivity (Serrato 2002).

To reduce anxiety and dissatisfaction with the process, the project coordinator will want to keep careful records of how decisions were successively made after the initial inventory of ideas. Even after all the choices are made and the design comes back for initial review, the CAO will be stunned to find how difficult it is to keep people from measuring space to see if they got their share, to keep people from labeling spaces for single usage rather than as shared space, and to negotiate with those who continue to argue for a special interest that is not reflected in the final compromise plan. The CAO plays a crucial role in reducing costs by encouraging shared spaces, for example, conference rooms and storage areas—a recommendation architects are reluctant to make to faculty.

Delays for contentious deliberation by faculty discourage facilities planners from consultation. Observers warn, "An architect who has little direct experience working in an academic setting may underestimate the amount of review time required by academic clients" (Kiil and Brandt 1990, 57). It takes patience to refocus attention on all the preliminary decisions, to revisit them briefly to be sure they turned out as expected, and then to move on. If academics want to keep their place at the table, however, they need to respond to the professional planners in a timely way. Use of project management software can keep everyone on track and aware of when windows for change close and the next stage begins.

Once the dreams are turned into plans, the bids come in, the plans are harmonized with the realities of funding, and the building is underway. Even then the CAO and other academic administrators cannot sit by and wait for the building to be completed. Planning the way in which the building will be used is primarily up to the occupants, and they face many decisions. Will there be bulletin boards in the halls? Who will schedule the common spaces? What kind of signage is appropriate? Will graduate students have keys to the building? Must all faculty have harmonizing furniture so it can move anyplace in the building or can they choose to furnish as they wish? The answers to these questions are not nearly as important as the way in which the answers are reached. The habits that are first established will affect the long-term culture of the building. If units that had no previous relationship are co-located, time must be spent getting to know one another, or the opportunities for collaboration and intellectual community will be lost.

The academic administrator and committee charged with overseeing the project will also need to keep a close watch on the final finishing of the building. Electricians without guidance may orient the front of the room so that students pass in front of the teacher. Similarly, tile layers, faced only with boxes of gray floor tile instead of the expected beige tile, may decide to disregard the final effect because they have a deadline to meet. The decorator may think color coding the doors in the new science building is a helpful guide, with blue for offices, purple for classrooms, and green for labs, yet because the facilities are intermixed on a single hall, the final effect may not be at all pleasing to the occupants.

Anyone who has built a new home knows the level of oversight required to turn the plans into reality and the importance of solving unexpected problems as they come up. One campus appointed a staff person to be the electronic point person to manage the concerns of faculty from six different units as concerns about the new building were raised. In this way, communication with the facilities staff could be limited to one integrated memo a week, replacing what might have been numerous daily complaining phone calls. In the end, one academic administrator must be identified as the final arbiter to work with the project coordinator from the facilities staff and make daily walks through the building to determine where corrections need to be made while also recognizing that not everything will match expectations.

Finally, the building opens and is dedicated with all the usual fanfare. The chief academic officer, recognizing the importance of an inclusive culture, should encourage celebration of the new building with a year-long series of events to help others on campus take advantage of the new facility. In that way, others on campus will be less likely to be envious or indifferent and will understand the project as a contribution to institutional progress. The academic administrator also has a responsibility to provide appropriate thanks to all those who made the project possible while also creating pride in the staff who will maintain it. One dean ordered monogrammed shirts for the faculty, staff, and maintenance staff to give them community identity. A department chair hosted monthly lunches for the several departments sharing the building. Creating a sense of community where there was none is not an insignificant task, nor is it one to be left to its own making. Ceremony and symbolic acts are part of creating the new culture and norms.

Designing a New Facility

- How will faculty and staff input be gathered and synthesized?
- In what ways will the facility reflect future needs, rather than address old concerns?

- Who will manage the academic interests and be point person with the overall coordinator of the building project?
- After the building is accepted, when does the academic coordinator sign off?
- Who will be responsible for establishing the new culture, managing the many small decisions about how to live in the building, and monitoring ongoing success?

THE HIGH PRICE OF SPACE

Built-in inefficiencies, due to three-day faculty schedules, classes bunched in the middle of the day, and virtually empty campuses in the summer, make managing the physical plant particularly challenging. While other institutions can establish metrics such as a bed occupancy rate of 90 percent for hospitals or 70 percent for hotels, the efficiency of classroom space may well be as low as 30 percent (Corbett 1998, 81). Public campuses must report on space utilization and legislators are increasingly reluctant to build additional infrastructure, noting that technology has changed and can further change the way students access higher education. Since the possibilities for the future are unknown, what appears to be stinginess may be good advance planning. Space utilization studies can help the chief academic officer understand where there are opportunities to increase efficiency and respond to changing demands.

All campuses recognize that unused facilities are expensive and develop activities and programs to increase utilization. They rent classrooms, auditoriums, theaters, recreation facilities, and chapels; open the cafeterias and libraries to the public; and create auxiliary enterprises such as amusement arcades and vending machines in unused spaces such as tunnels and hallways. Many campuses are also involved in commercial enterprises, including hotels, conference centers, and corporate research parks. Whether these many enterprises serve merely to prop up the budget or also contribute to the academic enterprise depends upon the degree of collaboration across the divisions that sponsor the activities. Savvy campuses design these activities around key themes and have enhanced the identity of the campus, for example, as serving adults in retirement or providing opportunities for outstanding high school students. The chief academic officer needs to work collaboratively with the other divisions so that activities such as continuing education, management training, and summer activities can also support enrollment development, fund raising, and academic program opportunities.

Managing costs of space is difficult, as most academics treat offices, labs, conference rooms, and classrooms as a "free good" and are ready to claim that more is always better. Indeed, academic-space wars and the techniques faculty use to claim space, including squatters' rights, political negotiations between departments, and midnight raids on offices and furniture when a colleague retires, are part of campus lore. Just as information is power, faculty think of space as power or at least a symbol of their relative importance on the campus. Administrators, too, have used space for political purposes such as marginalizing a difficult person by moving their office or commandeering larger space believing it an essential statement about their position and status. The types of collaborative committees described earlier in the chapter have gone a long way toward reducing conflict, increasing responsibility, and appropriately allocating space. They are less likely to analyze space costs.

Rational economists suggest behavior would change if space costing were used and all units were charged rent based on operating expenses and maintenance costs of their space. Being charged for all space would put a different set of incentives for efficiency into play and encourage units to set priorities. Campuses that have instituted space-costing models do experience a freeing up of space as many departments determine they can give back underutilized space and reallocate the resources to higher priorities. When units are allocated space according to what they can pay for, however, those units that have the potential for generating funds, either from uses of their space or external funding, have an advantage.

One approach to managing classroom space more efficiently has been to move away from the model of distributing classrooms around the campus under the control of departments. Under that model, the amount of general classroom space declined over time because when there was a need the department simply converted a classroom to an office and asked to have their classes scheduled elsewhere. As it became more and more difficult to schedule the curriculum, campuses chose to build generic classroom buildings to be used by the entire campus. In this centralized model, classrooms are a variety of sizes, belong to the registrar, and have a target utilization rate around 60 to 70 percent (Winicur 1988). Since there are no faculty offices in these buildings, lounges for faculty and students to meet are needed as well as technology support staff offices and study areas. Chief academic officers recognize that while creating one type of efficiency, the downside of generic buildings is that no one feels ownership nor a commitment to taking care of the facility, and there is less informal interaction among faculty and students.

When the business affairs division is solely responsible for utility and fuel costs or increased wages for cleaning staff, faculty resent not being able to regulate the heat in their offices or the schedule for vacuuming their offices. If faculty see painting or carpeting in response to individual pressures to refurbish, they lose confidence in the facilities management process. Making units fully responsible for their space and facilities, however, is not something most CAOs desire. It appears that the iterative processes that link space use with planning, allocation, management, and costs are the best way for campuses to achieve the balance between effectiveness and efficiency.

Managing for Cost-Effectiveness

- How well do enrollments match plant capacity?
- How do regular space utilization studies inform planning?
- How often is the allocation of space adjusted to match changes in the academic program?
- Have faculty been asked to review the space allocated to their unit to make recommendations for efficiencies?
- To what extent can facilities such as mailrooms and lounges be shared?
- Which programs might increase the usage of facilities and return revenues to the campus?
- To what extent can facilities be partially supported by user fees?

CAMPUS BEAUTIFICATION AND THE GREEN CAMPUS

As faculty see the inside of buildings remain in need of upgrading, they often question the attention given to external repairs and campus beautification. Well aware that a well-manicured campus impacts student enrollment, they still question why the tulip bulbs are being replaced or curbs being repainted. When an unseasonable spring ice storm left one campus a mess one week before Admitted Student Visiting Day, the president called on all staff, students, faculty, and administrators to rake, sweep, saw, clean up, and plant in time for the students' visit. Everyone had such a good time, Campus Beautification Day was turned into a spring tradition that builds community and commitment to the environment.

Participants note how often they find themselves checking "their" plants, pulling a weed, or picking up a piece of paper as they daily cross campus.

Many campuses have allocated funds for outdoor sculpture, inviting benches, memorial gates, light-pole flags, and unique emblems and statuary in order to create focal points and a sense of pride in the campus. One president used his own funds to place an unlikely bronze sculpture of a hippopotamus on campus and encouraged students to rub its snout for good luck before exams. The bright shine after a few years is ample proof that students quickly adopted the tradition. Investment in the physical environment has payoffs ranging from increased enrollments to greater enjoyment.

Adopting the principles of the "green campus" movement has even greater payoffs, including cost containment, positive impact on the environment, and increased student awareness of the challenge of sustainability. Although deemed essential when campuses responded to the energy crisis decades ago, most campuses remain committed to increased efficiency in lighting, water use, heating, and air conditioning as well as to environmental programs such as recycling. A recent survey of college and university environmental practices gives campuses high marks for these programs but notes far less commitment to integrating environmental issues into the curriculum. Most campuses recycle aluminum and paper, 49 percent encourage environmentally sound purchasing, 69 percent have programs to reduce the need for paper hard copies, and 55 percent have exchange programs for computers, furniture, office supplies, and lab equipment (McIntosh, Cacciola, Clermont, and Keniry 2001). Roughly a third of campuses are restoring ecological landscapes with native plants and natural habitats for birds, butterflies, and wildlife.

Compared to the "greening" commitment in operations and facilities management, however, campuses fall short on making environmental awareness a feature of the academic program. Forty-three percent of campuses offer a major or a minor in environmental studies serving only a small number of students and "only 8 percent of campuses require all their students to take environmental studies courses regardless of their major" (McIntosh et al. 2001).

As social institutions with a commitment to improving the future, colleges and universities have a unique opportunity to demonstrate innovativeness and commitment in environmentally sound practices in the management of the physical environment of the campus while also encouraging students through formal study to carry the environmental responsibility ethic with them into their future endeavors. As cost containment is not the rationale for academic commitments to the environment, the chief academic officer interested in the environment will need to work directly with faculty and students to find the rationale that is persuasive enough to infuse academic activities with the broad environmental ethic that integrates social and economic issues with ecological issues.

Environmental Review of a Campus

- To what extent is the campus green space in harmony with the natural environment?

- To what extent is energy conservation taken into account when renovating and building facilities? Do commitments go beyond requirements?

- How well understood by the campus community are the environmental concepts that undergird the purchasing, utilities, and recycling programs?

- How might spaces be returned to their natural state and serve as an outdoor laboratory?

- Through which programs and forms of communication might students learn about sustainability, conservation, and environmental responsibility?

SUCCESSFUL ACADEMIC FACILITIES PLANNING

Although chief academic officers often find themselves initially interested in facilities planning as a defense against arguments and complaints, further reflection would suggest that rational planning can go a long way toward maintaining alignment of the environment with academic needs. By making single faculty offices a priority, more faculty can work on campus. By providing comfortable furniture and up-to-date equipment, students will experience a more professional learning environment. Through planning for a variety of classroom types, innovative pedagogies can be encouraged. When facilities are left in the hands of others who have different concerns, these academic priorities may not be served well.

Because facilities planning and management are complex, it is essential that the processes for communication and decision making are systematic and well understood. The chief business officer and facilities staff must respect the leadership role of the chief academic officer with students, faculty, and staff in establishing a positive learning environment. The most often voiced complaint from academic administrators is that they are cut out of many aspects of facilities planning and management from priority setting to actual planning. Apparently well meaning staff in business affairs may believe that going directly to individual faculty and students is the best way to get input. When they do so, they eliminate any hope of an integrated, coherent, and shared academic facilities plan. If self-interest is to be brought together with institutional interest, the CAO must be given not just an opportunity for input but authority with the rest of the campus administration to speak on behalf of academic affairs. The CAO is in the best position to understand real priorities, forestall political maneuvering, and optimize the use of scarce resources for academic priorities.

If the CAO is to claim a clear role in ensuring that facilities and space fit the changing nature of academic activities, the CAO must have a broad understanding of emerging needs. Whether by walking the campus, conducting an audit through the departments, seeking information directly from individual faculty members, or using any one of the many strategies described throughout the chapter, the CAO will keep current on the strengths and shortcomings of the campus environment. The CAO can then rely on deans and department chairs for tapping the creative ideas of users, condensing information, suggesting priorities, and harmonizing competing interests. Campuses that fail to establish respected goals, roles, and procedures often rely on a "space czar" who is constantly embattled and, in either failing to consult or trying to make everyone happy, ends up pleasing no one. When administrators work together to gather information, create consensus on priorities, and prepare short-term and long-range plans, they make it possible for those charged with direct responsibility for the physical environment to do so in support of institutional excellence.

CHAPTER 4

Technology Integration:
Improving Learning and
Productivity

An advertisement from a technology consultant noted, "The five biggest problems in higher education information technology today are uncontrolled costs, unclear benefits, unstable infrastructure, unproductive information systems, and unhappy users" (*University Business* 2001, 61). At the end of this list was the simple assurance: "We can help." Although a consultant could help, the majority of campuses manage on their own. To do so requires effective campus leadership from administrators who understand information technology (IT), its applications, and its costs.

Despite widespread use of technology in teaching, research, and management coupled with higher education's commitment to institutional improvement and innovation, most chief academic officers (CAOs) face difficult decisions that require not just their expertise on academic matters but also increased expertise about technology. Yet, few CAOs are confident about their knowledge. Inundated by reports on the macro trends that argue that technology has changed the learning process and may well eliminate separate campuses and faculty centered curricula (Twigg 1995; Massy and Wilger 1998), many CAOs have difficulty determining the exact context in which they must manage technology applications on a single campus. Surrounded by advertisements for the latest hardware, software, and training options, these administrators feel an urgency to respond or risk being left behind. Questioned by parents, students, legislators, employers, and board members about technology capabilities and costs, CAOs become defensive when they do not fully understand the campus information technology capacity.

To gain greater confidence, chief academic officers are learning more about technology, what questions to ask of those with expertise, and how to implement a systematic approach to making effective IT decisions. Most CAOs will never be able to talk comfortably about plug ins, portals, security patches, or network routers. Thus on the majority of campuses, technology planning and resource allocation will remain primarily under the purview of the business area and the IT staff. Yet these nonacademic administrators are handicapped by little or no knowledge of issues such as pedagogy, curriculum development, and academic management needs. This bifurcated situation of two divisions with different expertise, different authority, and often separate budgets may have been viable in 1980 or even 1990 when the pace of change was more an evolution than a revolution. Today, however, chief academic officers who take a hands-off approach and defer to those with specialized technology knowledge, but not academic knowledge, lose the opportunity to provide essential leadership that is responsive to changing academic needs.

Higher education functions in a dynamic environment demanding flexibility and openness to new knowledge, skills, and strategies about information technology. All areas of a campus now rely on technology, including student affairs (e.g., admissions and registration), business affairs (e.g., personnel and capital planning), advancement (e.g., alumni records and donor prospecting), and academic affairs (e.g., research and extended campus programs). Observers confirm that most campuses are not keeping pace with other organizations, noting, "While the 'information revolution' has already transformed, eliminated, and created industries throughout the world, it has only scratched the surface of higher education" (Epper and Bates 2001, 2). To guide the further integration of information technologies requires creating a partnership among all administrators and engaging the right groups in planning so that user needs, infrastructure, and costs are systematically addressed.

Clearly, if the very administrators in a position to provide leadership are intimidated or lack crucial information, collaboration will be limited and progress slowed. This chapter aims to provide CAOs with the perspective and questions necessary to participate in addressing specific technology challenges, including planning, financing, organization, and training. In addition, it describes the accumulating wisdom about faculty involvement, improved learning, student technology competencies, and academic management applications. To begin to achieve the greater effectiveness and efficiency that new technologies promise requires that academic leaders learn from the experience of others as they face the myriad decisions related to fuller integration of technology into academic affairs. Understanding how widespread some of the challenges are can also be reassuring.

STRENGTHENING INSTITUTIONAL OPPORTUNITIES WITH TECHNOLOGY

Noting that the use of technology is now irreversible, Kenneth C. Green, director of the Campus Computing Project, warns, "As campus computing makes the transition from unique to ubiquitous, the 'right' decision is a moving target, less dependent on technology and more on strategy, mission, and niche" (Green 1996a, 5). Technology is so mesmerizing, new developments can divert energies and distract efforts from the central institutional focus, and technology enthusiasts can argue for more capacity than the campus needs. Thus, not only must CAOs evaluate the need for change but also assess the impact of new technologies in terms of other institutional and academic priorities expressed in the campus strategic plan.

Currently, academic applications of technology range across a broad spectrum from campuses limited to using technology to enhance traditional modes of instruction to the founding of wholly new virtual institutions. The applications can be classified in five major categories: minor changes (e.g., institutions moving from in-person registration to Web-based registration), major changes (e.g., institutions moving from the traditional supplier-client access to institutional data to data warehousing accessible to the entire university administration), step changes (e.g., institutions moving from a classroom format to asynchronous Web-based individualized learning), platform changes (e.g., institutions moving from face-to-face instruction to desktop delivery of live video-streaming lectures), and nascency (e.g., institutions creating new noncampus based approaches to education).

Institutions can also be categorized by the speed at which they adopt new technologies. Based on campus reports as well as on the diffusion of innovation theory, the rate at which campuses adopt information technology follows a bell-shaped curve over time (Rogers 1995, 243). About 3 percent of campuses are truly innovative and are the first to either create or adopt new educational technologies. These innovators are able and willing to take risks and incur higher costs in advancing technology utilization. Another group of institutions may not be the first, but are a close second in utilizing educational technologies. These campuses, less than 15 percent, follow the lead of lessons learned by the innovative campuses and try to avoid their mistakes. While costs are still high, some risks are reduced. The third group of institutions is more deliberate and takes a wait-and-see approach guided by detailed cost-benefit and value added analyses. This group, 35 to 65 percent of all campuses, often waits for technology costs to decrease before advancing. The final group of institutions may see insufficient advantages to changing the way academic business and student learning occur. These campuses will eventually adopt new technologies, but by the time they do, newer technologies will have already begun being widely utilized. This same process of diffusion takes place among the faculty on a single campus (Massy and Wilger 1998, 51).

To some extent the range of applications and the speed of adoption are directly linked to institutional mission as well as resources. Typically, community colleges need to emphasize up-to-date workforce training in technical fields. Comprehensive institutions may integrate technology applications into professional academic programs to meet accreditation requirements. Research universities stress both the development of new technologies and the application of technology to support research. Liberal arts campuses may emphasize integrating technology competencies into general education requirements as a foundation skill. Not all campuses are engaged in the same kind of change or in dramatic change.

Buffeted by market forces, all institutions need to consider new opportunities, new products, new programs, new sites, new students, and new services in order to remain competitive with their peers as well as the for-profit companies. The chief academic officer may feel unprepared for this highly entrepreneurial environment and be tempted to avoid what is somewhat puzzling. As change is inevitable, CAOs need to participate in technology discussions so that decisions are consistent with the academic goals and the institutional mission. A campus can then undertake new ventures, such as becoming a laptop campus, while avoiding being stampeded into areas that are not consistent with the mission and the students served. Technology goals must match the character and capacity of the campus. Sometimes being behind the curve is exactly where a campus should be.

At a minimum, all campuses need to use technology to improve student services in order to remain competitive. Students expect to search for colleges and apply for admission to a college electronically. Even the most traditional campus must market academics bundled with a broad range of services including cable television in residence halls, on-line résumé services through the career center, and complex Web sites so that students can walk the campus from their own computer to access advising, register for classes, order books, conduct library research, and access their grades. Comfortable with varied commercial on-line transactions, students assume the same convenience for campus services. They expect Web-based access, immediate response, and transparent staffing for all hours of the day. E-education and e-learning demand that higher education reexamine the assumptions it makes about students and alter the way it does business.

Student expectations are also a force driving curriculum change and degree requirements. Increased access and increased cost of higher education have created a more sophisticated consumer with less commitment to a single product or a single campus. Students can collect credits in many ways and orchestrate not just the kind of education they receive but also the price. In this environment, CAOs must be prepared to evaluate transferability of on-line course credits and consider moving into the arena of Web-based courses consistent with their institutions' values. Further, they must weigh the extent to which their academic offerings should be shaped by employer expectations or economic development needs. Many of these decisions will be based on business considerations as well as academic criteria.

Chief academic officers can neither go it alone in this dynamic environment nor depend on other campus administrators to guide academic applications. Nor can curriculum development and faculty development be left solely to individual faculty initiative as it has been in the past. Similarly, facilities planning and hardware standards cannot be left to business affairs. New forms of collaboration in decision making need to be established if opportunities are to be evaluated to fit academic needs and institutional capacity. Because each campus has its own culture, chief academic officers must be especially sensitive to faculty attitudes about technology. Indeed, a national survey confirmed that "keeping up with information technology" is among the leading stressors in faculty lives (Sax, Astin, Korn, and Gilmartin 1999). Although CAOs may feel a sense of urgency about the prospects for change, they must patiently build productive alliances and engage the campus community in careful discussions focused on the role technology will play in helping to design and achieve the future of the institution. In short, the integration of technology is dependent upon the shared academic vision held by the CAO and the faculty and endorsed by the campus administration.

Responding to New Opportunities

- How open is the campus to new products, new services, and new relationships?
- In the future, who will be the students and the target market?
- What varieties of pedagogy and delivery systems will be supported?
- Will the institution compete as a deliverer of distributed learning or be an importer to enrich curricular offerings?
- What expectations does the campus have for faculty use of technology?
- What models of improved efficiency and effectiveness of learning through technology are compelling to the campus?
- How will technology improve academic management?
- How will technology increase campuswide access to information to support decisions?
- How will technology deliver more academic services to students?

STRATEGIC PLANNING FOR TECHNOLOGY INTEGRATION

Planning creates the foundation for change in higher education; thus technology should be infused in many elements of an institution's strategic plan, including facilities, management, and instruction. In addition, campuses need a separate, but congruent, fully developed technology strategic plan. The Campus Computing Survey showed that, in 1996, 43.4 percent of campuses had such a plan (Green 1996b), and by 2000, 65.8 percent had a technology plan (Green 2000). Monitoring the gap between the plan and reality requires continuous attention, and it is particularly challenging given how fast technology changes. Even with inadequate planning, colleges and universities are changing their academic programs, services, and management. Although the process may not be as orderly as desired, student access, multimedia centers, smart classrooms, and technologically capable faculty are increasingly the norm.

A technology plan is no guarantee that the five problems identified at the beginning of the chapter will not emerge because, too often, the plan is based on unrealistic expectations or untested assumptions, for example, technology will save money, allow campuses to expand capacity, and improve learning (Frances, Pumerantz, and Caplan 1999). Most CAOs will admit to a nagging suspicion that they are not fully achieving the results expected from the investments they have made. To some extent, the fault may lie in not having a clear understanding of the goals to be achieved. More important, few technology plans include a systematic process for evaluating results and continuously revising and funding the plan. Finally, however, the most significant challenge is providing enough training and user support to realize the potential of the technology plan (Green 2001).

The accelerating pace of change, as well as imperfect information, makes both short-term and long-term technology planning and progress particularly difficult. On many campuses, more change has occurred in the last three years than in the previous decade. Continuously integrating technology requires CAOs to rethink their timelines for decision making and their styles of leadership. Intermittent attention and the slow committee-based deliberations, appropriate to many academic issues, are ill-suited to managing technology where advances occur in months, not years. At the same time, although prescriptive rather than participative decision making may be more fast paced, it would not suit faculty who want a say in matters that affect them directly.

To ensure support for institutional technology plans, most campuses involve students, faculty, staff, and administrators in the planning process and welcome perspectives from individuals with all levels of technology use and competence. When a broad-based effort, the technology plan may well be a compromise and essentially endorse already accepted modes of teaching, learning, and academic activities. In contrast, a future-oriented plan will result when the most imaginative thinkers and boldest users are involved. That result will be far more challenging and uncomfortable as it will reflect new perspectives on academic life, faculty roles, and delivery of instruction. In either case, the plan must be comprehensive and include issues as diverse as organization, networks, site licenses, intellectual property, acquisition, student fees, user support, electronic commerce, and personnel. Of particular interest to faculty are such matters as incentives, training, workload, and tenure guidelines. Because of the range of issues, technology plans are often written in segments by work groups with specialized knowledge but guided by a steering committee to bring coherence.

Even with conscientious planning, a disconnect between the technology plan and faculty readiness can occur if planning is guided primarily by IT experts who are unaware of the pattern of diffusion of innovations, particularly within the academic context. Just as with other academic innovations, there are lead users who readily adopt new technologies. IT professionals who interact only with the lead faculty may be convinced that everyone is ready for the entire portfolio of emerging technologies. When other faculty move more slowly, IT professionals may wonder what is wrong. Although the diffusion of technology within academia is moving faster than other innovations, those guiding the process must still be sensitive to the timing of adoption of applications, recognize the multiple stages of usage, acknowledge the reality of plateaus, and have a feel for how planning is both the push for change and the response to change.

One tension to be resolved with faculty is whether IT is in service to the current goals and processes of the institution or whether technology is the driving force for innovation in the learning process and academic services. A review of plans posted on campus Web sites suggests that on most campuses both purposes are being served simultaneously as faculty come to terms with the degree to which face-to-face activities should be supplemented or replaced. Although faculty have a role, most campuses believe it is up to the administration to set the direction for technology integration. Systematic planning, agreed upon goals, centralized coordination, and institutionalized change are essential if a campus is to realize significant institutional benefits connected to campus priorities, rather than just individual benefits, from investments in technology (Massy and Wilger 1998, 51; Golden and Kahn, 1998). Whereas once campuses were content to support individuals with specialized interests and innovative ideas and allow considerable decentralization, such an idiosyncratic approach is no longer manageable nor affordable for most institutions.

Developing a Strategic Technology Plan

- How will the campus be involved in the environmental scan, recognition of guiding assumptions, and identification of the goals of the plan (e.g., task force, standing committee, or survey of stakeholders)?

- What areas are to be included in the technology plan and how are they related to the university strategic plan and mission?

- What academic applications are specified in the objectives (e.g., student competencies, instructional methods, and research applications)?

- What administrative applications are included (e.g., separate systems and subsystems or integrated management information system)?

- Who sets the standards for creating and maintaining the infrastructure?

- Who supervises the organization of academic and administrative computing (e.g., business affairs, shared administration, or governance committee)?

- How are training goals for faculty and staff determined and supported (e.g., required competencies, on-line services, and workshops)?
- How is the authority for decision making shared across units?
- How is the plan costed out and budget support shared?
- How are new applications integrated into the plan (e.g., wireless networks, course management systems, and e-commerce applications)?
- How is the plan evaluated and updated?

FUNDING THE TECHNOLOGY PLAN

Realistic technology planning and integration requires understanding the cost implications and preparing a financial strategy to support the plan. Just as with the institution's strategic plan, if no budget model is linked to the technology plan, the goals may not be realized. Unfortunately, it is difficult for campuses to predict the costs of technology, upgrades, and support services (Oberlin 1996). Indeed, many CAOs suspect technology could be a bottomless pit. The percentage of the total budget allocated to technology has been significant on most campuses, yet campuses still report technology remains underfunded and the allocation to academic computing, especially for IT staff, is not keeping pace with needs (Green 2001). Funding will increasingly be a concern because "after a seven year cycle in which campus technology budgets increased dramatically," many campuses have hit a downturn mirroring the decline in technology investment across all sectors of the economy (Green 2001).

Novices in analyzing the planning and financing of technology will find help from resources such as EDUCAUSE (www.educause.edu) but will find that there is difficulty, if not reluctance, on the part of campus administrators, especially chief information officers, to identify full costs. Nonetheless, one longtime director of finance and planning for information technology notes, "Developing rational and viable financial strategies to accommodate technological change is an institutional imperative for effective information technology management" (Oberlin 1996, 10). His observations are still timely: "The fundamental forces driving the economics of information technology are: 1) the value of information technology is steadily increasing; 2) the demand for technology by institutions, faculty, and students is growing dramatically; 3) the acquisition price per unit of computing power is rapidly declining; and 4) the total cost of owning and maintaining technology is constantly increasing" (Oberlin 1996, 10).

The primary reason that budgeting and planning for technology have not been well linked is that technology has been treated, too often, as a one-time expense when it is a recurring cost and should be based on life-cycle assumptions. Only about half of all campuses have a financial plan for technology and rely instead on capturing resources as they can (Green 2001). Standard practice on many campuses is to acquire computers, software, and servers out of end-of-the-year funds or "budget dust" from many budget lines (Green and Jenkins 1998, 33). This has the effect of both constantly expanding capacity, with no operating budget for personnel or replacement, as well as confusing the total expenditure picture.

Even when there is an operating budget plan, the assumptions upon which it is established may not hold up. For example, the campus may have adopted a four-year replacement cycle yet find that a two-year cycle is more appropriate for certain programs in which students expect the program facilities and software to meet industry standards. Alternatively, through conscientious planning the useful life of a computer can be lengthened by a midcycle upgrade, thus harmonizing both user needs and budget capacity. Similarly, the campus may have converted classrooms for multimedia but failed to recognize the need for user support. Shifting dollars to personnel would increase the benefits of the hardware investment. CAOs need to be prepared to work with administrative colleagues to make midcourse adjustments in both plans and investments in order to optimize results.

With constrained resources as well as critics who question the efficacy of technology as a medium of instruction or vehicle for increased productivity, the chief academic officer must be able to not just cost out alternatives before making commitments but also be able to measure benefits. If technology remains an "add-on" and does not change productivity, a campus can neither justify nor sustain a continuing investment. Academic administrators may once have argued for continuous increases in technology funding because of fears of being left behind, but with good information, CAOs can be more judicious, evaluate opportunities, and encourage implementation of promising practices. Although it is difficult to do a full cost-benefit analysis of information technologies, the categories of benefits to be considered include enrollment, retention, learning outcomes, individualization of instruction, expansion of the curriculum, new faculty research, economic development, and reduction in physical plant needs (Norris and MacDonald 1993; Van Dusen 1997, 101–6).

Determining the actual dollar return on the results of technology is complicated by the need for a multiyear analysis. The payoff for an investment may not be realized in the same time frame as the expense.

Costs must be aligned to determine whether capitalization is sufficient to carry the initiative in its initial years and whether the eventual return is worth the investment. Although anticipating costs is difficult, the basic categories include: networks, hardware, software, maintenance, technical support, workstations per capita, classrooms, licenses, physical improvements, and consultants. Some items should be booked as continuing expenses and others as capital expenses. Budget worksheets can be used either by inputting the elements and adding up the cost or starting with the budget limit and working the equations backward (Green and Jenkins 1998, 36–37). However, not all costs and benefits can be easily measured in dollars.

Promising significant savings, creating unrealistic expectations when adopting new standards, or yielding to individual pressures to ignore institutional priorities in order to respond to special needs are as costly as having no funding plan. A murky budget picture and unrealized goals can lead to unexpected costs, to failures of confidence, and inevitably, to resistance to additional investments. One spill-over phenomenon of inadequate financial planning is that when central budgets are insufficient, colleges and departments are expected to contribute a share to the operation. Since the standard practice on many campuses is incremental budgeting, this reallocation effectively decreases expenditures on other priorities. Over time, this decentralization also masks the actual campus technology costs. To get a clearer picture of total costs, the chief academic officer could adapt the model of activity-based costing and restructure the operating budget to isolate aspects of integrating technology such as program development, instructional design, faculty training, or student services, rather than around units such as biology or the library.

To plan and manage operating budgets to sufficiently support technology requires rethinking standard budgeting principles and developing new approaches to analyzing fundamentals including asset management, amortization schedules, labor/capital ratios, marginal costs, unit costs, and total costs (Green and Jenkins 1998). In addition, administrators need to determine sources of funding, expected return on investment, and how technology initiatives fit into the overall picture of campus revenues. Many campuses, with varying degrees of success, have outsourced some functions such as repair and maintenance to achieve efficiencies. Others have used consultants as strategic investments in better management of IT resources. Leasing arrangements have appeal because they avoid large one-time expenditures and distribute costs annually. However, each of these can reduce control and flexibility.

At the same time institutions are conscientiously planning, selecting, funding, and implementing new opportunities, CAOs should also be seeking some risk capital where the return on investment may not be immediately realized. Obviously, it is far easier to experiment with new money than to determine what to stop doing in order to reallocate resources. Many institutions have benefited from external funding for technology through grants and bond measures. Students are routinely assessed a technology fee; however, if the fee is too high, students and parents rebel, arguing that they already pay a high tuition and expect to get Internet access, up-to-date labs, and support services at no additional charge. More and more campuses are making the hard decision to charge for services such as printing in order to contain costs. This taxation model may cover some costs or ensure a steady stream of funds for upgrades and replacement, but it has its limits for generating significant funding for new initiatives.

In the final analysis, chief academic officers need to work closely with business affairs and IT officers to reevaluate the budget needed to effect the technology plan with appropriate emphasis on academic applications. After so many years of experience with changing technologies, it is not defensible to take a haphazard approach, using end-of-year funds or department and student assessments, nor is it acceptable to maintain that it is too difficult to identify the total costs of technology. When costs must be contained by limiting printing, bandwidth, or free dial-up modem service, for example, CAOs must be consulted. The quality of academic programs and academic productivity relies on dependable technology support.

Analyzing Budget Implications

- What are the initial costs for hardware, software, and multimedia equipment as well as for upgrades?
- How is asset management planned for?
- What replacement cycle is optimal? affordable? appropriate to different needs?
- What are the expected benefits? How will productivity increase? Will increased effectiveness impact revenues such as through retention?
- What savings can be realized from increased administrative productivity?
- What efficiencies can be achieved through setting standards for procurement of technology products?

- What efficiencies in training and repair can be achieved by making hardware, software, and multimedia equipment compatible among all department and colleges?

- What share, if any, should units bear of the costs of training and system maintenance?

- What savings can be achieved through outsourcing? What factors need to be considered to make the relationship beneficial?

- What percentage of the computing capacity is being effectively used?

TRAINING FACULTY AND STAFF

While the integration of technology is clearly a priority in education, astute observers claim that technology has been oversold and underutilized; indeed there is evidence of declining use among once enthusiastic faculty (Cuban 2001). Campus conversations often estimate usage at as low as 15 percent of campus IT capacity although that does not appear to slow the demand for more and more powerful computers. The linchpin in widespread and effective integration of technology is training; however, because the industry moves faster than individual learning ever can, the gap will not be closed. Training can increase the pace of diffusion, enable individuals to make the right choices about technology use, and encourage continuous development of technology competence.

The same technology plan that provides for a computer on every faculty member's desk, software upgrades, and multimedia support centers must also address adequate support personnel for training and application development. Training and help on a just-in-time model appear to have more payoff than scheduled workshops. Individualized training with readily recognized payoff encourages development of skills. Support staff often have more opportunities than faculty to see the immediate results from their training as they apply new features of Word or desktop publishing to their daily work. For faculty, the results of PowerPoint, WebCT, or other applications to teaching are not always so evident. In any case, CAOs need to understand that both faculty and staff must significantly reorient their time in order to learn, practice, and adopt new technology skills.

When faculty development was first initiated three decades ago, academic administrators asked whether the program should be mandatory or voluntary. Primarily focused on teaching improvement for ineffective faculty, chief academic officers soon recognized that the programs could not make someone become a better teacher as faculty have the prerogative to ignore good advice. Faculty development for technology is now in a new role, however, where demand is great and campuses are challenged to keep up and create a coherent training program. Among the successful mandatory strategies that complement voluntary workshops are multi-level training that is provided when a faculty member gets a new computer; unitwide training to ensure minimum competency; focused training to meet requirements of specialized accreditation, such as National Council for Accreditation of Teacher Education (NCATE); and training required in order to use a technology classroom. The chief academic officer needs to find sufficient resources and incentives to support training or risk underutilization of technology.

To facilitate the integration of technology for teaching, and not just as a personal productivity tool, requires more than faculty development opportunities. Chief academic officers must encourage faculty leadership, reduce barriers to adoption, and support a campus culture that reinforces new approaches to the teaching/learning process. A recent book, *Teaching Faculty How to Use Technology: Best Practices from Leading Institutions* (Epper and Bates 2001) provides seven in-depth case studies revealing a number of themes leading to success. Technology adoption is facilitated, for example, by an administrator-supported institutional plan for technology, a high level of faculty ownership, comprehensive support systems for both faculty and students, and collaboration between faculty on actual teaching projects. CAOs can also provide incentives such as course releases or stipends for faculty to serve as consultants to colleagues.

As more and more faculty discover what technology can do, CAOs need good information on the degree to which faculty continue to teach as they have, but with technology enhancements, and the degree to which technology is constructing new modes of teaching and learning. Promoting a culture of experimentation results in both more use and greater diversity in applications (Hagner 2000, 27). At some point, the CAO must decide the extent to which variation can be fully supported. Just establishing a single classroom platform or limiting supported hardware and software can lead to heated faculty discussions. Over time, however, most campuses have recognized that they must resist the unmanageable variation that comes from bottom-up technology decision making and establish institutional norms in order to control costs and increase efficiency. Careful management need not stifle faculty innovation.

The assistance needed by faculty requires collaboration among several campus resources, including academic computing for technical expertise, programming, and network administration; the teaching development center for instructional design, pedagogy, and administration of a small incentive grants program; and the library for multimedia development and audiovisual support. Of particular interest to the chief academic officer are the financial underpinnings of these services and the relative costs of developing faculty expertise as opposed to making expertise available to faculty.

Despite widespread use of technology tools, only a fraction of faculty on every campus are deeply involved, and few campuses meet the definition of truly "transformed" education (Massy and Wilger 1998, 53–54). Even as more and more faculty are willing to experiment, others make only minimal changes. Many faculty report that keeping up with technology is difficult, and for some "not worth it." To reduce the possibility of creating a polarized faculty in terms of their outlook on technology and their skill levels, the CAO needs to walk a fine line between offering training and establishing incentives and between setting expectations and redefining evaluation criteria. Most faculty will use technology to supplement teaching materials and approaches, rather than have technology take their place.

Intriguing new questions have arisen about how to count teaching with technology in evaluation, tenure, and promotion decisions. Is the use of technology merely an alternative pedagogy or a genuine teaching improvement? Is it a new form of scholarship that produces new knowledge about learning? If the campus supports the work with a small grant or release time, is there a greater obligation for positive results? If the students do not give positive evaluations to the transformed course, is the faculty member penalized? If course materials such as a CD-ROM are peer reviewed does that make them more valued? What on-campus presence is required when teaching on-line or advising by e-mail? To answer the many questions, administrators and faculty will need to focus on learning and faculty productivity, not on technology.

Opportunities for Faculty and Staff Development

- How should technology training be included in orientation and support for new faculty and staff?
- To what extent are the strategies to meet individual needs scalable to institution-wide use?
- How can faculty and staff be given training options that meet various learning styles (e.g., on-line support, newsletters, staff support, workshops, and courses)?

- How much funding and support is provided for experimentation (e.g., through a faculty resources center, group work, team support, and release time for full-time faculty to support colleagues)?

- When a new high-tech facility opens, how might technical assistance staff be made available to support the creation of a new culture?

- Should there be campuswide curriculum design standards linked to technology competencies required of all students?

- What changes in formal expectations for evaluation, tenure, and promotion review are needed to reflect work on technology applications in teaching and scholarship?

- To what extent should position descriptions for staff reflect increased expectations for technology skills?

IMPROVING ON-CAMPUS INSTRUCTION

To ensure the fullest benefit of information technologies, chief academic officers must be persuasive spokespersons for an innovative environment that is supportive of technology not merely for enrichment but as an opportunity to effect a paradigm shift in ideas about teaching and learning (Massy and Wilger 1998, 50). As more and more faculty adapt technology to their teaching needs and weigh the time it takes to revise their courses, they appropriately ask about evidence that technology significantly enhances learning. The research data are not fully persuasive (Frances, Pumerantz, and Caplan 1999, 32–33; Jarmon 2002). Some research shows decreased failures and course withdrawals, perhaps due to frequent assessment. Some data suggest students are more engaged and involved in their learning when they manage the pace and selection of activities. Some data suggest that adults, rather than traditional age students, choose "consumer friendly" and "teacherless education" (Feenberg 1999, 4). A review of some 350 studies of distance courses suggests that "the instructional medium does not seem to make a difference," but rather it is "the design of the syllabus, the skill of the teacher, and the motivation of the students" that produces learning (Association of American Colleges and Universities 1999). Clearly, technology is not a substitute for good teaching, but rather a tool to create more powerful models of pedagogy that increase student engagement and student learning.

No matter what interest level faculty have in technology, they all recognize that technology has created a more discerning consumer. Raised on television and movies, students are no longer content with chalk and talk. They want color, sound, movement, and readily accessible class

notes. Used well, technology-mediated instruction can be highly inter-
active, engaging, and adaptable to different learning styles. By putting
students directly in touch with information and applications, technology
changes the teacher's role from authority to selector, guide, and co-
learner. Recognizing these principles has helped faculty shift their thinking about course design and faculty roles. However, faculty report it takes
considerably more time both to develop and to deliver courses with technology. CAOs faced with concerns about cost containment and faculty
resources must look for evidence that technology enhancements actually
increase student course success, improve retention, serve more students,
and can be sustained.

Faculty concerned about student learning have been attracted to course
design and learning management tools, such as WebCT and Blackboard,
in an effort to increase students' time on task, promote cooperative learning, and support regular assessment of learning. Ease of use has led to 73.2
percent of campuses using a course-management system (Green 2001).
With over a hundred e-learning vendors, chief academic administrators
will need help in keeping up with products, must review more than initial
costs, and recognize that upgrades will lead to price increases and additional training (Chnapko 2002). To help make the choice among products, the CAO needs to know the product's capacity to help faculty reflect
on the complex process of learning. Technology requires greater attention
to variations in how people learn. Thus the analysis of any instructional
software should focus on how the tool engages learners with concepts,
encourages them to probe and ask questions, provides prompt feedback,
supports their exploration of additional resources, encourages cooperation, and increases time on task—indeed, replicates the positive aspects
of both group and individualized instruction (Twigg 1996, 16; Hannum
2002).

The key question facing academic administrators in the long run is
which models of teaching should they encourage, as the models have very
different cost structures even if they do not have different learning results.
Adapting e-mail or Web resources to the traditional classroom enhances
current approaches to teaching and is similar to investments in lab equipment. Venturing into instructional design for Web-delivered rather than
Web-managed or Web-enhanced courses is a different kind of decision.
The latter model includes faculty labor costs with a teacher involved
through computer conferencing, on-line discussion groups, and regular
dialogue with students while Web-delivered courses, after initial design,
can achieve economies of scale, reduce labor costs, and reach new learners
in new locations.

To help make the decisions, new methods of isolating instructional costs for course development and course delivery can be applied to technology-based courses to demonstrate the cost-effectiveness of alternative forms of instruction (Catterall 1998). Large courses are particularly good candidates for efficiencies through technology support because the marginal cost is fixed, while marginal revenue increases with the enrollment. Many fear that faculty will resist replacing labor with capital because that appears to reduce the value of the faculty activity and alter the relationship with the students. Consequently, even though increasingly pressed to make choices about instruction based on cost and efficiency, most campuses continue to test their modes of instruction against their mission and faculty readiness for change.

Applying Technology to Learning

- What tools will increase student discussion, active learning, or participation?
- How can students become more discerning about Web resources?
- How can technology help students be better prepared for class (e.g., reading, asking questions, spending time on task, accessing information as needed, and drill and practice)?
- How might the Web support collaborative learning yet retain the role of individual contributions?
- How can technology improve writing and communication skills?
- What instructional design principles will help faculty improve their courses? individualize instruction? offer instruction in new modes?
- What technology skills do we expect of faculty? Are there institutional standards or program-specific skills?
- What is the appropriate balance between providing instructional designers to create courses and expecting faculty to have the necessary skills to redesign courses?
- What are the minimum essentials for technology-enhanced teaching (e.g., every classroom, a few "smart" classrooms, or portable equipment)?

PROMOTING STUDENT TECHNOLOGY COMPETENCIES

Not only will students learn through technology, they must also master a variety of applications as part of their undergraduate program. A decade ago, students attended college to be introduced to fundamental technology skills. Now they arrive with a high degree of comfort about basic skills mastered as part of the K–12 curriculum and expect to extend that learning. Unless a campus is very intentional about its expectations for student learning outcomes, both basic competencies and those essential to a field of study, it is unlikely to realize fully the educational benefits of investments in technology. Nor will it turn out graduates who are competitive in the job market.

As faculty plan the curriculum and specify technology outcomes, they must take into consideration that there is still a considerable range in the skills and aptitudes of a diverse student body. Many campuses conduct assessments of their entering students in order to learn more about their technology background and information literacy skills before establishing course expectations and student services. Whether given during freshman week or on-line as a part of registration, a typical survey will ask students to rate their skill levels in a variety of areas, identify those areas they want to learn more about, and describe their preferred learning mode. Such information can tell college writing instructors, for example, whether they can count on word-processed papers, free of spelling errors. The data can also identify what remedial opportunities are required for students with skill deficiencies. As one might expect, when asked what they would like to learn more about, the interest survey will show that students are far less interested in research or data analysis skills than they are in making their own Web page or downloading music to a CD. Faculty must set expectations rather than respond to student interests alone.

As technology competencies achieve the same status that writing, oral communication, critical thinking, and quantitative reasoning skills have as fundamental to a college education, campuses need to specify the competencies in some detail so that they can be assessed. To provide greater guidance on how information is related to the new technologies, the American Library Association has published Information Literacy Competency Standards for Higher Education 2000. Several states now require regular assessment reports from campuses on students' information literacy as a core concept in general education (Sellen 2002, 115).

The importance of these technology skills is well understood by parents, employers, and legislators. Employers in all fields—not just technology fields—consider computing skills among the most important qualifications for all types of jobs, and an applicant's knowledge of these skills is important in their final hiring decision. Conducting a survey of employers through the on-campus career center can provide up-to-date assessments of expected skill levels. Similarly, campuses can review the accreditation standards for professional programs and redesign curricula to ensure that the competency levels in the curriculum keep up with external demand. Based on current information, CAOs must then determine the efficacy and cost of alternative methods for developing competencies. Will these technology skills be mastered through general education courses, the major, self-paced modules, a single information literacy course, or any of several other methods? With the high cost of faculty expertise, the addition of a single course for all students may be prohibitively expensive compared to the development of self-paced on-line modules that have a reduced unit cost every time they are accessed.

As most students report they learn through trial and error and from their colleagues, simply making computing resources readily available could enable the majority of students to meet the competency levels, while formal instruction could be reserved for students who need help. Reports from lap-top campuses confirm the value of total immersion (Sargent, Heydinger, and Jorgens 1997). With computers required for all students and faculty, and technology applications embedded in all courses, availability and expectations reduce resistance and produce high skill levels. Because of the great variation in technology applications in different fields of study, students do criticize the uneven use of their laptops depending upon their major. However, they agree that basic tasks such as note taking, accessing class assignments, and keeping up through e-mail are all second nature after the first few weeks, and they would not willingly return to pencil and paper, handouts, and phone calls. To promote systematic development of competencies, many campuses map the curriculum to track both effectiveness and efficiency in developing technology competencies across all course work.

Identifying and helping students acquire the competencies, however, are not nearly as difficult as assessing whether students have mastered them. The options for assessment are many, including self reporting, embedded assessment in courses that are part of general education, independent assessment, degree-related exit competency tests, required or voluntary on-line testing, and assessment embedded in the major. Campuses that require assessments not connected to graduation requirements express concern about how to get students to show up and take the exams seriously as well as the cost of managing such a large-scale program. Campuses that rely on testing as part of course work worry about uneven learning due to differing faculty interests and variable course requirements. Those that use external certification programs are concerned about their match with the campus instruction; for example, the campus may give attention to applications such as spreadsheets whereas the test requires skill in troubleshooting hardware and software problems. Thus not only must CAOs provide leadership in evaluating the cost-benefit of different models for producing these competencies, they must also be responsible for assessing the cost-benefit of different approaches to measuring outcomes.

Assessing Student Technology Competencies

- How is the portfolio of competencies developed (e.g., by state mandate, accreditation requirements, employer expectations, or faculty selection)?

- Are technology competencies focused at theoretical or conceptual understanding, knowledge building, skill development, or application utilization?

- What value do faculty place on technology competencies and information literacy as compared to other skills such as written communication and analytical reasoning?

- How are technology competencies integrated into the curriculum (e.g., general education courses, the major, self-paced modules, or a single information literacy course)?

- When the curriculum is mapped to show which competencies are developed in which courses, is there even distribution and level of mastery throughout the curriculum?

- To what extent are students expected to use increasingly sophisticated technology competencies within their coursework?

- How is competency assessed (e.g., pre-post assessment differences between entering freshmen and graduating seniors, post-course assessments of technologies learned, at the time of graduation only, or some other method)?

- Should assessment be focused on the student body as a whole or be focused at the individual student level?

IMPROVING ACADEMIC MANAGEMENT WITH TECHNOLOGY

In addition to the teaching and learning applications of information technologies, chief academic officers are also interested in how IT can improve day-to-day decision making and managerial tasks ranging from hiring to course scheduling. Chief academic officers need accurate, timely, and useful information, yet they too often struggle with unproductive information systems. Unfortunately, many academic administrators rely on building their information databases on their desktops or using single-purpose software because their campus cannot afford to invest in one of the fully integrated management information systems (MIS).

Although these commercial products are relatively new, campuses have been dealing with administrative information systems for decades. What is new is their capacity to meet the overall information requirements of the institution and support decision making through easier access. These administrative information systems are designed to manage all of the major information needs of a campus, ranging from alumni records and registration to human resources and financial transactions. Once a student enrolls or a faculty member is employed, for example, a record is created that is accessible from multiple points on a campus with various levels of security. Technology can dramatically change the way in which information is gathered, stored, and made accessible to decision makers on a campus if there is adequate training.

When CAOs with a new management information system get together, they share their frustrations with the project management, installation support, time spent on training, and challenge of customizing the programs to what they perceive are unique needs of the campus. Perhaps what is most challenging about implementing one of these products is that the programs dictate relationships and ways of working that may not match the habits of a campus. One campus, for example, had personnel and payroll reporting to two different divisions and ran into staff resistance when the product required a changed sense of who owns information. Despite initial complaints about the time necessary for successful conversion to a single system, CAOs also recognize the enormous efficiencies of an integrated management information system.

Campuses that still use several proprietary systems know that each one has idiosyncratic ways to store information. Consequently, the systems cannot easily work together. When the CAO wants to address a particular problem, it may be necessary to call a systems administrator to load a tape or call on someone with the skills to use SQL (Structured Query Language) to extract data from one database and import it to another one. Unfortunately, that cumbersome process must be done over and over each time the study is conducted. A faculty workload report, for example, cannot be automatically updated. In addition to efficiency, the increasing reliance on up-to-date information for decision making is a strong argument for an integrated system.

To fully use any integrated management information system requires careful thinking about the kinds of activities, reports, and decisions that must be made to manage the institution. Which records should be held electronically? What information needs to be secure? What information can be available to others throughout the campus on a "read only" basis? Do all administrators need to be trained to do their own report generation? Anyone who has been through the bidding process, the decision-making process, or the implementation process will tell you that the questions are endless, the learning curve is steep, and the results are directly related to the level of campus commitment to taking full advantage of the system. Full advantage, one of the suppliers notes, is roughly 20 percent of capacity on average. To take greater advantage of the information system requires on-line help, user groups, and a continuing relationship with the vendor.

To address issues of timeliness, accuracy, and the ability to note trends, campuses develop data warehouses to collect, structure, and make accessible institutional information. The first step in developing a data warehouse is establishing the data definitions, and in most cases they will match criteria established by standard reporting requirements such as the U.S. Department of Education Integrated Postsecondary Education Data System (IPEDS) and state performance measures. Policies and procedures will lay out how data is maintained, secured, and made accessible. Whenever possible, those who will use the data should be consulted about what data they currently and potentially will use.

The data warehouse can be used for both standard reports as well as customized projects. Users can run queries and reports based on the particular variables they identify. To be effective, the system must be easy for many across campus to use. Training and support for users is essential to maximize usefulness, as units cannot afford to rely on a single staff member to run reports or answer questions. When the system is working well it eliminates the need for maintaining redundant sets of data, provides accurate descriptive data, and allows for ad hoc report generation. To facilitate the transformation of a campus from distributed and proprietary systems to a more fully integrated and community shared information system, CAOs need to collaborate with other administrators to ensure that information, interdepartmental interfaces, and faculty and staff interactions are all being effectively managed to maximize productivity.

Evaluating a Management Information System

- How can senior university administrators develop a better
  understanding of the potential applications to institutional decision
  making?
- What are the perceived or anticipated management information needs
  of academic deans and department chairs?
- What are the specialized skills that staff throughout the institution
  need in order to use the system?
- Does the CAO need to have an individual on staff or rely on the
  institutional research office to facilitate the administrative uses of
  technology?
- What steps will clarify and simplify the structure of pathways to
  information?
- What training will help deans and department chairs to use
  information in such areas as strategic planning, financial planning,
  staff appraisal, and program review?

ORGANIZING INFORMATION TECHNOLOGY

Organizing information technology on a campus is idiosyncratic. As many campuses use a decentralized model as use a centralized approach, each with variations in reporting lines and involvement of the CAO (Roth and Sanders 1996, 24). There are campuses that split administrative and academic computing, campuses that integrate them with the library, campuses with a vice president for technology, and campuses with an information officer reporting to the president or the administrative vice president. Although communication and decision making are affected by structures, successful leadership for integrating technology depends far more on relationships than on reporting lines to overcome fragmentation and ensure coordinated support for the information technology priorities the institution has established. Advisory committees can overcome territoriality and bring focus to both strategic and operational issues. Without collaboration among IT professionals and campus stakeholders for both academic and administrative computing, campuses are vulnerable to the problem of unstable infrastructure, not only in capital but also in personnel.

Ultimately, the organization must be flexible enough to reflect changing needs and thus may not remain fixed (Golden and Kahn 1998). Although faculty have little interest in the structure that supports functions such as student billing or admissions, they do have a stake in an adequate level of support for instruction. They will not rethink their courses and their pedagogy if administrative applications displace support for academic applications. Since both structures and resources affect priorities and responsiveness, chief academic officers often argue for greater control over academic computing and the attendant budget to guarantee support for academic affairs. CAOs may argue for greater control of IT but also recognize the necessity of collaboration across divisions because they all depend upon the same infrastructure and services for their success (Coffman 1997).

A particular challenge in providing dependable support is finding IT personnel who have technical expertise as well as an understanding of teaching and learning. Consequently, the chief academic officer will either need to collaborate on the selection of institutional IT personnel or hire personnel to serve within academic affairs who have both IT skills and the ability to work with faculty. One successful model invests in technology coordinators who have a broad academic background and technical skills to support academic program clusters. Another model invests several years of training in full-time faculty before reassigning them to academic technology support. Under both models, these academic-affairs based IT personnel provide training and applications support while also bringing their expertise to institutional planning committees.

Students are increasingly an important addition to the IT support staff as they install hardware and software, monitor labs, provide training to other students, and develop applications for faculty and their units. From time to time, campuses find students lock the Web sites they maintain, claiming authorship, promise more expertise than they really have, or take advantage of their access to information, but overall campuses are happy with the skills and contributions of their students. Providing internships, work study, and formal employment opportunities are all positive responses to the growing need to "grow your own" because of the shortage of IT personnel.

Another area in which to achieve better organization is in provision of and support for general-purpose and specialized labs. Many campuses initially developed numerous discipline-based labs spread all over campus in academic buildings as a complement to academic programs. Faculty ownership seemed important, and they believed the labs could be managed and supervised by faculty. Although that approach encouraged units to integrate technology into their programs, once the innovative stage was past, few faculty were willing to continue to maintain the labs and few departments had funding to upgrade the labs in later years. As more students had computers and libraries increased their work stations, the need for general-access labs decreased and the many satellite labs could be integrated into a centralized facility eligible for institutional funding and efficient management (Golden and Kahn 1998).

No matter how the technology resources are organized, responsiveness to academic concerns will remain the chief concern of CAOs. They will want a say about support for specialized college or department needs, such as computer-aided design labs, multimedia and video production facilities to support course development, availability of instructional designers to facilitate translation of courses from traditional mediums to technology delivery systems, and design of smart classrooms. At the same time, however, it is counterproductive to challenge those who are tasked with IT leadership on the campus. Many campuses find that a cross-divisional IT advisory group is an effective way for concerns and priorities to be addressed. Many institutions have found it inefficient to manage such a diverse array of needs and have outsourced some services. These third-party arrangements increase the need for good communication and coordination. In the end, the tensions in organizing technology resources can be resolved most successfully if the goals are clear, the organization can be changed and reshaped as needs evolve, and there is commitment to consultation and collaboration.

Assessing the IT Organization Structure

- To what degree are resources organized to match goals, functions, and services, rather than department or division lines?

- How well do staff with IT responsibilities across the campus work together regardless of organizational lines?

- How responsive is academic computing to faculty needs? student needs?

- How well does the director understand the priorities of various users and provide integrative leadership for the campus?

- To what extent are faculty involved in selecting course-management software and other applications?

- How well are IT staff trained, supervised, and able to take feedback from users? Who do they believe they work for?

- How well are the needs for planning and control balanced with needs for change and responsiveness?

SUCCESSFUL TECHNOLOGY INTEGRATION

Clearly, there are no guarantees that a campus can avoid the challenges of "uncontrolled costs, unclear benefits, unstable infrastructure, unproductive information systems, and unhappy users" (*University Business* 2001, 61). The chief academic officer can join with fellow administrators in auditing the technology status of the campus on a regular basis to identify problems that need attention and new opportunities to improve learning and student services. A review of most technology plans does not make clear who will be responsible for such ongoing assessment of technology integration, but rather relies on unit annual reports on technology activities and individual initiative. This can easily be corrected by establishing specific goals, timelines, and reporting structures focused on technology integration. Although it is often enough just for a campus to keep up in a rapidly changing environment, tracking the macro view on a regular basis will reveal the degree to which the institution as a system is progressing.

Just as an audit of the institution is important, so too is a regular technology audit of faculty, their skills, and their comfort level. Of particular interest to CAOs will be the opportunity costs associated with integrating technology as faculty have many choices about how best to use their time. Technology offers a dizzying array of ways to compete, offer better services, provide greater flexibility, and stimulate innovation, yet requires significant investment of time to realize results. Faculty enthusiasm for new opportunities is always balanced with caution, especially if sufficient support and incentives are not available. Recognition, course releases, small grants, and awards to support faculty innovation can only go so far. In the end, faculty spend time on what brings personal and professional rewards. It is up to the chief academic officer to ensure that the institutional environment brings such rewards so that the commitment to technology integration is sustained.

CHAPTER 5

Financial Resources: Aligning Budget with Academic Priorities

Three longtime college presidents, asked to compare the major issues faced in their first presidency with those in their current term, all identified the same issue then and now—money (Lowery 2002). Whether leading higher education in the 1970s, 1980s, 1990s, or now, they claim the struggle for sufficient funds has always been with them. Undeterred, they raise money, invest in quality, and take on new concerns such as technology and diversity. Faculty and administrators without a long-term perspective often question the financial management of their campus. Their lack of confidence may be due to inadequate information on sources of funds and expenditures or confusion about the roles of the chief academic officer (CAO) and the faculty in developing the budget. But the greatest concerns, by far, arise when choices must be made among competing priorities.

Understanding the external forces of a declining economy or reduced state support can help administrators and faculty focus on the need to pursue productivity and contain costs in order to meet the educational mandate of the institution. Learning more about the budget development process can assuage concerns about allocations and create broader campus confidence. When faculty are not informed about the challenge of generating funds, they are likely to blame the administration for the increasingly straitened campus budget. Yet, even when faculty understand these matters as well as the impact of increased health care costs or the effect of tuition-discounting policies, many faculty will still want more money allocated to instruction and academic affairs as they equate funding with quality.

Higher education is affected not only by economic, political, and societal forces but also by changing aspirations and new opportunities. This environment requires continuous rethinking about how to generate and manage financial resources for future strength. This chapter focuses on the specific role of the chief academic officer in budget planning and management at both the institutional and divisional levels. This overview includes the purpose of the institutional budget, sources of revenues, the academic affairs budget-planning process, sources of flexibility necessary for effective management, strategies for cost containment, and the challenge of reallocations and reductions. On most campuses, the academic affairs budget is over 50 percent of the institution's operating budget; thus, financial expertise is essential for the CAO.

UNDERSTANDING THE INSTITUTIONAL BUDGET

The chief academic officer with limited experience may find it difficult to understand the different types of institutional budgets, the financial statement, the audit report, and the many other documents that reveal the financial situation of the institution. Although few faculty want the CAO to be an accounting expert, tossing around terms such as mandatory transfers, debt service, accrued liabilities, or quasi-endowment, they do want some confidence that the chief academic officer understands the principles, if not all of the details, and can be an active participant in overseeing the financial well-being of the institution. As most campuses struggle with insufficient resources, the CAO must face these economic realities and assess the consequences of the compromises that are inherent in today's higher education environment.

Just as the CAO collaborates in setting the priorities in the strategic plan, the CAO must collaborate in shaping the institutional budget that translates that plan into action. To do so effectively requires understanding the principles behind the various academic budgets, such as instruction and student support, as well as the nonacademic budgets, such as the auxiliary and capital budgets. The CAO needs to understand how resources come to the university, how they are internally distributed, and how to advocate for the resources necessary to meet the academic mission of the institution. It cannot be left to the chief financial officer (CFO) alone to make the hard budgetary decisions affecting the entire institution and, more specifically, academic affairs. Nor can the CAO risk being locked in a battle of wills with other administrators over how best to systematically align resources with institutional expectations. Demonstrating compromise and trust among administrators, especially with the chief financial officer, is the best way to defuse faculty concerns about whether academic priorities are understood and valued.

Reviewing the budget documentation and procedure handbooks for the campus as well as asking questions can build the CAO's budgetary expertise over time. Most institutions follow the same accepted accounting principles and financial practices outlined by the National Association of Colleges and University Business Offices (NACUBO) (Grills 2000); however, they may use slightly different terms and report structures. Many campuses are trying to simplify their reports to help both the board and faculty understand the financial condition of the campus. Understanding fund accounting, for example, is deemed far less important than being able to track key indicators of institutional performance such as total real net worth (Winston 1994). The chief academic officer should focus on measures of the well-being of academic affairs such as net tuition revenue, instructional expenditures as a percent of net revenue, administrative expenditures as a percent of net revenue, and the total number of active faculty lines. Indeed, when budgets are tight, these latter trends are what faculty scrutinize for indications that academic affairs is sufficiently funded and can maintain quality.

Fundamentally the institutional budget is the annual operating resource plan, structured and controlled through the computer-based budget management and accounting information system. The institution's strategic plan should provide the framework for the allocation of resources to specific programs and supporting activities for the annual academic year as well as for the redistribution and realignment of resources over the three-to-five-year strategic planning period. If an institution had more money than it needed, many of the stages of budget development where difficult choices are made could be eliminated. It is never possible, however, to eliminate the many budget management processes, as the institution is subject to an annual review of its accounting and financial controls through an independent external audit. Thus the twin purposes of planning and accountability are the foundation of every budget with the expectation that revenues and expenditures will balance.

On many campuses, the chief academic officer sees only the academic affairs expenditure budget arrayed by object codes and may not fully understand all budget categories. Typically, the total institutional expenditure budget is structured around several program categories including: Instruction (e.g., faculty and department support), Research (e.g., research centers and cost sharing), Public Service (e.g., external services),

Academic Support (e.g., advising and academic computing), Libraries (e.g., staff and materials), Student Services (e.g., registrar and disability services), Institutional Support (e.g., executive management and public relations), Operation and Plant Maintenance (e.g., utilities and campus security), Scholarships (e.g., staff tuition benefits and fellowships), Auxiliary Enterprises (e.g., intercollegiate athletics and food service) and Mandatory Transfers (e.g., debt service) (Meisinger 1994, 6–8).

Unless using a multiyear strategic budgeting approach, the annual operating budget is typically based on expenditure patterns of previous years with the actual line item amounts in each budget appearing to many deans and department chairs as more important than the distribution of the entire institutional budget. Taking a strategic perspective, however, the CAO should question whether academic affairs has adequate resources to support its contribution to the institutional strategic plan and whether resources might be reallocated across divisions in the future. Significant restructuring of budget allocations or reallocations across divisions, rather than incremental budgeting, requires a strong hand and persuasive rationales from the president and chief budget officer as no one wants to make "unpopular decisions" (Newton 2000, 38). Most campuses use a representative budget committee to provide input, but the hard decisions inevitably come from the administration and the board.

With little new funding, CAOs committed to effecting any change need the courage to reallocate within the academic affairs division. Few CAOs make those decisions alone. They work with deans and department chairs to identify priorities and consider the implications of reallocations. Some campuses use budget advisory committees at every level from the department to the central administration to consider issues such as tuition increases and salary goals, although the general view is that this takes time and does not always build consensus. Nonetheless, when budget development is collaborative, based on both top-down and bottom-up planning, there is a greater chance that the budget can be aligned with the strategic plan and be based on both an annual as well as multiyear perspective (Newton 2000; Chabotar 1999, 20–22). And when budgets must be reduced, the trust developed through an open process is critical.

The operating budget, once developed, serves as the spending authorization that allows many throughout the institution to disperse funds. However, unlike having funds in a checking account, the funds are carefully categorized and can only be spent as designated, unless the budget office gives permission to transfer funds. The degree of centralized involvement in budget management varies from campus to campus, but usually the rate of spending if not the specific expenditures are closely monitored.

Too often, the many reports the budget office believes are helpful to those with budget oversight responsibilities are left unread because their purpose is not clear to the budget managers. A budget-to-actual monthly report on year-to-date expenditures as well as an historical actual expenditures report are useful for understanding the current needs of the unit and for developing future plans. The CAO who wants to improve the use of such reports in the management of current funds and the development of the next year's budget can conduct annual training sessions with unit budget managers and budget office staff. To promote creative thinking about resource reallocation, the CAO will not want to micromanage but rather be sure the deans and department chairs understand their responsibility and authority for budget management with the clear understanding that overspending is not an option.

Even with an established budget for the year, any change in revenues during the year will require an adjustment in expenditures. Depending upon the habits of a particular campus, there may be continual adjustments, unexplained adjustments, or midcourse corrections due to circumstance such as a tuition shortfall, a drop in endowment income, a change in benefits costs, or a reversion of state funds. Because of the impact reductions have on faculty confidence and morale, many chief academic officers try to effectively insulate the units by holding back some funds in order to manage minor budget adjustments centrally. However, a significant reversion of state funds or enrollment shortfall cannot be handled transparently.

In addition to operating budget changes due to revenue adjustments, several internal campus practices, such as when raises go into effect, when indirect costs are distributed, or whether the budget office sweeps unexpended funds during the year, will also change the unit operating budgets throughout the year. Therefore, unit budget managers must understand not just the policies but the budget practices in order to anticipate changes and minimize misunderstanding. Many CAOs, interested in productively engaging academic units in budget responsibility, press the CFO for more information but less control from the budget office. Some large campuses have moved to an entirely decentralized approach, "responsibility centered budgeting," to facilitate unit responsibility for both revenues and expenditures as well as to calculate allocations of their share of institutional overhead (Whalen 1991).

Chief academic officers need to help faculty understand how strategic budgeting and a multiyear perspective facilitates change. Presenting the annual budget with additions or reductions listed separately makes it easier to understand budget changes. Having a clear sense of the two different calendars for decisions and actions, one for the management of the current year's budget and the other for the development of the next year's budget, also helps faculty and administrators participate knowledgeably in the budget discussions that are ongoing throughout the year. For public campuses, there is still a third calendar to follow in developing the budget requests for state funds. In that case, to collaborate with the CFO on the detailed budget requests, the chief academic officer needs a clear sense of what the state is likely to support and how special initiative funding could advance the institution's plans.

Understanding the Institutional Budget

- How is the budget clearly linked to the strategic plan, with each year a part of the multiyear effort?
- What basis is used to determine whether divisions and units are adequately funded?
- How often is the distribution of the budget adjusted to match changing needs?
- For a public institution, what basis is used to determine whether the campus is funded adequately from the state as compared to other institutions in the system?
- How much of the budget is continuing obligations and how much of it is available for reallocation to reshape the institution?
- How does the fiscal collaboration between the CAO and the CFO contribute to or detract from faculty and unit-head confidence in budget planning and management?
- What training do those with budget oversight responsibility need and receive?

UNDERSTANDING REVENUES

When faculty talk about budgets, their main contention is that resources are not sufficient to support instruction and academic quality. With little understanding of sources of revenues, this claim may be naïve in the context of competing demands, rising costs, and the mandate to "live within one's means." Many CAOs address this issue by holding an annual faculty forum with the CFO to explain the current financial condition of the campus, the process for forecasting institutional revenues for the coming year from each source, and the variables that have the greatest impact on revenues, for example, enrollment and financial aid.

To begin the annual budget development process, the budget office provides the preliminary estimates of expected revenues from all categories based on such analyses as tuition, annual fund giving, or state appropriations. The previous year's revenues are the best guide to anticipated revenues. It is not uncommon, however, for an institution to determine what it would like to spend and then ask what enrollment will be required, what increase in tuition will be needed, what increase in fees will be tolerated, or what increase in housing costs will generate a surplus. These increases may aim to make up for deficits in other areas such as state support or be targeted for new initiatives. Although the budget must be a match between revenues and expenditures, a surprising number of colleges run operating deficits.

Tuition produces a large portion of an institution's revenue with some private institutions being 90 percent tuition dependent so that they are extremely vulnerable to even small changes in enrollment (Chabotar 1999, 25). Institutions have routinely raised tuition at twice the rate of the Consumer Price Index to generate additional revenues to cover expenses (Greene and Greene 2002, 19). The increases have been used to enhance programs, recreation facilities, technology, and a variety of amenities deemed essential to remain competitive with other campuses. To offset the tuition increases for needy students, tuition discounts through financial aid have also increased and cut into those revenues, with some campuses learning that marginal revenue actually decreased as they expanded and diversified the student body. Public campuses face a different challenge as several states have capped tuition, rather than allow institutions to transfer increased costs to families via tuition increases.

Fees are determined primarily by the actual cost of the service and are usually designated for the unit providing the service. Typically, academic affairs does not receive much of a share of fees. Students often protest specific fees, such as for student activities, claiming that they do not benefit from that service. Others argue that services such as health clubs and cable television should be paid for by the users and not wrapped into a comprehensive fee. Fees represent a substantial portion of the budget; therefore, students are not allowed to pick and choose among the fees. When CFOs and boards review the tuition and fee structure for possible increases, they look at several comparisons, including the Consumer Price

Index, the Higher Education Price Index, and market comparisons with competitors, in an effort to understand what the tolerance level of students might be for increases. CAOs and faculty are particularly concerned about the impact of cost on access and diversity of the student body.

Auxiliary enterprises are activities that generate funds through sales, services, and rentals from the users including, for example, residence halls and campus stores. Entrepreneurial efforts to increase revenues have tested some town-gown relations as local businesses claim unfair competition with their restaurants and bookstores. Chief academic officers should retain oversight for the variety of educational services and facilities made available to the public, such as speech clinics and child care centers, and understand how the revenues are allocated.

Endowments are permanent funds established to provide a source of investment income for the institution. All campuses adhere to a spending rule of roughly five percent in order to preserve principal. For the majority of campuses, the actual amount of endowment income is very small and only a fraction of revenues. In addition, endowment income does not always provide budget relief to the institution; for example, funds designated for scholarships go into the tuition pool as a replacement for funds from students. The real benefit of endowed scholarships, however, for many institutions has been the ability to attract outstanding students resulting in an increase in the overall academic quality of the institution. This in turn attracts additional students and increases tuition revenues. CAOs should collaborate with the development office in identifying projects and activities attractive to potential donors and corporate partners.

Gifts represent a small source of operating revenue for most campuses and are not very predictable. The gift may be earmarked for specific activities or be unrestricted. Even if restricted, such as a corporate gift for technology, a gift can provide budget relief if it is for an activity that is a priority of the campus and would have been funded through other institutional sources. Many campuses receive gifts of art, books, and even working farms that actually cost the campus to preserve. At times it is difficult for CAOs to help development officers, deans, or department faculty understand that a gift designated for an academic area should not be accepted if it fits neither the academic affairs budget nor the academic priorities.

Grants and contracts provide support for designated activities including research and training activities. This is a significant resource for major research institutions that carefully track changes in federal support and actively seek corporate partners. Many foundations and agencies fund only direct expenses. When indirect costs are allowed, the campus sets internal policies for the allocation of those resources and how they will be included in the operating budget. CAOs are particularly interested in finding ways to let the departments and principal investigators have a share as an incentive for continued proposal writing. However, they are cautious about required matching funds if the potential revenue would come with an added expense requiring reallocation within the academic affairs budget.

Investment income can be generated from any surplus in operating funds. When revenues are collected with some lag time before disbursement, the surplus is invested on a short-term basis and the income is added to the total revenues for the campus. For example, a foundation grant for program development may be received in full at the start of the project but then disbursed over a longer period. Savvy CAOs ask the CFO for a share of such earnings.

Budget development discussions focus on both the decisions about generating revenues and the principles for allocation of funds to expenditure categories. At this stage, key administrators will be asked to verify revenue projections and determine whether there can be increases in revenues. Increasingly, CAOs and deans have a direct role in enrollment, grant activity, and fund raising. The CAO may ask academic units to set realistic but higher targets for research support and gifts in an effort to find budget relief or to support new activities. The chief academic officer should be especially concerned about how changes will affect academic quality. For example, will an increase in tuition and fees impact the diversity of students? Will an increase in faculty on grants reduce full-time teaching resources? With a focus on academic quality, CAOs must evaluate potential sources of new revenue and their long-term effect.

Alternative Policies for Generating Revenues

- If there is unused program capacity, how can an increase in enrollment increase marginal revenue but not marginal cost?
- To what extent should student user fees cover more of the costs of institutional services?
- Should academic programs carry differential tuition to reflect their differential costs?
- For which academic programs should fees cover materials and special services?
- Which academic programs can be offered to new markets or new populations?

- Should the number of credits covered by the full-time tuition rate be reduced?
- Could a greater emphasis in fund-raising for unrestricted gifts provide budget relief?
- Should indirect costs on grants go to the institutional budget or be shared with departments and principal investigators?
- Should some of the auxiliary budget that results from increased enrollment be targeted for academic activities?
- Are there assets such as art, land, or buildings that should be sold?

STATE SUPPORT FOR HIGHER EDUCATION

In addition to the institution-specific revenue categories discussed above, public institutions receive appropriations from state governing authorities, usually referred to as general funds. Most citizens assume that public colleges and universities receive their entire operating funds from the state; however, state support represents only about a third of the operating budget of most public institutions (Lissner and Taylor 1996, 7). As a proportion of total revenues, the percentage of general fund support has declined so significantly for many campuses that they no longer refer to themselves as state supported but merely state assisted or more wryly as "state located" institutions. State budget deficits are so severe that continued reductions are likely.

State governing boards and state legislative bodies expect funds to be used to promote their public policy agendas, for example, economic development and workforce training. Because funding of higher education is quid pro quo, accountability is critical and campuses are required to show that they are a good investment for tax dollars. Assessment of student achievement and "report cards" on institutional effectiveness are important to legislators who want to authorize higher education appropriations based on demonstrated quality assurance.

Higher education must also compete for limited resources with other state agencies. Legislators increasingly expect campuses to manage without additional state support because there are more pressing needs to be funded, and they see universities as being able to add to their operating budget through tuition increases. University administrators argue that state appropriations have not kept up with inflation, enrollment trends, or with increasing expectations to expand higher education's basic mission. Flat appropriations as well as recent budget reversions are cited as causes for reduced academic quality due to overcrowded classrooms, greater use of part-time faculty, and continued deterioration of facilities and equipment. Despite declines in funding, states have increased institutional accountability for quality in academic performance (McKeown and Layzell 1994). Thus, chief academic officers of public institutions need to understand the basis used for their institution. Whether the institution receives funds based on a formula (e.g., enrollments or peer group equity) or measures of performance (e.g., graduation rates), CAOs must understand the accountability measures being used, ensure that their institution meets the standards, create an academic affairs budget consistent with the method used, and advocate responsibly for adequate funding both internally and externally.

Formula funding is the oldest and most widely adopted method for determining higher education appropriations and links resources mathematically to an institution's characteristics, mission, and credit-hour production. Formulas vary from state to state and are becoming increasingly complex as they make use of peer data (McKeown and Layzell 1994). Most funding formulas are based on discipline-specific productivity expectations that take into account aspects such as the clinical nature of the program, out-of-classroom supervision, and student/teacher ratios for instruction at lower, upper, masters, and doctoral levels. Whereas the use of formulas promotes equity and minimizes political influences, there are disadvantages: the formulas "perpetuate inequities," do not provide sufficient funds for new initiatives, lag behind enrollment increases, fail to provide predictable funding, and are "only as accurate as the data on which they are based" (McKeown-Moak 1999, 103).

CAOs need to be able to explain funding formulas to faculty and, if not block funded, how differences in disciplines, full-time equivalent students, and credit-hour production affect both personnel and nonpersonnel appropriations to the university. They must also be able to explain to faculty the basis for internal allocation of funds to colleges and departments. Some institutions apply the state's funding formula, others consider institutional and programmatic goals and objectives in allocations, and still others rely on a more political and advocacy-based approach.

Performance funding, another widely used method for determining appropriations, is often used in combination with formula funding. Performance funding shifts the focus from enrollment- and credit-hour-based measures to other indicators of institutional value and reflects the increased accountability expectations. Direct performance funding, usually in the form of bonuses added to the formula or incremental budget, rewards institutions that achieve or exceed certain performance goals. Although the intentions of the funding models are appropriate, institutions have questioned the high cost of measuring and documenting performance across multiple measures when the amount of performance funding is relatively low. The CAO may find faculty have difficulty understanding performance funding, as the measures can be confusing. In some cases the measures are contradictory; for example, faculty productivity as measured by a high student/faculty ratio is a positive indicator of productivity at the same time that small classes are a positive indicator of quality. Even if chief academic officers feel they have little influence over actual state support for their institutions, they can benefit from the measures of institutional effectiveness by endorsing the values of quality and efficiency as priorities for academic affairs.

Two other approaches, target and incentive funding, affect institutional priorities. Targeted funding permits legislators, governors, and college and university leaders to advocate for special-purpose funding in addition to base budget appropriations. These legislative initiatives or budget line items are used to fund activities such as centers, institutes, and economic development initiatives that address specific regional, state, or national needs (Marks and Caruthers 1999b, 9). Target funding is often tied to strategic planning and helps lay the financial foundation for redirecting or reinforcing the institution's mission. For that reason, the CAO must understand the process for submitting legislative funding requests, the limit on the number of initiatives, and how the campus will set priorities among the possible initiatives linked to the strategic plan.

Incentive funding, often used in combination with performance funding, aims to encourage specific activities that support the agenda of the general assembly or other state funding agency. For example, a state might use this method to encourage inter-institutional cooperation between four-year and two-year institutions and to optimize efficiency by funding distance-learning degree-completion programs (Marks and Caruthers 1999b, 9). Although the chief financial officer and the president take the lead in seeking additional state funding, they cannot do so successfully without the collaboration of the chief academic officer, who helps identify potentially successful opportunities and provides evidence that the institution is a good investment.

Understanding State Funding

- To what extent do faculty understand the basis for state appropriations for the campus?

- If enrollment driven, how were the formulas created and how often does the state make adjustments? Is the campus meeting its targets?

- How should enrollment adjustment funding be distributed to serve the additional students?

- If performance based, how can the measurement processes be analyzed to determine how the campus can optimize its performance?

- If initiative funding is available, how can the state priorities be linked to the campus strategic plan priorities?

- How should proposals for initiative funding be developed?

- How should the cost of sustaining an initiative be factored into the institutional budget?

- What funding initiatives match institutional priorities (e.g., technology enhancements), can serve as budget relief, and allow reallocation?

DESIGNING THE ACADEMIC BUDGET DEVELOPMENT PROCESS

Once the total academic affairs base budget allocation is made, the CAO begins the work of developing the unit allocations and aligning resources with the institutionally approved priorities established by the strategic planning process. Despite the fact that most of the operating budget is locked in through continuing faculty and staff positions and programs, most CAOs still use a participatory process to build the budget, allocate open positions, and support specific needs. Ideally, additional funds are available to cover strategic priorities; however, as most budget development relies on internal reallocation, CAOs recognize how important it is to have a reliable two-way process for communicating needs and making decisions.

Most academics are not accountants nor do they wish to be, but faculty do expect to be informed about the budget-development process in terms they can understand. If faculty do not understand the guiding principles and methods for determining how funds will be allocated to the division and then to colleges, departments, and programs, they will question the integrity of the process and resist implementation of any progressive changes derived from the strategic plan. Although the CAO has final authority over budget allocations within academic affairs, a budget development process that is open and participatory has the greatest potential for credibility and appropriate representation of unit needs.

Depending upon the size of the institution and personal preference for consultation, CAOs use a variety of approaches in budget development, for example, relying on a faculty budget advisory committee, holding open budget hearings for faculty and staff, or working directly with deans and department chairs. Although some assume that budgeting should be simple with funds being allocated where they will have the greatest impact, the budget process remains political and contentious on many campuses. However, campuses that have collaboratively conducted strategic planning have a better track record of collaborative budget development. In those cases, the credibility of the budget is derived from the systematic evaluation of operations and programs, the allocation of resources according to the relative priority and performance of programs, and a broad understanding of the principles that guide budget decisions, including reliable and consistently applied data.

As the academic affairs budget and its allocation to units will ultimately impact other divisions, the CAO must also consult with administrators outside the division to ensure that decisions made in academic affairs do not negatively impact another division's ability to meet its annual or strategic goals and objectives. Similarly, the chief academic officer should expect the other division heads to share their initial plans to verify that together the division budgets support the institutional priorities. Failures to consult can cause unexpected consequences for others. For example, cutting the advertising budget for the office of admissions could reduce the tuition income from transfer students, or reducing student wages could impact the supervision of technology labs. Depending upon the practices of the campus, the CAO may also need to review the division's budget with the university-wide planning and budget advisory committee or the president, as the annual budget serves as a management tool.

To maintain faculty confidence in budget development, the process should be assessed regularly. However, most campuses do not critically review budgeting principles and procedures until there are complaints. For instance, faculty will argue that departmental budgets are not based on actual performance when they remain flat despite increases in the number of hours taught, number of students advised, and expectations for research. Deans express concern that department chairs look at their budget as an entitlement and make little or no effort to find program efficiencies or increase program revenues. Department chairs explain that there are no incentives for either saving or increasing revenues because they may not directly benefit. Even when the budget process is assessed, unless a collaborative review is undertaken and the rationale for changes to allocation principles are clearly communicated, both the CAO and the process will be criticized. Departments receiving less will claim they are being penalized, but not know why. Departments receiving more will not know why they are being rewarded. CAOs who want to systematically address the budget process and improve it will need to do so between cycles and in collaboration with deans, department chairs, and the chief financial officer.

Designing a Participatory Process

- How are individual faculty, unit, and college interests represented?
- To what extent do faculty and unit heads perceive that their contributions make a difference?
- How much of the budget information is available across all units?
- How is consultation across divisions and units facilitated?
- What is the role of the administration in setting priorities or indicating constraints?
- What incentives are there for collaboration rather than competition for resources?
- How are the process and the principles critiqued and regularly improved?

DEVELOPING THE ACADEMIC AFFAIRS BUDGET

Typically each campus establishes a calendar to systematically guide the budget development process, although many CAOs admit it is difficult to ensure that each stage is completed fully and in a timely way. Rather than be distracted by due dates for documents, they find that the more important guide for developing the academic affairs budget is agreement on accepted guidelines or foundational principles. When there is broad agreement on principles, the time required for discussion can be reduced. When units are not faced with an adversarial budgeting process, they can be advocates on behalf of all of academic affairs. The following principles are relevant whether distributing additional funds, making incremental reallocations, or managing a budget reduction.

Make Student Services and Program Quality a Priority

The academic affairs budget should be based on a fundamental commitment to front-line services to students and program quality. By adhering to this principle, especially when there are no new resources, the CAO can help units understand how to make choices between competing priorities, for example, more full-time faculty or higher salaries. Reallocations across units or reductions in budgets are guided by data on the impact on student learning. Information from academic program review is essential in developing the strategic multiyear approach necessary to make readjustments caused by changes in enrollments, plans to strengthen programs, or the decision to phase out a program.

Allocate Funds Based on Centrality

Universities evolve and programs once important to an institution are replaced with new ones to keep pace with evolving areas of study and student and employer needs. The CAO, through program review, can identify those programs central to the vision and mission of the university, growing in demand, and competitive for faculty and students. Resources must be used in the most effective way possible, growing some programs while reducing or completely eliminating funding for others. However, the CAO should never use incremental budget reductions to slowly debilitate a program to the point of not being viable. When a program is no longer contributing to the mission of the institution, the phaseout should be intentional with the action initiated through the program review process or other internal governance process.

Recognize Differences among Units

Budget allocations must reflect unit differences based on: type of program offered (e.g., nursing programs have smaller class sizes and greater costs for supplies than a history program), level of students taught (e.g., student/faculty ratios for doctoral courses must be smaller than general education courses), mix of faculty and staff (e.g., more credit hours require more faculty, but more majors require more advisors), unit obligations to public service and outreach efforts (e.g., extended campus operations are more costly than on-campus programs), potential return on investment (e.g., expanding a music program will cost a campus more than expanding the business program), and economies of scale (e.g., psychology departments can achieve economies that are not possible for small departments). Because faculty seldom have an overview of all programs in academic affairs, the CAO and deans need to explain how unit differences impact budget-development decisions.

Determine Base Budget Adequacy and Make Regular Adjustments

Every effort should be made to annually determine the funding necessary for a unit to fulfill its approved mission. Base-level budgets for staffing may be established using student/faculty ratios, faculty workload comparisons, state productivity guidelines, or professional program accreditation standards. It is more difficult to determine equitable allocation principles for nonpersonnel funds and to encourage units to create efficiencies such as by sharing copy machines and administrative staff. One university uses a model that calculates a base level for standard amenities per unit, adds a budget factor for each full-time faculty member, and then includes an adjustment for unique aspects of the program such as labs and studios.

Establish a Multiyear Approach

Deans and unit directors need some sense of stability; thus, the budget development process should not result in significant or unexpected increases or decreases from the previous academic year's budget. Annual budgeting provides the opportunity for units to strategically realign budgets (Marks and Caruthers 1999a, 4). However, if budget development is limited to a one-year look-ahead model, little institutional change will take place. Multiyear budgets allow for greater stability in effecting plans. Change can only occur if all parties understand the strategic direction being taken by the institution and units can anticipate that budget allocations will be based on increments necessary to effect the long-term vision. The CAO must help units understand that a budget is not a continuing entitlement but will be conditioned upon successful implementation of unit strategic plans and reallocations that align resources with results.

Reduce Administrative Expenses

Most campuses claim that direct service to students is their highest priority, yet there is evidence of a steep increase in administrative expenses "during the last 20 years as a percentage of total institutional costs" through the unsystematic addition of positions (Lenington 1996, 113).

That trend can be reversed by reductions, especially at the middle-management level, through job redesign. Campuses have successfully combined colleges and departments of similar mission, eliminated services that do not add value, consolidated functions, and reduced the number of assistants and associates at every level from the vice president to the department. A budget advisory committee charged with reviewing the entire division can often identify administrative expenses that could be eliminated without diminishing student support and program quality. With that guidance, the CAO can make appropriate decisions.

Avoid Budget-Driven Personnel Reductions

Nothing is more painful when trying to contain costs or balance a budget than targeting positions for elimination; thus staffing plans must have built-in flexibility. A comprehensive position authorization system can guide the reallocation of faculty and staff positions over time from low-priority areas to high-priority areas. The CAO cannot rely on retirements and voluntary separations for reallocation opportunities as the open positions may have an uneven impact on academic operations or not align with priorities. Maintaining a certain number of positions as temporary and part-time provides essential flexibility to adjust staffing as needed. One guideline for a four-year campus would limit the total credit hours taught by part-time faculty to 15 percent and the total credit hours for any unit to 25 percent (American Association of University Professors 2001, 85).

Maintain the Academic Infrastructure

Too often, budget constraints lead to reducing funds that are not attached to specific personnel or a well-defended academic department. As a result, funds for library purchases, graduate assistantships, or science equipment become an immediate target for reduction or reallocation. Libraries have suffered from both inflationary impacts on materials budgets and budget reductions, leaving collection gaps, overworked staff, and inadequate technology when they should have been a priority. The base budget for activities that are essential for academic quality, regardless of enrollment, should be protected according to the same principles as other budgets.

Invest in the Future

Strategic budgeting calls for both resource reallocation across units and set-asides for risk capital. Both planning beyond the immediate year and targeted funding are investments in the future. To stimulate new initiatives some campuses require that every unit annually reduce their expenditures to guarantee a pool of funds for which units can compete (Newton 2000, 41). The CAO must have a clear and collaborative process for determining investment priorities as support for a new initiative means less support for other programs. Programs that have potential for moving the institution into a stronger strategic position and also require no upfront funding are easy to support, but cost-free initiatives are not often encountered by a CAO. Making a distinction between start-up costs and continuing funding is essential. Typically such investment funding is used to start new programs that are projected to fully recover costs through improved retention or additional enrollments. Committing to selective investment and rewarding excellence should be major considerations in budgeting at the CAO level because these academic investments are critical to the achievement of institutional goals.

Evaluating the Budget Development Process

- How is the budget development process linked with strategic priorities at all levels?
- How is information about budget development shared before final decisions are made?
- To what extent is institutional data (e.g., credit hours, workload, and enrollment) reliable and consistently used?
- What are the conflicting needs for budget adequacy, stability, change, and innovation, and how are they reconciled?
- What balance is sought between positions that sustain the quality of the institution as it is (replacements) and those that move the institution in new directions (new positions)?
- How systematic is the approach to getting the right number on the right lines (e.g., circulating the draft budget for unit-level review, final authorization of the academic affairs budget from the CFO, and interaction with budget office support staff to make final adjustments due to unsuccessful searches or late separations)?

IMPROVING BUDGET MANAGEMENT

Once the academic year budget is in place, it is the responsibility of the chief business officer to manage the institutional operating budget, holding all budget managers responsible for using the funds as established in the original budget. The chief academic officer, also committed to achieving the goals for which the budget was intended, is often less rigid about what constitutes good budget management. One business officer flatly claimed that the budget is not "an authorization to spend," approvals should be required for every expenditure, transfers between accounts "defeat the purpose of variance analysis," vice presidents are responsible for bringing the budget "back into line if there are variances," and everyone should be committed to "under spending the budget" (Lenington 1996, 52–53). Chief academic officers who believe in decentralization argue instead that rigid adherence to the "planned" budget effectively eliminates adjusting to changing circumstances throughout the year and discourages responsible management and cooperation at the unit level. Good budget management requires flexibility. The majority of campuses are small enough that they do not need responsibility center budgeting but they can take advantage of the incentives for efficiency that come from trusting units to manage their own affairs. The following suggestions meet the need for both accountability and flexibility.

Decentralize Budget Management

Approaches to budget management systems range from highly centralized to highly decentralized, but during the past decade the movement in higher education has been toward greater authority and responsibility for budgetary decisions at the college or department level. The prevailing view is that the authority for decisions should be aligned with accountability for performance, and the best decisions will be made by those closest to the activities. Rewards and sanctions can be developed to operationalize this relationship; resource-expanding incentives are preferable to resource-constraining barriers; and outcome measures are preferable to input controls (Strauss and Curry 2002, 7–8). While decentralization of the budget has many advantages, it can lead to diminished collegiality and a strong sense of entitlement. Most approaches to budget management lie somewhere between the extremes so that institutional change is not held hostage to unit financial interests.

In times of prosperity, the academic affairs budget is often much more decentralized, whereas in times of budget reversions or diminished fiscal flexibility, the chief academic officer asserts more control. As campuses move from good times to bad, the shift in control can lead to frustration and misunderstanding on the part of department chairs and faculty. However, the CAO is responsible for the welfare of the whole division; thus some actions contrary to previous procedures may be necessary to preserve the viability of all units and keep the division on the path to meeting its priorities.

The chief academic officer has considerable latitude in how the budget will be managed at the division, college, and unit levels. The level of control exercised is a matter of CAO personal preference and institutional history. Some chief academic officers believe the best way to maintain their authority is through the budget, and they monitor it regularly, authorize special requests, and offer incentive supplements throughout the year. There are other CAOs who trust a goal-oriented approach and expect to leave units alone once the budget for the year is established. They may still review the expenditure patterns on a quarterly basis, but they recognize that expenditure patterns are uneven and responsible budget managers at the unit level are accountable for not over-spending the budget. The more the budget is decentralized, the more units are responsible for good budget management and have less need to return to the chief academic officer with budget requests.

If faculty have been used to "begging" for special needs or "shopping" the campus for resources, decentralized management requires some reorientation. Department chairs need to share the budget with faculty to show how resources are linked to the academic goals in the unit strategic plan. As needs arise or new ideas emerge, units can seek efficiencies and reallocate to their highest priorities throughout the year as a continuous adjustment process, rather than a once-a-year budget development activity. CAOs who trust that the budget, unit plans, and the institutional strategic plan are aligned can reallocate the time once spent on day-to-day budget issues to other matters and only step in when there are unexpected issues that need their input.

Find Strategies for Pooling and Rolling Forward Funds

The ability to pool funds and roll forward funds changes the spending psychology of units. Instead of trying to spend money fast, out of fear that the budget office will take it, or wait and spend in an end-of-the-year rush, budget managers can set priorities and be thoughtful about expenditures. A complete review of the budget in January and again in early spring allows the CAO and deans to identify resources that might be used to advance a strategic initiative that was not funded at the beginning of the year. If funds can be moved among categories, institutions will find faculty willing to save and pool funds for lab equipment and instructional materials. If state requirements restrict rolling forward funds, the chief academic officer can use the monies in the current year, for example, to prepay standing library purchases, leases, and membership dues, and then add back the funds to the units in the next budget year. Some campuses allow balances to be banked and allow deficits to be charged against the next year's budget.

Establish Personnel Variance Pools at the Unit Level

The greatest variation in budget commitments during a year is in personnel dollars. In many institutions, lapsed salary funds from faculty resignations, grant-funded time, or unused part-time funds are transferred to the chief academic officer, or in some cases, the excess personnel funds revert back to the general university budget. While this has advantages in times of very tight budgets, it impairs the ability of units to make decisions about midyear replacements and part-time faculty in a timely way. If a midyear resignation can be covered with part-time faculty and the units can offer some additional courses, the full-time faculty are more willing to pick up the additional advising and committee work. If units can be the beneficiaries when a colleague is on a grant, for example, they are more supportive of the activity. At the same time units reap the benefits from lapsed salary funds, they should also be responsible for covering replacements for sick faculty and separation payouts.

Managing for Both Control and Flexibility

- If funds are moved from one budget line to another, how can historical trends be preserved and used to analyze budget needs?
- If there are variances in budget lines, when can funds be moved to other needs?
- If units save money, how can they be the beneficiary of their prudence?
- Should the next year's budget be put together based on budget or actual figures from the previous year?
- How often should the department or unit head consult with the dean about spending patterns (budget-to-actual)?
- Can spending patterns be best understood on a monthly basis, or quarterly basis, or in reference to the previous year's pattern?

MANAGING A BUDGET REVERSION

In recent years, many public institutions have faced reversions of some portion of their operating budget caused by shortfalls in state revenue projections. The same national economic circumstances have hit private institutions causing fewer donations and dramatic declines in endowment income, which also require adjustments. Because the economic conditions that cause these reversions were not anticipated, the impact is greater than when reductions are planned. Ideally, campuses have contingency funds and reserves to cushion the blow. However, in most cases these resources have already been tapped in previous years without enough good years to rebuild the funds.

Given the short time frame to effect reductions, some chief financial officers argue for across-the-board reductions as both expedient and equitable. In fact, the impact is not equitable because many activities cannot be eliminated and must be added to the load of others. Not only does this situation have a psychological cost to the campus as measured by declining morale, thoughtless reductions can do real harm to a campus. Others argue for opportunistic cuts and immediately freeze all open positions and discretionary spending such as travel funds. Because not all positions and not all activities contribute in the same way to academic quality, it makes more sense during times of crisis for all university constituencies to work collaboratively to identify, evaluate, and implement short-term solutions based on their impact on the institution. The goal of this collaborative effort should be to ensure that university operations can continue with minimal disruptions while looking to restructuring for the longer term.

Campuses have successfully managed reductions using both the top-down and the bottom-up approaches. In the first instance, the administration makes cost-cutting recommendations to a representative committee for their review and reaction. In the second approach, a committee makes recommendations to the administration for their review and action. Either approach will be successful if the guiding principles for reducing the budget are the same as those that built the budget in the first place, with highest priority going to preserving academic quality and service to students.

When budgets must be reduced midyear, typical immediate steps include freezing unfilled positions; eliminating nonessential instructional support, such as speakers; reducing discretionary spending, such as receptions; reducing facilities maintenance; using electronic delivery to reduce printing charges; reducing hours of service; and delaying purchases. These temporary solutions provide time to assess the situation, determine funds available, and begin to identify areas for permanent savings. If the crisis is truly a one-time occurrence with no long-term base-budget reduction required, then the task is simply to find cash in the existing operating budget. If the campus fails to recognize when there needs to be an actual reduction in the base budget, this crisis management process might be repeated again and again. Each time it will be harder to bring the budget into balance and also weaken the institution that needs to be restructured to preserve quality.

After more than a decade of worrying about budgets, most of the quick fixes have already been instituted; thus many CAOs are looking for more than a holding action. Short-run cost-cutting strategies can be reviewed to determine how to develop long-term cost-containment ideas. By providing full information on the urgency of the financial situation for higher education, colleges and universities can tap the creativity of faculty and staff to redesign what they do and how they do it in an effort to preserve quality of education, service to students, and quality of life for employees. If the chief academic officer does not assure faculty that they will have a say, faculty will resist rather than help.

Turning Cost-Cutting into Cost-Containment

- Rather than eliminate all midlevel management, how can management responsibilities at all levels be restructured?

- Rather than indiscriminately reduce staff, how can duplicative functions be consolidated?

- Rather than cut all elective courses, how can the curriculum be redesigned?

- Rather than eliminate faculty salary increases, how can the total number of faculty be gradually reduced?

- Rather than eliminate sabbaticals, how can units redesign course offerings while the faculty member is on leave?

- Rather than eliminate some student services, how can they be provided through technology?

- Rather than pay overtime for staff, how can other staff be cross trained to help at peak work times?

LINKING BUDGET TO LONG-TERM CHANGE

Many CAOs would argue that it is far easier to make necessary adjustments or undertake restructuring when there is a perceived crisis or external pressure. In tough times, rather than trim a little here and a little there, weak programs must be cut and unimportant activities eliminated. But waiting until a crisis occurs divorces budget from institutional plans. Regardless of increasing or decreasing revenues, the budget should be aligned with both operational and strategic plans. Many small private campuses that ran deficits for years, which eroded endowments, only found the courage to restructure for viability when closing was imminent. Indeed, some waited too long and did not survive.

The chief academic officer must develop a conversation within academic affairs that is not crisis oriented, but rather is responsive to changing circumstances and strategic priorities. For that to happen, faculty must be able to hear two messages at once. The first is the need to reconsider how resources are generated, allocated, and used while the second is that the very activities that create the quality of the campus—excellent teaching, thoughtful research, and service to students—are still supported. The faculty perspective that quality is linked to money can be a barrier to their understanding of budget matters. Nonetheless, the chief academic officer must have the courage and the facilitation skills to help faculty accept responsibility for being more productive and more innovative in the face of clear data on resource limitations. The goal is not survival but comparative advantage in a competitive environment. Such redesign cannot be mandated by a CAO but rather is a shared responsibility with the faculty.

Unfortunately, the stakes are high because no restructuring or significant budget reduction can be handled without touching personnel. Recognizing that not all services need to be available when there are few students around in the summer, many colleges and universities have established 9-, 10-, and 11-month staff appointments (e.g., cafeteria workers and counselors). Many campuses have hired faculty on continuing contracts to serve primarily in the classroom and carry no research responsibilities. After a decade of adding to the faculty research support effort through reduced teaching loads, summer grants, and additional funding for graduate students, many comprehensive campuses have reflected on their priorities, reasserted the importance of undergraduate teaching, and begun to reduce research support with a concomitant reduction in research expectations of faculty.

Campuses are also well aware of the many ways to put less pressure on the budget, for example, holding enrollments at the current level, not developing new programs, reducing non-need-based scholarships, and postponing facilities projects; however, these actions can have long-term negative consequences. Many campuses, seeking permanent positive changes, have been courageous in carefully eliminating programs that no longer are in demand nationally or no longer attract students. Some campuses have reduced or eliminated "at the margins" programs in order to protect their core academic mission. Most have implemented productivity improvements including greater use of technology, reductions in paperwork, and outsourcing. Real restructuring will be marked by a mix of planning and experimentation, constant evaluation, some setbacks, and renewed commitment to reform (Myers 1996, 70–71).

The prospect of no relief from budget constraints appears to jeopardize academic innovation. Campuses question whether they can afford to continue to staff a service learning office, provide supervision for interns, offer faculty development programs, subsidize study abroad programs, or maintain small classes for the honors program. To some extent, faculty point to these programs as candidates for elimination because they are not department based and do not affect all faculty and students. However, as many of these initiatives contribute to academic quality and attract enrollments, the chief academic officer must ask whether the campus can afford not to have these programs. Such decisions must be based not just on direct costs but also on evaluation data about the benefits to students. Costs should not be disaggregated from benefits as neither alone is sufficient basis for decisions.

Ultimately faculty and academic administrators must address how to sustain academic integrity, stimulate innovation and change, and not just do cost cutting. The chief academic officer must be sure that the decision-making bodies working on long-term financial planning for the institution include deans, department chairs, program heads, faculty, and students who are interested in considering new ways of educating. In addition, close cooperation among all divisions, but especially between the CFO and the CAO, is essential if academic quality and fiscal considerations are to be integrated. The agenda calls for adjustments in enrollment planning, facilities planning, academic innovations, instructional services, and student support activities. Just as businesses have to spend money to make money, success in the long term will depend upon using some resources for investments in quality that will bring a return to the campus.

The chief academic officer needs to be able to evaluate new ideas that challenge prevailing ways of conducting business for the campus. These approaches may include, for example, participation in inter-institutional agreements to share resources (e.g., library consortia), regional cooperation (e.g., degree completion on community college campuses), avoidance of program duplication (e.g., graduate study centers), and new research and supplemental income arrangements with faculty (e.g., business/research parks and clinical work) (Simpson 1991). Each of these arrangements has financial aspects that need to be carefully analyzed. However, few chief academic officers have the technical and legal expertise necessary to negotiate rental agreements, supplementary pay plans, or patent policies. Collaboration with business affairs is a necessity.

Institutional redesign must also be a collaborative effort. The role for the chief academic officer is to ask how each of these new arrangements might extend academic programs and services, meet quality standards, and either be self supporting, revenue enhancing, or lead to reductions in current expenditures. To be sure that these new arrangements continue to have integrity, the chief academic officer will also want to establish processes for regular reports, systematic review, and renewal of agreements as these new models fall outside of most of the standard review processes of the campus.

Restructuring for Long-Term Strength

- What changes will increase revenues (e.g., recruit more out-of-state students, raise tuition and fees, and increase unrestricted gifts)?
- What actions will reduce the pressure on the budget (e.g., freeze enrollment at its current level or manage the curriculum more effectively)?
- What changes in behaviors will conserve current resources (e.g., energy conservation and greater use of e-mail)?
- How might resources be used more effectively (e.g., return administrators to the classroom and reduce financial aid budget by giving students wage positions)?
- How might resources be used more efficiently (e.g., cross-train staff and increase use of technology)?
- What new relationships might enhance services, provide savings, or increase revenues (e.g., consortia and business incubator)?

SUCCESSFUL BUDGET PLANNING AND MANAGEMENT

Budget planning and management requires clear thinking, solid principles, and predictable processes. No matter how dedicated and diligent the chief academic officer is, a past history of competition and entitlements cause many faculty to resist or mistrust collaborative thinking about budgets. Once allocated, budgets often create divisions as deans and department chairs feel that they "own" resources that they believe must not be shared, given up, or traded off. Once allocated, budgets often look like expense accounts requiring record keeping, but not accountability, for how the funds are used. To change past habits and gain trust for new ways, the CAO must encourage an environment of shared responsibility and mutual accountability. The goal of the CAO should be for each dean and department chair to have a clear understanding of what resources they can expect from the university, what resources they can expect to generate themselves, and how those resources can best be used to achieve institutional goals.

To some degree, the management of money is not a totally rational process and many CAOs find it disheartening to see the games their colleagues play with institutional funds. Clearly, it is far easier to understand accounting rules than to penetrate the psyche of the department chair, dean, or budget officer as they work with the budget. The first provides a rational method of accounting for resources; the second may reflect emotional issues that shape decisions about money such as the desire to be liked, to impose penalties, or to exercise control. Experienced CAOs note the need some have to inflate real need, to hide funds in unlikely places, to pad budget lines as a contingency, to respond to budget requests from friends while denying others, and to want to have some money to give away to buy support—the list could go on. It is neither useful nor possible to determine why individuals behave as they do nor to study every budget. It is more important to recognize that individuals learn what is acceptable behavior.

The budget system on a campus can create negative behaviors or reward positive behaviors. Individuals will emulate the behaviors that are effective. The chief academic officer can set the tone for openness, collaboration, fair-mindedness, and putting institutional needs first. The CAO should be mindful that the principles that guide the budget process become the "rules" by which the game will be played. Principles for allocating funds have powerful effects on an institution; for example, if budgets are primarily based on credit hours generated rather than an historical entitlement, units will become more responsive to student interests in planning their course offerings. Ultimately, to provide effective and consistent leadership, the CAO must be aware of his or her own attitudes and behaviors with regard to budgets.

CHAPTER 6

Academic Entrepreneurship:
Marketing Intellectual Capital

Broader expectations for higher education, increased competitiveness, and financial challenges require chief academic officers (CAOs) to be academic entrepreneurs. Entrepreneurship is a difficult orientation for many CAOs and faculty, however, because thinking of academic programs in terms of profits and losses or viewing intellectual activity as a commercial product are antithetical to the traditions of the academy. Nonetheless, a stronger future depends upon those in academic affairs understanding higher education as a highly competitive enterprise to be managed with a focus on product identification, customer service, and financial well being. To thrive in a competitive environment, new ideas, new markets, and new revenues are a necessity, and faculty creativity and energy must be the driver.

Unfortunately, when resources are tight, campuses feel vulnerable and conservative—yet, that is exactly the time when innovation and calculated risk taking are called for to generate new revenues. Higher education is fundamentally risk averse and slow to change, and chief academic officers are not encouraged to gamble. Instead, CAOs are held accountable for successfully meeting institutional goals with well-thought-out initiatives. Even when encouraged to be innovative or move quickly, most CAOs have little entrepreneurial experience to draw upon. Those chief academic officers with an entrepreneurial spirit have long understood that a constantly changing environment offers revenue opportunities ranging from extending continuing education and expanding research and development activities to offering on-line courses and creating partnerships with industry. In addition, entrepreneurial CAOs understand the importance of providing an outlet for the creativity of faculty in nontraditional forms such as training programs, inventions, and new product development.

Not all new ideas can be profitable. To create successful entrepreneurial operations alongside traditional activities and ensure that the projects are revenue producing, the chief business officer must give both financial guidance and budgetary freedom to the CAO. Chief academic officers need a realistic understanding of what risk capital is available, how to account for all costs, what rules govern off-budget activities, and how revenue sharing can provide sufficient incentives for faculty participation. The budget models for entrepreneurial activities must ensure more than a break-even return. The campus that jumps too quickly to innovation, whether in programming, delivery systems, products or partnerships, assuming "if we build it, they will come," may find the innovations too costly to be sustained.

The campus that is responsive to a changing environment and is willing to experiment with new instructional modalities, new roles in the community, and new forms of faculty activity can compete effectively. This chapter suggests processes for developing new academic products, examples of outreach offerings and potential partnerships, and guidelines for evaluating the budgetary implications for these new academic activities. The ways in which campuses fund research and development activities through grants and contracts, market their intellectual capital, and extend their impact through activities such as community service relationships and corporate parks are also analyzed. Whether a small campus with a single weekend adult degree program or a major research university committed to business incubation and technology transfer, the foundation for academic entrepreneurship is effective collaboration among faculty, academic administrators, and business affairs staff to ensure that entrepreneurial activities have both financial and intellectual integrity.

CREATING NEW ACADEMIC VENTURES

While new venture development does not have a single best approach, consciously or unconsciously, higher education has adopted many of the same considerations, steps, and procedures as are used in business in order to identify and evaluate the merits of new academic activities. Current institutional strengths can provide a firm foundation to support new ideas, but entrepreneurial activities must tap new markets and new customers rather than compete internally. The design and implementation process must make it possible for the institution to be nimble enough to move a product to market quickly, create relationships without bureaucratic hassles, and appropriately compensate faculty for their ideas and time. Decision criteria at each step help identify those opportunities that will provide the greatest return.

Establishing the New Venture Team

No new venture creates itself. Many institutions rely on individual initiative for new ideas; however, the more entrepreneurial campuses are proactive, harness group energy to stimulate creativity, and provide a supportive environment. To make entrepreneurship an intentional rather than a sporadic process, the chief academic officer needs to create a new venture team charged with identifying needs and opportunities that match the institution's strengths and mission. Their work will rely on the environmental scan and academic strengths identified through strategic planning, but they will also conduct additional needs assessments and work with a greater sense of urgency and freedom. The capacity to see the institution and higher education from a different perspective must be combined with the ability to work collaboratively and efficiently toward a coordinated strategy for the institution.

The chief academic officer must work closely with the team to clarify purposes, processes, criteria, resources, and policies for each stage of the development process. In addition, new decision-making structures, if not the standard curriculum review process, and new organizational structures, if not the colleges and departments, must be designed to support the entrepreneurial activities. Formalizing a coordinated institutional strategy for entrepreneurship should not crush individual initiative. However, CAOs will want to make clear that individual initiatives that are congruent with institutional priorities will receive a more favorable hearing. Similarly, the new venture team should not supercede governance processes, yet the CAO will want to make clear that entrepreneurial activities are on a fast track and must be brought to fruition expeditiously rather than debated endlessly. Many campuses already offer courses under experimental numbers or provide an interdisciplinary degree rubric to facilitate innovative curricula and provide an outlet for individual creativity. The coordinated institutional strategy strives for that same streamlined approach from idea to implementation but requires more planning, investment, and accountability.

Looking for Opportunities

New venture teams are charged with scanning for new student interests, new markets, and emerging careers in order to enhance existing programs, create new programs, and provide academic access for new populations or new locations. The traditional portfolio of academic offerings can be considered for new formats, new calendars, new content, new teaching/learning modalities, new purposes, new locations, or nontraditional staffing. Many of the models will require different pricing structures, client relationships, and accounting for costs and revenues. To continuously generate ideas, each member of the team should be charged with tracking a different source, ranging from electronic job listings to the advisory board members for the business college. The challenge is selecting the right opportunities that will serve students and the community, be interesting for faculty, secure a revenue stream, and enhance the reputation of the institution. Successful innovation may help transform the campus.

Identifying the Target Population

Often, when a campus first begins to think entrepreneurially, development efforts focus on programs rather than markets or customers to be served. In the traditional academic environment, programs are created and then promoted to potential students based on the assumption that faculty know best what students and employers need. Business works the other way around, letting the market drive product development and working backward from what people want or need to what the business can do about it. One campus identified a large number of computer specialists in the community who had dropped out to join the dot-com boom of the 1990s and needed efficient degree-completion programs to enhance their career mobility. When the educational needs of different market segments are the focus, the institution becomes responsible for markets, learners, and outcomes, instead of for courses, credits, or programs and is freed of preconceptions about the content and format of academic offerings.

Determining Needs

Once the target customers are identified, the team must determine ways to capture their specific educational needs, including how important the need is, how it might be satisfied, and what the return will be to the institution. Methods for conducting a needs analysis range from qualitative personal interviews and focus group studies to quantitative surveys and questionnaires. Faculty in areas such as marketing and psychology can consult with the CAO and advise the team on the most appropriate methods. The market data collection system must be continuous, not episodic, in order to provide accurate, up-to-date information to support product development, pricing, and marketing strategies.

Creating and Screening Concepts

Moving from needs assessment to creating concepts requires determining the worth and feasibility of the project. Criteria used include: congruence with the mission, vision, and values of the institution; whether the new venture duplicates existing programs at nearby universities; ability to establish a market niche; and projected time to reach maturity. Feasibility of the concept can also be measured against such criteria as the extent to which the risks of initiating the venture can be shared with other institutions or other partners; availability of resources to support the new venture; and the expected return on investment. An example of shared risk and resources is the design of a program based on documented employer needs for Web design and electronic marketing. One four-year institution linked its expertise in English and art to the technology programs at the community college. The innovative two-plus-two program took advantage of facilities and equipment at the community college, which reduced costs for the four-year institution, allowed the community college to host a degree-completion program, and provided the skilled employees that employers needed.

The new venture team needs to be empowered to both recommend creative program development and consult at the early stage of their thinking with all those on campus who have a stake in the initiative. To facilitate further consideration and initial approval, the team can ask a department to develop a short concept paper rather than fully developed curricula. Based on the unit's analysis of how they can respond to the market needs, resources required, and measures of quality, the team and the CAO can provide a realistic assessment of whether the idea fits the mission and capacity of the campus and should be developed. Some campuses divide these responsibilities and rely on the administration to determine feasibility. However, if the administration turns down too many ideas as unworkable, the new venture team may give up, believing they are a token and that the administration will ultimately do what it wants.

Ensuring External Approval

Programs offered out of state, at remote locations, or delivered using distance-learning technology may require approval of the institution's governing board, state academic oversight council, and/or regional accrediting agency. The CAO must provide the new venture team with all the relevant external constraints at the outset. If the campus mission is limited to serving the region, an initiative aimed at students beyond the service area would not be approved. If the accreditation requirements place restrictions on off-campus programs, they need to be met. No venture should be initiated without the necessary approvals, even on a pilot basis. However, many entrepreneurial activities are not subject to the same external oversight as degree programs.

Determining Viability

Before launching any entrepreneurial venture, the operating budget with full costing and anticipated revenues must be developed. The initial budget will include both instructional costs for faculty, staff, and equipment as well as noninstructional costs such as advertising and publications. Depending upon the administrative model the campus uses for these ventures, overhead costs for space, libraries, and administrative support may be allocated to the program. Some start-up capital may be invested with the expected return delayed. If not a degree program, most campuses establish expected return on investment ratios and revenue sharing principles, for example, a 2:1 income-to-expense return with all additional revenues to the sponsoring unit. Revenue distribution is an essential incentive for faculty and units to participate in new ventures. However, running too many programs off-budget or with little return well beyond their start-up phase raises red flags with the business officer, especially if the program competes with an on-campus program and diverts potential tuition revenues from the institutional budget.

Initial Offering and Pilot Testing

To move a concept into action quickly, it can be tried first through a small-scale implementation to discover any conceptual or organizational flaws before too many resources have been committed. For example, one university wanted to develop extended campus graduate programs for a rural area. In piloting the first program, faculty learned that staffing by faculty overloads ensured quality in the short term but would lead to burnout in the long run. The CAO discovered that the budget model did not account for high first-year course enrollments (significant revenues) followed by subsequent years with smaller course enrollments (costs exceeding revenues) due to accreditation requirements for the advanced clinical supervision courses and electives. The ability to anticipate and resolve such issues increases when there is a standard protocol that includes a multiyear analysis of the costs, potential internal resource reallocation, and impact on current programs, faculty, and facilities.

Establishing Policies

Efficient management of entrepreneurial activities requires specific, and often standardized, operational and academic policies on such matters as student admissions, faculty extra earnings, control of content, credit toward faculty evaluation, and unit sponsorship of activities. Standard policies would include, for example, required credentials of the instructor and the maximum number of contact hours per week for a credit-bearing course taught in a compressed format. The use of new technologies requires clarifying the intellectual property rights of faculty who develop courseware. Other policies directed at ethical obligations would include, for example, a prohibition on instructors generating business or clients through their campus entrepreneurial role and diverting them to their own independent training and consulting activities. It should always be clear who has authority to make agreements on behalf of the campus and individual units. Policies should be brought together in a single policy document and approved through the governance processes of the campus. If policies are not clear, constant negotiation, monitoring, and misunderstandings take valuable staff time and divert energies.

Refining the Budget Model

Once the new ventures have passed through the concept, feasibility, and prototype gates, they must be assessed in terms of the resources necessary to continue the development and implementation. Support for a new Web-based program might include low-cost items such as library access as well as high-cost items such as computer service staff time for adding video-streaming elements. The budget model must accurately distinguish between development costs and recurring costs and estimate the number of offerings before the market is saturated. General overhead, such as upkeep and maintenance of distance-delivery classrooms, must be accounted for. The CFO needs to decide whether classroom rental is a direct, an indirect, or a waived cost; whether each program must cover all costs through charge backs; or if institutional funds will support an off-campus center.

Turning the New Venture over to an Academic Unit

In order for the new venture team to continue to explore ideas, they must turn new activities over to a unit for implementation and management. The unit is responsible for the initiative, approval through accepted internal governance processes, staffing and management, marketing, evaluation, and continuous improvement. Typically, degree offerings are handled through departments and most campuses do not allow ideas to go forward without an academic unit sponsor to ensure a strong connection with faculty interests and priorities. Departments, however, are not experienced in the kind of marketing, outreach, and service necessary for many entrepreneurial ventures.

Because there are so many business issues presented by entrepreneurial activities, many campuses organize these activities in a single unit with experienced staff. The success of entrepreneurial projects depends upon a high level of responsiveness to clients; thus special attention is paid to customer service. Support staff must provide logistical support and a full range of services ranging from advising and delivery of books to troubleshooting on technology issues and assessment. It takes particular skill to support faculty as well as clients and not get in the middle. To maintain quality control, the CAO should establish an advisory board for these new academic ventures to review their viability and academic quality at regular intervals.

Establishing an Entrepreneurial Process

- How can the energy behind academic inquiry be cultivated into entrepreneurial thinking?

- How might a new venture or innovation team work effectively on behalf of the campus?

- What resources are available to the team such as data on environmental scanning, administrative priorities, competition, national trends, and workforce needs?

- Is the time frame for development responsive to changing conditions yet not so fast as to inhibit quality results?

- What institutional criteria for effectiveness and efficiency must programs meet (e.g., comparative advantage, repeatable, economy of scale, or self-supporting)?

- How are experimental programs moved into the regular portfolio of offerings when appropriate (e.g., competes with regular offerings and stable enrollments)?

- What are the appropriate financial models and policies for a variety of types of offerings (e.g., continuing education, executive training, workshops, and on-line courses)?

- What administrative structure and staffing is appropriate to support different models of entrepreneurial activities?

- Are there sufficient incentives to involve faculty while at the same time not distracting them from regular academic offerings (e.g., department profit sharing, faculty development funds, overload pay, or credit toward tenure and evaluation)?

- If regular faculty are not providing the program, what methods of supervision and evaluation will be used?

RESPONDING TO COMMUNITY AND WORKFORCE NEEDS

Higher education has a long tradition of adult education, including continuing education, noncredit programs, conferences, and special institutes. Initially, ideas for outreach efforts were generated from faculty interests or client interests in personal enrichment. Increasingly, institutions are narrowing their focus to a more intentional assessment of community needs in order to offer specialized workforce training aimed at stimulating economic growth. As institutions accept greater responsibility for serving their community, they analyze skill deficits and changes in local industry. Although many continuing education programs still offer enrichment opportunities, the majority of revenue-producing activity has shifted to community, economic, and workforce development. Community colleges provide a significant proportion of customized job training, but any campus can seek partnerships and compete in nontechnical fields where start-up costs are low (Young 1997).

Clients are looking for quick response and value for their money. Thus, to be successful, campuses must match their strengths with a strategic needs analysis, select appropriate agencies with whom to partner, plan with stakeholders, provide start-up funds, design pedagogy appropriate to an increasingly diverse clientele, and commit to a quality product. Based on well-documented workforce needs, campuses design innovative health care management programs in collaboration with local hospitals and provide in-service training and preparation of teachers' aides through effective partnerships with schools systems.

Technology training, although in great demand, is among the most challenging needs to respond to because of the uncertain economy, rapidly changing technologies, high cost for training personnel, and considerable competition from for-profit training operations. In addition, many communities do not have the infrastructure, employment opportunities, and human resources necessary to support ongoing training and provide consistent economic development energy sufficient to take advantage of new technologies (Walshock 1997). Nonetheless, linking continuing education, economic development, and business incubation is a priority for a number of public institutions and community partners who hope to transform their regions. Reviewing case studies of exemplary entrepreneurial institutions, described in *Innovation U: New University Roles in a Knowledge Economy* (Tornatzky, Waugaman, and Gray 2002), can help CAOs understand the challenges and opportunities of new relationships. To provide effective leadership for such entrepreneurship, CAOs must get off campus and spend time with community leaders and major employers.

Benefits from these new relationships and the new workforce training focus go well beyond those of a specific program. Colleges and universities strengthen partnerships with the business community, share resources, and support community change. Traditional students have opportunities to work in the community and apply their classroom learning. Faculty have opportunities to study social, economic, and public policy issues from the inside. Unfortunately, these measures of success are open ended and cannot be documented in the short run except in terms of participation and good will. As entrepreneurial activities, the financial return must come sooner; thus the campus and community must see education of the workforce as a business venture in which both partners invest. Institutional resources can only be committed where there is real need and sufficient demand to produce profits. CAOs may need to insist that industry partners guarantee enrollments or support a program on a fixed contract. Contract education is low risk for the campus. For community partners and corporate clients, the return on their investment is in the increased availability and skill levels of the workforce.

As states encourage public institutions to make a greater commitment to economic outreach efforts, but do not provide additional resources, many chief academic officers are challenged to provide staffing. CAOs are understandably reluctant to move regular faculty from their role as educators to that of trainers. As a result, they may suggest that programs developed to respond to workplace shortages and skill needs be handled by instructors with different training and career aspirations. The availability of trainers and the relationship with community colleges are among the criteria for evaluating an institution's capacity to respond to training needs.

For any project, the planning team and faculty must work directly with industry professionals in order to adapt standard academic programs to be more directly relevant to the workplace or be willing to create wholly new offerings. Education is not the same as training. To ensure an institution-industry match, CAOs can require signoff by partners, involve industry leaders in planning sessions, or sponsor faculty-industry placements. Technology and business programs, especially, need partnerships with technology companies, collaborative arrangements with business partners to transfer knowledge, and opportunities to exchange expertise through executive-in-residence programs. These ideas are also useful for traditional academic programs, but their outward orientation is essential for training activities.

Workforce and community development activities range from a non-credit institute to a degree program, from a single session to a multiyear program, and from serving an intact cohort to open enrollment. Some activities will be offered on-site. Consequently, pricing of training activities, conferences, courses, and continuing education can be complicated. The formula always is based on direct costs, administration, overhead, projected revenues, and profit with the goal of increasing participation and the operating margin while bringing down the development and production expenses through subsequent offerings.

Among the issues the CAO needs to consider are whether each activity must meet a specific revenue target, whether activities can be summed together to determine unit profitability, whether an activity should be offered with low enrollment to recover at least some of the development costs, how to link pricing strategies to the market, and how to increase value without increasing cost. Helpful resources to answer such administrative questions and improve profitability and quality are available from the Learning Resources Network (LERN) and the University Continuing Education Association (UCEA). One rule that has held up over time is that to be competitive when working with business and industry, "the best strategy is to build the finest program possible and price the program to generate sufficient resources to support top quality" (Fischer 1987, 63).

Providing Workforce Training

- What level of commitment to community needs is appropriate for the institution?

- How much are community partners willing to invest in workforce activities?

- What role does the client play in design and development, and how is that reconciled with faculty views of academic freedom?

- How have the needs of the target population and the service area been identified?

- What credentials and specialized training do faculty need to provide these programs to new populations and with a different orientation?

- Do the activities need to be credit bearing? degree related? or credentialed by continuing education units (CEU)?

- How will quality assurance be established?

- How can contract activities as opposed to open enrollment offerings reduce risk?

DESIGNING NEW FORMATS

Dramatic changes in the students pursuing traditional forms of education has created demand for credit-bearing academic programs that are more tailored to varied student needs. Compressed time schedules, evening and weekend schedules, short courses, and certificates, for example, are all designed to make education accessible and manageable. These programs are also advantageous for campuses because they can get greater use of the physical plant, offer faculty additional income, use part time faculty, and attract students who may start in a certificate program or as a non-degree student and then decide to enroll in a degree program.

Developing Certificate Programs

Among the fastest growing new program models are certificate programs designed to signify that the student has developed special expertise in an applied area. Certificates may be given based on a few instructional hours or several weekends of study, but typically are at least the equivalent of a semester of credit-based work (Patterson 1998). Certificates are low risk as they are based on a cluster of already existing courses and require limited institutional investment for a significant return. Pricing is the same as for other credit-bearing courses. The CAO can assess the potential for expansion of the certificate program into a full degree or conversion of certificate students to degree status in another program already in place. The appeal for students is credentialing in a short period of time.

Certificate programs are not new to academia; however, with an increased emphasis on continued learning and the need in many industries for specific skills and abilities, certificate programs have begun to flourish in areas as diverse as nurse practitioner and hazardous waste management to provide specialized training beyond the bachelor's degree. Many certificate programs are very technical, such as forensics, whereas other certificates are more general, such as organizational management, and can serve the needs of varied careers. Some certificates are specifically designed to respond to a shortage in a profession such as a graduate certificate in educational administration. Unlike traditional degree programs, certificate programs often bring together intellectual resources across the university without regard to disciplinary silos (Cooper 1998).

Certificate programs are also relatively easy to establish. Most states have protracted processes for approving new degree programs but do not extend that approval process to certificate programs. Therefore, even though the internal curriculum approval processes applied to certificates may be the same as applied to new degree programs, the exclusion of external review and approval significantly shortens the overall process from conceptualization to implementation (Bernstein 1998). Similarly, certificate programs that decrease in popularity, demand, or professional need can easily be discontinued without external notification or approval. The low risk, ease of development, and flexibility appeal to both faculty and chief academic officers.

Designing Cohort Degree Programs

Another successful and fast-growing model is the cohort degree program, primarily at the graduate level. Executive M.B.A. programs, for example, are often designed in a compressed format with intensive weekend study to match the needs of the students and with content tailored to an experienced clientele. Education programs are offered in intensive summer formats to match the schedule of teachers. Cohort programs, designed to keep the students as an intact group throughout the course of the program, produce high levels of learning as the students benefit from the close working relationships with other motivated professionals. In addition, they take the curriculum in an intentional way that almost guarantees degree completion.

Faculty enjoy working with highly motivated students, yet sometimes need to add professionals as part-time faculty to ensure currency of content. The campus also benefits as it has a reliable student base, efficient use of resources, and predictable revenues. Many such programs carry a higher tuition than the traditional program because of the extra level of services, special mentoring, exceptionally qualified instructors, and the likelihood that the students are sponsored by their employers. Because the cost is high and the students motivated, CAOs must be sure there is a dynamic and respected cohort leader who can serve as both an advisor to students and marketer to both individuals and sponsoring employers.

Directors of such programs know that one of the first topics to be addressed must be "managing your career" in order to set the expectations and support systems in place that will make both the students and the program successful. Students are often surprised by the sacrifices they must make to keep up with the intensity of the programs. Cohort programs have difficulty meeting the needs of a student who must stop out of the program because of some life event or career change, although institutions often make provisions for the student to pick up the course through regular campus offerings. Campuses, students, and employers benefit from cohort programs because the fixed time period guarantees a predictable return on their investment.

Designing Programs to Meet New Student Needs

- What types of flexible structures can be tailored to adult student needs?
- What efficiencies are created when regular courses can be offered in a new format?
- How realistic are the programs as opportunities to advance students' careers?
- How available are faculty for advising and to support specialized student needs?
- What kind of staff support is necessary to market, coordinate, and assess the programs?
- Can students who start as nondegree convert their coursework to a degree program?
- How are the marginal costs for the program calculated if there is erosion in the cohort?
- What expectations do employers have when they are partners in these programs?

- What indicators should be used to measure the success or failure of programs?
- How often should cohorts be started to maintain a continuous presence in the market?

TAKING ADVANTAGE OF TECHNOLOGY

Of all the entrepreneurial opportunities available to colleges and universities, the use of new learning technologies for both campus-based curricula and outreach programs has caused the most controversy, trepidation, and financial risk. Public systems are under pressure to increase efficiency and access by moving to distance or distributed learning. Legislators threaten to freeze capital projects believing service to a greater number of students can be achieved through technology. Private institutions interested in capitalizing on student demand for accessible educational opportunities have also been attracted to the new technologies. Institutions with large off-campus enrollments have quickly converted to Web-based instruction. Even with the deterrent of large investments and uncertain returns, technology has been a force for educational innovation.

Although the number of students interested in accessing higher education through a model of "any time, any place" is steadily increasing, distance or distributed education is still not cost-effective for many campuses. Best estimates are that it is already too late for a campus without substantial resources and distance-education experience to become a major player as a provider. After initial institutional high expectations for distance education, many institutions have had to scale back efforts. Among the causes of failure are insufficient planning, rushing ahead believing that one had to get in early or be left out, underestimation of start-up costs, overly optimistic projections of the number of students who would pursue a degree this way, the unanticipated impact of the economic downturn starting in 2000, the recent collapse of several companies that promised to provide technical support, and the increased competition from companies providing training for their own employees (Carlson and Carnevale, 2001; Mangan 2001). Nevertheless, the rapid growth in technology-based instruction utilizing a variety of distance-education modalities has changed the university from a place for learning to a hub for learning.

Campuses that carefully plan based on understanding their market, learning modes, and cost structures have come to different conclusions about distance education. Many campuses are choosing a hybrid model of instruction that retains the best elements of both face-to-face and distance delivery. Others have taken a lesson from business, decided not to over-diversify and offer products that are not their strength, and made only a limited investment in technology. They import courses from other providers and integrate them with their own offerings in order to save design and infrastructure costs. Even more cautious campuses are content to stay on the sidelines, let a new industry emerge, and watch with interest as for-profit ventures such as the University of Phoenix and Caliber Learning Network develop. The principle behind each decision is to match technology projects to campus mission and capacity.

These new opportunities raise many questions to which CAOs need to respond. Business officers wonder whether the cost of delivering to remote sites can be justified when there are already fixed costs associated with underutilized campus facilities during evenings and weekends. Deans and department chairs question whether faculty members should be allowed to teach their entire load on-line and seldom be on campus. Faculty unions legitimately question whether students added to an on-campus class through compressed video transmission from another site constitutes an unauthorized increase in workload. Some faculty ask whether it would be easier to simply mail a videotape of their on-campus lectures and work with students through e-mail, rather than take the time to redesign their course and learn the new skills required to teach on the Web. Board members and state legislators who envision solving cost and access issues by having every faculty member teach hundreds of students through technology confront faculty resistance based on a different concept of quality education. Obviously, the many issues related to increasing access through distance or distributed education must be resolved in the context of the impact on the total organization.

In addition to the financial considerations in delivering via new technologies, CAOs face issues related to course ownership and incentives. Faculty are resistant to third-party involvement in their courses and resent control by program developers and instructional designers. Some campuses have boldly hired a totally different faculty to teach their distance courses through a separate college. Although separate units, and in some cases units independent of the parent institution, can protect the image of the core activities and expectations of faculty, faculty resentment is still not completely defused. CAOs need to systematically address such policy and culture issues and make an early decision that regular faculty will or will not be involved. Up-to-date intellectual property policies are a must to clarify who owns the course, what "work for hire" means, or how many times a telecourse can be offered without remuneration to the faculty member who developed it. Once distance education becomes a business decision, rather than an academic decision, it calls for different timelines and different outcome measures.

Responding to a Changing Learning Environment

- To what extent should distance education be handled as a marginal and entrepreneurial activity, and to what extent should it be integrated into all offerings of the campus?

- What are the implications for funding, management, technical support, student services, and enrollment for a successful distance-education operation?

- How should total costs be calculated for alternative modes of delivery?

- How should faculty be compensated for development and delivery of instruction with technology?

- Should formal agreements be signed to clarify institutional ownership of intellectual property when faculty are employed to create and deliver distance education?

- What skills do students need to access and be successful in distance learning?

- What are the implications for faculty hiring if the majority of one's work will be on-line?

CREATING NEW RESEARCH AND DEVELOPMENT VENTURES

Whether leading a small campus with modest research and sponsored program activity or one of the major research universities, CAOs must also provide entrepreneurial leadership for stimulating and managing this intellectual activity to the benefit of individuals, the institution, and the community. Among the issues chief academic officers deal with are how to enhance the intellectual capacity of the faculty with internal resources, how to market the campus capacity for external support, how institutional priorities and individual entrepreneurship can be coordinated, how to assess the contribution of these activities to institutional quality, and how to develop partnerships with government and industry. Because grant activity is an important source of direct revenue for the campus and has potential through licensing the results, good communication and collaboration with the chief financial officer (CFO) is essential to manage the fiscal and legal matters related to sponsored activities.

The increasing opportunities to turn new knowledge and new research techniques into commercial ventures has dramatically changed the role of higher education and blurred the traditional boundaries of the campus. Few campuses can even dream of matching the success of Gatorade and the $76 million dollar return to the University of Florida based on a 20 percent share of the royalties (Huntley 2002). On a smaller scale, however, many campuses are able to turn the ideas of faculty and students in areas as diverse as new drugs, software, and soybean varieties into patents, licenses, and start-up companies from which they receive royalty income or equity in the new business. Marketing the intellectual capital of the campus benefits the individual faculty member, the institution, and the community.

The increasingly entrepreneurial approach to research activity is not without consequences. For example, when funded by industry, academic researchers are pressured to streamline research goals, reduce the time between discovery and application, and may be prohibited from publication. CAOs worry about the propriety of accepting funds from companies with questionable reputations and how certain areas of research such as cloning may reflect on the image of the campus. CFOs worry about expanding activities through increased dependence on soft money. The philosophical questions about whether institutions should eschew commercialization and maintain their traditional role in openly sharing new knowledge rather than selling it must be resolved for each campus; however, the trend is clearly toward entrepreneurship and expanding commercial opportunities. Most CAOs have confidence that their campus can strike the right balance as they know that academic researchers have long relied on government support of their activities with limited negative consequences.

Faculty who are engaged in commercial opportunities to share their discoveries appreciate the support of their campus in sorting out complicated relationships so that they can spend their time on the research. Despite the best efforts of campuses, however, faculty note a number of barriers, including slow action from technology transfer offices, limited institutional funding for the patent process, and difficulty getting companies to recognize the commercial potential of really cutting-edge ideas (Blumenstyk 2002). To play a facilitative role in this complicated and unfamiliar environment, CAOs need to address directly any skepticism, encourage faculty, learn more about potential institutional relationships, make sure campus policies are appropriate, and hire sufficient staff experienced in commercial ventures.

Developing a Research and Development Plan

Many campuses have aggressive strategic plans for research development and do not rely merely on faculty initiative and a benignly supportive environment. In the same way new academic ventures are developed, potential research ventures need a coordinated approach. The research development team scans for opportunities for funding including foundations and corporations as well as federal and state agencies, aims to match funding priorities to faculty strengths, conducts capacity assessments to determine not just individuals but faculty who can form a research group for large-scale projects, and recommends incentives for faculty. Typically the sciences, engineering, and medicine are the drivers for attracting millions of dollars in revenues for basic and applied research. Education and health and human services have potential for attracting resources for training, curriculum development, and community-based projects.

For a research plan to be strategic and entrepreneurial it also needs to focus on strengths and opportunities that are not bounded by traditional disciplines. Increasingly, research breaks down boundaries, requires collaboration, and creates new partnerships beyond the campus. That is not to say that campuses should abandon faculty who pursue their scholarship alone or in a leisurely fashion, but that activity is not the focus of the institutional research plan. The CAO will need a degree of tact to guide the development of a culture where there are well understood institutional priorities without making it appear that faculty members need to fit their research into that mold (Karr and Kelley 1996, 35).

No CAO wants to be perceived as stifling the interests of individual researchers through a proactive approach nor would faculty stand for top-down management of their intellectual work. What CAOs can do is encourage activities that bring faculty together, promote collaboration, and result in strong research groups. An option is to ask all department chairs to host a series of faculty lunches with faculty from other units with shared interests with the goal of one collaborative grant from each department. Another is to take a portion of the indirect costs from grants and distribute it to departments based on collaborative activities designed to strengthen the research capabilities of the faculty. Having risk capital available can prime the pump.

Role of Research Offices

How campuses organize to support sponsored activities depends upon their size, volume of grants, management philosophy, and amount of oversight required by sponsoring agencies (Norris 2000, 18:5). Typically, the research office is a service center responding to inquiries, finding sources of support, helping with proposal and budget development, negotiating and managing awards, and overseeing compliance activities. The individual faculty member, not the institution, is the client, and the amount of grant activity depends upon faculty interests. Consequently, many campuses find that both the level of support and the number of faculty writing proposals remain roughly the same from year to year.

The CAO who wants to increase grants and sponsored programs will need to help the grants office add proactive strategies to complement the responsive approach and review the incentives and barriers for faculty involvement. Many grants offices have expanded their service capacity through technology and teach faculty to do searches, maintain faculty interest data banks, and rely on e-mail to increase communication with faculty. Proposal workshops, analysis of effective proposals, revision based on reviewer comments, and resubmission are all activities that move a campus from merely supporting sponsored activities to improving the rate of success. Accountability is based on both client service and institutional outcomes.

Many research support activities take place with little direct involvement of the CAO. However, the overall picture of who is seeking funding and how successful the proposals are must be analyzed by someone other than the grants office in order to effect an institutional strategy. For example, the grants office can submit hundreds of proposals and appear to be doing a good job, but the data might look far different from an academic perspective. One CAO new to a campus inquired as to why the majority of the proposals submitted were for less than $100,000. The director of the grants office was deliberately holding cost down hoping to improve the chance of getting funded since he was accountable for the number of successful proposals not the amount of funding. When the CAO changed the goal to total research dollars, the scale of grants changed immediately and suffered no less success.

Internal Research Support Programs

For research activity to be a significant revenue stream for the campus, position the campus in the larger research environment, and promote high levels of performance, it must have a focus and a center of gravity. To attract funding, both the campus and individual researchers must be known as a good investment. Analyses of awards show that funding goes to those with the capacity to deliver and a good track record. Because it is hard to break into the ranks, new investigator awards allow assistant professors to compete at an appropriate level. Many campuses use internal funds to build capacity, as well as to continue to support individuals whose work does not fit the institutional strategy.

Typical internal initiatives include travel funds, summer grants, equipment monies, release time from teaching, additional graduate students, laboratory space, and sabbaticals. The support may be managed centrally, at the college level, at the department level, through a faculty senate committee, or any combination. CAOs who want to increase the likelihood that these institutional investments pay off have clear requirements, require a research plan, use review panels to help allocate the resources, consult external experts, and hold faculty accountable through final reports describing both the outcomes and the dissemination plan. Although faculty do not like competition and peer review, the process helps faculty learn how to develop research proposals to meet standards similar to those of external competitive grant programs.

Campuses use various approaches for calculating how much support to give, how large each grant should be, and how best to distribute it. Internal support programs may be funded as a percentage of the regular operating budget as part of the faculty development effort, through the campus foundation from funds designated to support student and faculty research, or with a portion of the indirect cost recovery on grants and sponsored activities. Although many faculty believe resources should be distributed equitably and automatically, because faculty have different needs and not all are engaged in research, few campuses rely on per capita distribution except for travel funds. Whatever the level of support or however managed, most campuses hope that internal support will help a faculty member initiate a line of research, take risks in new areas, and eventually strengthen the faculty member's ability to attract external funds. In fact, the specific goal of many seed grant programs is to provide sufficient funds to do a pilot study or to initiate work with the clear expectation that a major grant proposal will be developed.

Most campuses use faculty committees to manage these internal resources, although deans and department chairs also have some discretionary funds. When funds are limited, campus committees are willing to establish selective criteria, for example, giving high priority to junior faculty, limiting eligibility to every three years, or reviewing the outcomes from the last research project for which the faculty member received support. If required to contain costs, the CAO may cap the total amount for travel, summer support, or the number of sabbaticals in a given year but would be reluctant to stop support altogether. When faculty are involved in managing internal funds, they are sensitized to institutional issues and are better able to advise the CAO on research policies and how to strengthen the research environment of the campus.

Incentives for Faculty

Real rewards, ranging from space and staff to increased income, are necessary for faculty to participate in grants and sponsored projects. Sometimes it is enough that an idea is funded, but far too many faculty are discouraged by the paperwork, restrictive policies, and bureaucratic hassles of grant management. When it is too difficult to do their work on campus, they turn to consulting or take a leave to work with industry. Many CAOs try to facilitate faculty work by improving grant management and carefully explaining policies on indirect cost rates, cost sharing, and regulations on faculty time and salaries, all areas of concern to faculty. Major research institutions set up technology transfer offices to pursue business development, contact venture capitalists, arrange licensing agreements, and provide technical and legal expertise on matters such as intellectual property protection, patents, and income and equity sharing.

Role of Students in Research

Graduate students play a major role in the research activities of a campus. In some fields, such as the sciences and engineering, doctoral students and post-doctoral students are supported by industry and do their research for a company under careful agreements about disclosure and publication. The students may be torn between an academic or an industry career if they are in fields such as medical physics. Faculty, recognizing that they are training students for both types of careers, work hard to create and sustain industry relationships, recognizing benefits to both parties. Increasingly, graduate faculty recognize that "successful and resilient academic professionals are 'intellectual entrepreneurs'" and aim to train graduate students to understand their marketability (Cherwitz and Sullivan 2002, 23). CAOs must encourage these relationships as the support keeps the graduate programs strong by funding highly able students, reduces the claim on institutional support, and provides career opportunities for students and faculty.

Undergraduate research is increasingly recognized as a significant contribution to both student learning and institutional research capacity. Faculty on liberal arts campuses who wanted to continue their research were the first to recognize the potential for involving undergraduates. To avoid conflicts of interest, CAOs need to be sure policies on student involvement in research are clear, especially when the faculty member is being paid for a project. Many policy handbooks prohibit double dipping and also make it clear that it is inappropriate for students to pay tuition to do work as a course requirement that the faculty member is also paid for as a consultant. Students should not have their grades dependent upon the faculty member's capacity to meet the sponsor's standards. When the undergraduate works with the faculty member on an unfunded project as part of a capstone course or independent study, there is no conflict. Careful oversight of new relationships developed through entrepreneurial activities can ensure high ethical standards.

Preparing the Research Plan

- To what extent do current academic programs and faculty strengths match the areas where funding is available?

- Is the campus recognized as a good investment for government and industry interested in new knowledge, inventions, and training activities?

- What percentage of the faculty are interested in developing proposals?

- How might project teams be put together to strengthen projects through collaboration?

- How might partnerships with other institutions strengthen proposals?

- What support services are available to help faculty develop and manage proposals?

- What role can deans and department chairs play in stimulating grant and contract activity?

- How can the staff of the development office and the grant office work together to establish realistic goals, additional contacts, and greater visibility for the campus?

- What is a realistic investment for the campus to make in expectation of generating new revenues to support research activities?

- What services are necessary to turn faculty research into entrepreneurial ventures?

DEVELOPING AN INTERDISCIPLINARY RESEARCH CENTER

When a group of faculty share research interests that cross disciplinary lines they often want to establish a center to provide greater visibility and serve as a vehicle for generating additional funding. Such centers are advantageous for both faculty and the institution if, after some initial support, they capitalize on the interests of the faculty, become highly entrepreneurial, and attract funding to sustain their efforts. Shared space, faculty fellows identified with the center, the resources of graduate students, and opportunities to host visiting scholars or produce publications lead to a breakdown of department and disciplinary boundaries. Centers should be established through a formal proposal that includes a clear mission, a well-thought-out plan for activities, agreement on responsibilities of the director and affiliated faculty, and a financial plan that conforms to all institution policies, overhead costs, and revenue goals.

Unfortunately, many campuses are littered with inactive centers, which confuse the image of the campus. Having stationery, a sign on the door, and a budget account number does not ensure the kind of intellectual activity appropriate to a forward-looking campus. Centers that are established at the whim of a single faculty member, cobbled together from departmental resources, housed in the faculty member's office, and engage few faculty colleagues simply do not have the infrastructure to thrive nor any accountability. Similarly, centers started based on a single donor's initial interest, but with little planning and accountability, are hard to sustain.

Too often, the CAO does not recognize that the center is a drain on the budget or believes that continuing to invest is necessary in order to get some return on previous investments. By establishing a center through a formal agreement for a fixed time period, with a clear budget, and measures for fiscal and intellectual performance, the CAO is in a better position to monitor the results. If a center is not able to meet its goals or becomes inactive, the agreement is not renewed. Without that formality, centers are as difficult to close as academic programs.

Creating a Research Center

- What activities have already been conducted that suggest a center is needed and why is a formal center more appropriate than the regular academic structures of the campus?

- How will the goals and activities of the center support the priorities of the institution's strategic plan?

- What staff, facilities, and affiliated faculty are appropriate for the center?

- What measures of intellectual effectiveness will guide the performance of the center?

- After start-up costs, how will the center become self-supporting?

- What measures of financial performance must be met to continue a center?

- What types of activities, for example, conferences, publications, and consulting, can add to the prestige and revenues of the center?

SEEKING GOVERNMENT SUPPORT FOR RESEARCH

Not all campuses receive government research support; however, for many it represents a significant source of support and sustains their ability to create new knowledge. Recognizing that the significant intellectual capital of campuses can be tapped to contribute to society, both federal and state agencies support pure research and applied research as well as program development and training efforts in areas as diverse as transportation, agriculture, health, housing, and the environment. Because grants, contracts, and other sponsored agreements can be an important source of revenue to a campus, CAOs need to understand how highly competitive grants are, recognize that funding priorities shift as administration priorities shift or the economy changes, and develop a diversified portfolio of research strengths and sponsors.

As competition for government support increases and indirect cost-recovery rates decline, the pressure on campuses to fund an increased share of research expenses leads observers to conclude that "institutions seeking to ensure the continued quality of their research in the face of this reality will have to become more creative, coordinated, and focused in their quest for research dollars" (Karr and Kelley 1996, 33). An institutional strategic research plan can reduce the inefficiencies of individuals, unit chairs, or deans working in an ad hoc way and help develop a reliable portfolio of sources of support. At the same time, CAOs and faculty must guard against letting sources of funding distort research interests.

Some institutions have increased their efforts to seek direct federal support through earmarks. Although highly criticized as "pork barrel" projects not subject to peer review, campuses cannot ignore that, in the

2002 fiscal year, $1.837 billion in federal funds went to higher education without competition, most of it for research (Brainard 2002). A recent analysis of the relationship between institutional lobbying and success in getting noncompetitive grants revealed that the amount spent lobbying was not as important as whether the institution was from a district with a representative on an appropriations committee and from the party in control (Brainard 2002). Many campuses are also successful in lobbying for direct support at the state level; however, CAOs need to be careful to protect faculty autonomy from political agendas.

Gaining Government Support for Research

- How can faculty with strong credentials related to funding agency priorities be identified and supported to seek external funding?
- Are there particular areas of research activity that the campus supports? is known for?
- What types of grants are appropriate to the capacity of the campus and might lead to continuing rather than one-time-only funding?
- What types of correlated projects are appropriate for funding from a variety of sources?
- Can small projects with small amounts from several sources add up to make up a significant research effort?
- What kinds of relationships with funding agencies increase success of proposals?

DEVELOPING PARTNERSHIPS WITH INDUSTRY

Collaborations with industry are often criticized as if receiving money for research taints the faculty member and the institution. With $2 billion annually from industry to support large-scale basic science research, universities cannot afford to ignore this source of support (Kirp and Berman 2002, 40). Major research institutions, funded by both the government and industry in three-way partnerships, are producing path breaking work in areas such as biotechnology, semiconductors, and genetic engineering of agricultural products. The partnerships are equally important to industry, as alone they could not sustain this type of work.

Running research like a business, however, takes a different mindset from traditional academic research. CAOs must be cautious and not let research programs depend upon a single source of support that could make them vulnerable to both criticism and continuation. CAOs also need to find appropriate ways to evaluate faculty performance when limited disclosure agreements prohibit review of work products. As this secrecy goes against the publication norms of the academy where it is expected that one learn from the work of others and that experiments are to be replicated and extended, many faculty prefer an open environment and will choose only the kinds of collaborations that allow them to share results. On the other hand, among the benefits that accrue to campuses through corporate partnerships are new labs and equipment, new science buildings, graduate fellowships, and named professorships funded by companies that have benefited from the work of students and faculty on their products.

Workload arrangements vary. In some cases a teaching faculty member is reassigned to a full-time research appointment to head up a research center, thus keeping the activities under the control of the institution. In other cases, the faculty member is given a reduced salary contract with full benefits, with salary replacement coming from the partner business. In that case the faculty member has two bosses. In other cases, the faculty member keeps an institutional affiliation but works full time for the industry or government partner with an arrangement much like for sabbaticals and relinquishes control of the work product. In still other cases, a university is able to lure someone from industry to head up a university research center, hoping that the significant reduction in salary is offset by the access to graduate students and research colleagues that cuts across institutional boundaries (Kirp and Berman 2002, 39). Although some arrangements may be individually tailored, the CAO must be sure all arrangements match campus personnel and sponsored research policies.

Many campuses invest in and house faculty entrepreneurial projects hoping they will develop into successful businesses. On a large scale they may develop a corporate research park, although it is estimated to take several million to start a corporate research park and a half a million to maintain it (Sausner and Goral 2002). Hoping to create jobs and have the businesses stay in the community, universities provide staff to help small start-ups develop a business plan, do market analysis, introduce them to potential investors, and sometimes put in their own venture capital. These universities are "hoping to leverage their relationships with business incubators to bring in research funding, attract entrepreneurial faculty and students, strengthen local economies, and bring in revenue from licensing research discoveries to startups" (Sausner and Goral 2002,

30). There are different ways to manage university-business partnerships, but it appears that the more independent they are, the more entrepreneurial they are.

Strengthening Industry Relationships

- What changes in the academic culture are necessary to take advantage of business-related opportunities?
- What expectation is there that if faculty generate funding to support their research, graduate students, and equipment needs that the campus will help market the results?
- What types of financial arrangements will allow both the faculty and the institution to share in the profits?
- Who is responsible for losses when the business incubation project is not successful?
- What are the limitations imposed by confidentiality agreements, and how can faculty document their work for tenure and promotion?
- How might a campus protect itself from the impact of the economy on industry's capacity to continue to support research?

SUCCESSFUL ACADEMIC ENTREPRENEURSHIP

In the present and foreseeable future, the CAO must go well beyond leading for long-term evolutionary change and confidently seek ways to identify, develop, implement, and learn from entrepreneurial opportunities. However, even when the CAO, deans, department chairs, and faculty collaboratively endorse a posture of innovation and development of new academic ventures and new research relationships, change may not come easily. Each institution has an organizational culture developed over decades through good times and bad times. Leadership and institutional well-being have a significant effect on faculty willingness to try new things.

If leadership is top down, the environment may not feel open enough to new ideas. If leadership is too parochial, the campus may look to others for ideas rather than tapping their own creativity. If resources are limited, the atmosphere may be too cautious for any risks. The fortunate campuses have an open-architecture style of leadership where change is led by people who have confidence in their contributions regardless of their formal position. New ideas are encouraged and innovation comes naturally in this environment. To guide an entrepreneurial and rapid-response organization, the CAO and other administrative officers must be committed to experimentation themselves and recognize both the risks and opportunities they face.

Entrepreneurship does not immediately result in significant revenues or a totally different campus. CAOs must be realistic about the life cycle of entrepreneurial ventures from introduction and growth through maturity to decline. Some ventures will be sustained and integrated into the mainstream of the campus. Thus, over time entrepreneurship can produce intentional and long-term changes in how the campus reaches new markets, serves more students, and impacts the community. These innovations can be the foundation for redesigning higher education to be more productive in a challenging environment. To become more entrepreneurial, the contemporary chief academic officer will need to create like an artist, experiment like a scientist, and risk like a venture capitalist.

CHAPTER 7

Program Review: Pursuing Academic Quality and Cost-Effectiveness

A t a time when campuses are judged by students, parents, employers, and legislators; when competition among campuses is intense; when funding may be linked to performance; and when limited resources need to be used to advantage, chief academic officers (CAOs) need more than the tools to measure effectiveness. They also need the courage to take actions to improve programs as well as eliminate programs that do not measure up. The tools designed to strengthen institutional effectiveness, namely, strategic planning, program review, assessment, and performance indicators, all have different histories, different methodologies, and different purposes. Thus, CAOs need to understand these processes separately, as well as the interrelationships among them, or risk being lost in a morass of documentation and reporting to many different stakeholders. Equally important, CAOs must be able to convince faculty of the efficacy of evaluation processes in promoting quality.

Campus administrators are often asked by those unfamiliar with their institution, "What is your campus known for? Which are the outstanding programs?" The vice president for academic affairs might name the most selective programs or those with recognized faculty. The vice president for student affairs might describe programs that are popular with students and increase applications. The vice president for financial affairs might cite the largest programs because of their importance to tuition revenues. The vice president for development might list the programs that are most appealing to donors and visible to the press. All will have difficulty answering the questions with any certainty because their measures are a mix of disparate variables, including demand, visibility, size, and reputation.

To determine quality with confidence takes agreement on a systematic evaluation process, relevant data, and judgment based on common criteria. Most campuses rely on academic program review as the basis for understanding effectiveness and on assessment to document student learning. Periodic program review has become a significant corollary to strategic planning as the process can identify strengths and weaknesses, set priorities for strategic investment, and link accountability to goals (Barak and Sweeney 1995; Eaton and Giles-Gee 1996).

Evaluation is no longer just an internal process as higher education is increasingly driven by accreditation standards and external expectations for accessible comparisons among institutions on key performance indicators (Gaither, Nedwek, and Neal 1994). Indicators of institutional effectiveness are as diverse as campus crime statistics, student loan defaults, extramural funding, graduation rates, and alumni giving. These many forms of evaluation, for both internal and external constituencies, serve multiple purposes, including improvement, resource allocation, accountability, consumer choice, and as the basis for public trust.

For any evaluation process to have credibility and actually bring the expected results, it needs to be carefully designed by those subject to the results. In the case of program review, faculty must be directly involved because they are ultimately responsible for developing and implementing programs and are directly affected by changes. Key administrators and boards must be involved because they are responsible for making difficult choices such as closing a program or changing funding priorities. The specific challenge for the chief academic officer is to create and sustain a faculty culture that recognizes that the future depends upon setting priorities, continuously adapting to a changing environment, and vigorously pursuing quality.

As campuses increase their understanding of how to plan for and measure effectiveness, program review remains the central strategy in the portfolio for academic quality management. This chapter provides advice on how to make program review more effective and suggests opportunities to link program review with other decision-making processes, including planning and budgeting. CAOs who want quality academic programs need not just connect these processes but also clearly communicate to faculty and other administrators the critical importance of communicating results and "closing the loop" by acting upon the findings. In this way, program review serves as a basic tool of good resource management and a stimulus for continuous program improvement.

DEFINING THE TERMS

Higher education has a long history of evaluation as the rational basis for measuring effectiveness. Over time, processes have developed ranging from voluntary accreditation to mandatory state audits for external constituencies to annual reports, program review, and assessment for internal purposes. No matter how carefully designed or how important these processes, evaluation is a sensitive matter and faculty often claim they are overevaluated and underappreciated.

Program review has been defined as "the process of defining, collecting, and analyzing information about an existing program or non-instructional unit to arrive at a judgment about the continuation, modification, enhancement, or termination of the program or unit" (Conrad and Wilson 1985, 10). Not structured as research inquiry, program review began as more of a description of what is. It is similar to "goal free" evaluation in that many aspects of it are nonprescriptive, allow for discovery in the evaluation process, and are focused on advocacy. Increasingly, program review has required clear goals set in measurable terms, and both qualitative and quantitative methods are used to look at inputs, processes, and outputs.

The process varies widely on campuses and is perceived differently by stakeholders as they often have different goals (Mets 1995). Faculty view program review as an internal process to assert their quality and make a case for more resources. Administrators see program review as a way to strengthen programs and build institutional competitiveness (Conrad and Wilson 1985, 11–14). States mandate program review hoping to reduce program duplication and eliminate unproductive programs. Despite widespread use of program review, critics argue that it still gives too much emphasis to intentions while providing inadequate information about real outcomes and comparative priorities (Dickeson 1999, 48). Campuses are challenged to make program review both formative and summative.

Assessment began in the 1980s in response to demands for greater accountability and clear evidence that the institution makes a difference in the lives of students. Assessment defines academic quality in terms of student learning and development, either as outcomes or value added. Assessment data for internal purposes is primarily formative and used for instructional and program improvements in a variety of academic and student affairs areas, including teaching and student support services. Because assessment provides direct measures of program success, it has become an essential part of academic program review rather than a separate process and in many states is used for accountability. Both program review and assessment are criticized by external stakeholders who care more about absolute comparisons among institutions on key performance indicators, such as retention and graduation rates, than about internal integrity, that is, "Did you accomplish your goals?"

Unfortunately, when resources are limited faculty are not motivated to do program review. Claiming little return, they resent the time spent. Faculty who fail to see assessment as an integral part of their work claim it is an add-on to an already busy schedule. Not only do CAOs face faculty resistance but also, too often, the many evaluation and accountability strands on a campus appear disconnected. Annual reports celebrate activities with little analysis of inhibitors to continuing success. Accreditation takes place unrelated to program productivity considerations. Program review focuses on student credit hours and faculty productivity rather than on student learning. Assessment, left to faculty discretion or the institutional research office, fails to be a continuous, coordinated, and integrated part of the planning processes of the campus. Strategic planning makes limited use of program evaluation findings as a basis for setting budget priorities. State reporting requirements emphasize easily reported quantitative measures to compare institutions and seldom follow up with processes that encourage improvement. When multiple evaluation efforts are ongoing and independent of each other, guided by administrators in different divisions, and used for both internal and external decision making, they can become unmanageable and counterproductive. Worse yet, faculty avoid, ignore, or fear them.

Whether internally or externally motivated, however, campuses must respond to the undeniable mandate for quality and accountability and help faculty understand that evaluation processes are no longer discretionary. Stakeholders need to see real connections between data and quality, as assertions are not enough. CAOs who can put findings into context are better able to help others recognize how data collection and analysis can lead to informed decisions and action plans for systematic improvement. Faculty resistance is reduced when they are active participants in the process and can see positive benefits. CAOs who provide recognition to individuals and programs and show how reallocations of time and resources make a difference can strengthen the impact of evaluation. The most important investment a CAO can make to promote quality is in working with faculty to develop credible and supported evaluation processes for individuals, programs, and the institution. Ultimately, the goal is to make evaluation and continuous improvement part of the "institution's fabric" (Schilling and Schilling 1998, 72).

Integrating Evaluation Activities

- Does the institutional strategic plan have specific academic goals and measures of achievement?

- Does each college and program have a strategic plan with a clear mission, goals, and outcome measures that are integrated with the institutional strategic plan?

- How does the annual report from each unit serve as the basis for both assessment of progress and recognition of achievement?

- Does each program have an ongoing outcomes assessment process and make use of the information to improve?

- How are faculty evaluation and program quality measures linked?

- How do institutional accreditation, specialized accreditation, and external program reviews inform the campus of its strengths and goals for improvement?

- Does the institutional research office have a regular evaluation program (e.g., senior surveys, alumni surveys, and employer surveys) and share the information with the campus?

- How does the campus make use of results of program and institutional rankings (e.g., *U.S. News and World Report* and the National Research Council)?

DESIGNING THE PROGRAM REVIEW PROCESS

When faculty are asked about their reaction to program review, they often respond, "We groan, we think of avoidance strategies, we recall past experiences being forced to 'account' to accrediting agencies and administrators" (Anson 2002). When seen as a task with no return for the time invested, it is a chore or a burden. Thus, whether designing a process for the first time or revising a process, the challenge for the chief academic officer is not merely helping faculty determine what to do and how to do it but also clarifying why they need to do program review and how to make the results meaningful. Program improvement, curricular integrity, resource management, verification of quality to others, or advocacy for state funding call for different types of information and analysis. Once the process is collaboratively designed by administrators and faculty to match the purpose, it is also up to the chief academic officer to ensure credibility by linking the process to the governance procedures and helping to solve the inevitable problems that arise in any process. Even the best paper process will fail without strong leadership and faculty support.

The chief academic officer guiding a campus review of the academic program review can consult the many good descriptions (Barak and Breier 1990; Dickeson 1999), case studies, and critiques of the processes (Conrad and Wilson 1985; Haworth and Conrad 1997) as well as a review of the literature on program review (Mets 1995). In addition, many campuses post their processes on the Web, including useful worksheets and calendars. What has changed in recent years, however, is the future orientation for program review resulting in closer links among strategic planning, resource allocation, and program innovation. Even outstanding programs are expected to have an action plan for future development.

Selecting Common Criteria

A fundamental principle underlying program review is that all programs are measured against the same criteria in order to ensure fairness and objectivity. Campuses may select different aspects to emphasize, add elements that reflect program variation, or elaborate on the criteria, yet the basic categories remain: importance, demand, quality, and cost (Dickeson 1999, 53–55). Achieving agreement on the criteria is easy. Weighing their relative importance, understanding how the criteria are interdependent, and doing a comparative analysis of programs are all far more challenging yet critical to producing institutionally significant results.

To be strategic, program review requires "portfolio analysis," rather than reviewing programs in isolation (Keller 1983, 154–55). A program might have strong student enrollments and require few new resources, yet be at a declining stage of the discipline. If continuance is based on current viability or a good cost/revenue ratio, the program would be kept. However, if program continuance is based on trends or on its ability to satisfy future demands, when compared to another developing program it might be phased out. Similarly, a program could represent a discipline for which there is nationally high demand, yet at the institution there is low demand, high unit costs, and no indication that growth will occur. Using the portfolio approach, this program would be seen as not living up to its potential and a candidate for elimination from the institution's inventory of programs. Not infrequently, administrators and faculty have different agendas with the former wishing to refine the portfolio and the latter wanting to keep all programs. For both parties to have confidence in the process and decisions of program review, both the criteria and their relative importance must be agreed upon at the outset.

Importance

Typically, in the category of need or importance are issues of *centrality* or *essentiality* to the institution's mission. Each program identifies how its curricular offerings, scholarship, and service support the institutional mission. Liberal arts colleges have protected small programs such as classics on the grounds that certain disciplines are essential to the very definition of liberal arts. The matter of centrality can be clouded, however, by forces external to the campus. For example, the state might provide incentive grants to encourage all campuses to provide teacher training. In that instance, it is hard for the claim of centrality as defined by the mission to be distinguished from the effect of external resources. The chief academic officer must determine which factors serve as justifications of centrality and which might not be defensible. Centrality also can be confused with core competencies. As an institution evolves, it generally does so from strengths, developing new programmatic offerings to satisfy the needs of new constituents. In some cases, a new program such as information systems may seem marginal in the beginning because of low demand yet grow over time fueled by external opportunities. The CAO needs to help faculty understand the distinction between programs central to the university at the current time versus programs that may be central to what the institution is trying to become as set forth in its vision and its strategic plan. Fundamentally, the test for all programs is whether the program can advance the vision of the institution.

Demand

A second set of criteria are related to *demand* for the program, usually defined in terms of student enrollments but, more recently, also in terms of employment opportunities and national trends. Many campuses have been caught off guard by changes in student interest resulting in massive movements away from traditional fields such as history and sociology and into new fields such as communications. Although faculty may believe students are fickle and unfocused, external demand always reflects a changing society and employment opportunities; thus environmental scanning has become an important part of program review.

Internal demand must also be measured. Aware of the factors that drive up student credit-hour production, departments may resist changes in general education requirements or major requirements to protect their status. The CAO can clarify internal demand by providing data based on an induced course load matrix (ICLM), which shows program interdependencies. With a credit-hour matrix made up with disciplines as rows and programs as columns, this array will show the enrollment generated by the department and the credit hours consumed by the department (Meisinger and Dubeck 1984, 213–19). The ICLM might show that demand for a program is primarily for general education courses and prerequisites for other programs. The CAO may ask whether continuing the major is justifiable; however, faculty will be very resistant to being only a service department. For a multicollege campus, contribution and consumption reports are often the basis for levying taxes and reallocating resources under a responsibility center budgeting process.

Quality

Centrality and demand are necessary, but not sufficient, conditions for maintaining or investing in a program; meaningful evidence of quality is required. For years, campuses were comfortable with using "inputs" as indicators of quality, for example, SAT scores, number of faculty holding a terminal degree, and percent of courses taught by full-time faculty. Many program review processes still emphasize these descriptors, but they are more indicators of potential than of quality. Unfortunately, many of the external ranking systems reinforce this input notion of quality as they rely on such indicators as student selectivity, faculty/student ratios, and size of the endowment. Some campuses emphasize distinctiveness of a program, although if it is merely a descriptor, such as an English program that emphasizes technical writing, distinctiveness will fail as evidence of quality. Program review should require more extensive evidence of quality, yet CAOs cannot ignore the influence of external rankings and need to monitor all measures that enhance perceptions about the institution's reputation.

Outcomes are the more important measures of program quality. A variety of indicators of results are used, including student scores on standard examinations, faculty publications, awards received, graduate school admissions, employment of graduates, consultant reviews, and accreditation results. On many campuses, departments are expected to have a continuous assessment program of student learning outcomes and show evidence of program changes based on the results, which are then reported as part of the periodic program review. Similarly, they may be expected to show evidence of increasing faculty productivity and effectiveness.

More difficult than selecting the indicator of quality, however, is selecting the comparator. For example, what does a first-to-second-year retention rate of 67 percent mean? It can be measured against the previous year's rate, if improvement is the goal. It can be measured against the predicted rate for students of a particular ability level, if meeting the benchmark is the goal. It can be measured against peer group data, if being best in class is the goal. Similarly, what does a faculty publication rate of one journal article a year on average mean? Compared to an internal measure of expected unit productivity, it can provide evidence of overall unit success. Compared to an individual productivity goal, it can reveal faculty who are not meeting the target. Compared to the average for all faculty in schools of a similar type, it can provide a peer ranking. In short, the strongest case for quality comes from placing the outcome measures in context.

Many campuses use different criteria for reviewing graduate programs. Masters level programs are often quite cost effective and not highly selective, with enrollments in terminal programs moving in inverse relationship to national trends in employment. Doctoral programs, with high unit costs, are held to particularly high standards in terms of student selectivity, completion rates, national rankings, employment market, and faculty productivity with the assumption that unless the faculty are active scholars they cannot provide adequate training to their doctoral students. Recent initiatives have added a focus on quality of training for teaching as well as research (Gaff, Pruitt-Logan, and Weibl 2000). Professional programs such as business or social work rely on specialized accreditation as additional evidence of quality.

The latest thinking about program quality focuses on the processes that produce quality results, primarily on forms of faculty and student engagement. Many program review models use process data such as student evaluations of teaching, ratings of services such as advising, and evidence of innovative pedagogy. What has been missing until recently is a demonstrated link between process and quality outcomes. Engagement theory focuses on how student learning is enhanced by interrelationships among students and faculty. For example, research findings show that students who work directly with faculty have deeper understanding, students who are supported in taking risks are more creative and imaginative, and faculty mentoring builds student confidence (Haworth and Conrad 1997, 31–39). The National Survey of Student Engagement (NSSE) allows a campus to survey the degree to which undergraduate students are engaged with campus activities, the community, faculty, and other students, all elements that have been identified as reinforcing learning (Kuh 2001). Documenting faculty and student engagement as it relates to accomplishing significant program goals clearly has meaning for formative evaluation that is aimed at program improvement. It also has meaning for consequential decisions about funding or continuance as the institution is obligated to provide adequate resources for faculty, facilities, and student support, but the department must demonstrate that the resources are used to support engagement such as undergraduate research and collaborative learning.

Cost

The role of cost, although given prominence in most program review processes, is not altogether clear. A survey of states in 1986 indicated that "demand, quality, program duplication, need, mission compatibility, and costs (in that order) were the crucial criteria" for review of undergraduate programs (Seymour 1988, 41). A decade later, much of the writing on the use of program review by states emphasizes productivity and cost about equal with quality and student outcomes as the critical factors in making decisions about program continuance (Eaton and Giles-Gee 1996). To reduce cost per program graduate, campuses increase class sizes, streamline curricula, offer the curriculum on a multiyear cycle, and increase the use of adjunct faculty. The program review experience on most campuses, however, reveals just how difficult it is to make decisions based on comparative cost of programs because factors such as class size and faculty salaries are not comparable across units. To have meaning, cost data must be set in context by comparison with similar program costs on peer campuses. Programs identified as being more than 20 percent more expensive than the same program on another campus might be flagged for further analysis.

Often boards, legislators, and state council members have unrealistic expectations about the cost savings to be achieved through reducing low-enrollment programs. They fail to recognize that as productivity declines, campuses gradually reallocate budgets and faculty positions. For campuses to achieve significant cost savings through program reductions would require cutting faculty positions (difficult because of tenure), taking space and facilities offline, reducing program interdependencies, and eliminating administration and support staff. Although such actions do take place opportunistically, such as not refilling a position when a faculty member retires, a campus cannot expect to pursue program quality only through sporadic and unplanned reallocations. It takes courage based on real cost analyses to undertake the kind of necessary campuswide and then system-wide restructuring that results in better alignment of programs and re-sources (Dickeson 1999, 23).

The role that cost plays in program review decisions is complicated because programs are not just cost centers. Programs generate revenues for the institution. Some programs attract highly qualified students with external sources of financial aid, others attract grants and sponsored pro-ject funds, others benefit from alumni fund raising and bequests, whereas others provide courses to other programs thus directly subsidizing them. Program support grants for health services pay for faculty and expanded learning opportunities for students. Other programs might serve students from community colleges thus creating the efficiency of 2 + 2 college com-pletion programs. CAOs may calculate income/expense ratios or net costs as a basis for internal comparison, however, few challenge the complex system of cross subsidies that allows expensive programs such as nursing and music to be supported by the institution.

Few program review models are designed around this kind of financial analysis nor are program review committees experienced with how to weigh these factors. At least one campus has agreed to separate program review into two phases. The first phase deals with quality assessment with strong faculty contribution and external expert reviews as well as cross-discipline collaborative review. The second phase is the responsibility of the deans and CAO and focuses on the financial side with the relative merits of programs being assessed in light of the institution's mission, its costs, cost comparisons with peers, and its position in the portfolio of programs. This has the advantage of underscoring that the quality of programs in terms of curriculum, teaching, scholarship, advising, and as-sessment rests with the faculty while the institution is responsible for ensuring adequate resources. The drawback to this approach is that it insulates faculty from responsibility for the effective management of re-sources and the difficult local choices about how best to use limited re-sources to accomplish their goals.

Calculating Program Costs

- How many faculty are assigned to the program (e.g., full time, part time, temporary, other units)? What anticipated changes in mix might increase or decrease salary costs?

- What is the current total for faculty salaries and benefits? How is the total affected by the demographics of the unit (e.g., age, rank)?
- What anticipated faculty salary costs are associated with the program? How will this be affected by market competition?
- What is the average class/section size? Will the faculty/student ratio change in the future?
- What is the average faculty load (e.g., number of courses and credit hours)? Is it above or below the institutional average?
- What portion of salaries is associated with teaching responsibilities? What portion is reassigned for research or service responsibilities?
- What is the current staff salaries and benefits total?
- What are the program noninstructional costs?
- How do the unit costs differ when they are allocated by general education, majors, masters, and doctoral programs?

MAKING PROGRAM REVIEW MANAGEABLE

The program review process must be perceived as systematic, impartial, data-driven, manageable, and productive. Typically, the process takes a year or more to provide time for data gathering, analysis, committee review, design of an action plan to respond to recommendations, implementation, and follow-up. Depending upon the size and complexity of the institution, these stages may first be at the college level and then institution-wide with recommendations to decision makers also at several levels including various academic administrators, the president, board, or state council. Some campuses expect programs to gather data for several years culminating in a self-study or portfolio submitted at a specified time. As more institutions develop data warehouses and relational databases accessible by department chairs, the program review process becomes an ongoing assessment rather than an every five-year report card.

Program review usually is selective and periodic, with a set of programs being reviewed at a time on a five year to seven year schedule. Campuses that review every program at the same time find this extensive effort time consuming and disruptive of other activities. Proponents of total review, however, argue that it is imperative to establish a common baseline for all programs and consider the entire program portfolio in the same time frame and budget context in order to set priorities (Dickeson 1999, 48–49). Only by reviewing the entire portfolio, with strong leadership and faculty involvement, can a campus hope to overcome the politics, protectionism, and complacency that resists tough decisions. Critics of full-scale review, however, note that not only do faculty resist restructuring but also they burn out from the overload of full-scale program accountability. In that case, they see the activity as an administratively imposed burden rather than an activity that promotes institutional quality.

Periodic review of a limited number of programs at one time, the preferred model on most campuses, also has limitations. When program review is either irregular or on a five year to seven year cycle, the timing in the history of the program or the financial trends of the campus can cloud reality or make the fate of the program more precarious than expected. One program might benefit from the halo effect of some special event while another is caught at a moment when it is particularly vulnerable. For example, a program might have just received a large grant that justifies hiring a faculty member whereas another has had several retirements and looks like a prime candidate for being phased out. In both cases, if the programs came up for review a few years earlier or later, the recommendations on continuation or elimination might be very different. The chief academic officer who exercises caution in taking advantage of unusual internal circumstances and retains oversight for a program can always wait to make appropriate decisions in subsequent years (Ferren and Barnard 2001).

External events can also affect program review decisions. A set of programs might come up for review at just the time when a statewide recession leads to a budget reduction making it appear to necessitate stern recommendations. To dampen the effect of situational criteria, campuses review all of the sciences or all of the arts in the same year so that the decisions are not just about individual programs but are comparative and in the context of the whole division. Campuses have also found that reviewing all masters or all doctoral programs at the same time allows them to judiciously winnow or develop programs based on changing external needs.

What constitutes a program, usually based on Classification of Instructional Programs (CIP) codes from the Integrated Postsecondary Education Data System (IPEDS), how many programs can be reviewed, and in what order they should be reviewed must be determined. Many campuses begin with the department as the unit of analysis and review all separate degree programs and options within the department. Some campuses want to have the benefits of program review for university-wide programs such as honors, general education, and study abroad. Some campuses design program review to coincide with specialized accreditation to reduce the work and achieve complementary results. Others put program review and accreditation on different schedules so that the one process suggests improvements that result in a stronger case for reaffirmation of program accreditation. There is no one right way; however, the schedule must define a manageable amount of work, give units advance notice, ensure sufficient time to conduct each part of the process, establish deadlines, and be congruent with the working culture of the campus.

Although timing and scope are important, the more serious concern about program review is that it is mere ritual and effects little change because the steps for implementation and evaluation of changes are unclear. Many campuses include a formal process with clear timelines for responding to recommendations rather than leave departments on their own to effect improvements. Deadlines for developing action plans and reporting on progress are set for appropriate intervals for both the units and the academic leaders overseeing the continuous process. The CAO is responsible for planning budget reallocations and holding departments harmless if there is no discretionary money for immediate use. In some cases, a program might be recommended for full review again, earlier than the expected cycle, because its situation requires greater attention. Reviewing the process regularly, tracking the results, and requiring interim reports are all critical to counter inertia and ensure ongoing institutional development.

Managing the Process

- Who is responsible for overseeing the process, informing units of the schedule, providing relevant data, and receiving documentation?

- What role do faculty, department chairs, deans, and other administrators play in the process? How are they oriented to the process goals and possible decisions?

- If there is a program review committee, how is it related to internal governance?

- What standardized multiyear data sets are available to support trend analyses? Can the unit arrange for additional studies?

- If external reviewers are used, how are they oriented, and what documentation do they receive? What standing will their report have compared to those from on-campus entities?

- How is face-to-face consultation between the program faculty and the program review committee facilitated? Is the consultation aimed at advocacy or clarification?

- How much time needs to be provided for each stage of the process?
- After recommendations have been made, who drafts the action plan? What financial commitment does the institution make to the action plan?
- How will implementation of recommendations be monitored and evaluated?
- How much of the information (e.g., self-study, committee report, CAO response, and action plans) will be made available to the whole campus?

PREPARING THE PROGRAM SELF-STUDY

In order to ensure comparable information as a basis for judgments, the study period should be specified (usually three to five years) and the office of institutional research (IR) should provide a common data set related to the established criteria for each of the programs being reviewed. The standardized information would include descriptive data such as enrollment histories, faculty staffing, and credit-hour production as well as more complex analyses such as program costs. IR staff should also be prepared to provide data on quality, such as major field achievement test scores, career placement data, and alumni satisfaction. Program faculty will supplement this data with additional evidence of quality such as faculty publication records, grants received, and evidence of external recognition. Some departments err on the side of too many data elements if a set of guidelines is not specified.

A self-study is strengthened by involvement of all department faculty. Faculty may assume the self-study is the chair's responsibility because the chair typically writes the department's annual report. The chair should resist acceding to past habits because the strongest reviews are those that are guided by faculty and carry their language, values, and aspirations. The department chair can then provide leadership for harmonizing individual faculty perspectives and testing departmental thinking against the realities of college resources and priorities. The chair also can maintain a liaison role with the dean throughout the process so that the dean's recommendations, though independent of the faculty's, will reflect understanding of the department and programs.

A typical criticism of self-studies is the faculty tendency to write pages of persuasive rhetoric with limited analysis of the data. Because a committee is usually made up of faculty from many disciplines who are unfamiliar with the program and must make recommendations based on the self-study, faculty need to present data in charts and graphs accompanied by analyses based directly on the information. The analyses should be more than self-comparisons that note trends. They should be anchored by meaningful comparators such as similar programs on the campus and programs at other institutions that are comparable. Documenting the processes such as student recruitment, curricular revision, department planning, or faculty development that lead to the results in the graphs can also provide appropriate context. When a study is inadequate, the committee may find it difficult to send it back for revision; however, they will find it even more difficult to make appropriate recommendations without a good basis.

Perhaps the most difficult challenge for the department chair and dean is to persuade faculty that it is in their best interest to tell the whole truth, to identify weaknesses on their own, to address resource needs realistically, and to propose strategies for improvement. If the self-study is candid, faculty can learn from the review, align their findings and recommendations with the department plan, and take charge of change rather than feel program review is a bureaucratic process that is being done to them. When it is clear that the program review results in institutional actions, faculty are motivated to try to shape the results.

One section of the self-study should address how realistic the aspirations of the department that houses the program are given the institutional context, the extent to which the department plan has been accomplished, and any impediments to success that need to be addressed. Sometimes the link between the department's strategic plan and program review is unclear since they are often produced at different times and for different audiences. A unit may have well-established goals and action plans but fail to use the program review process to identify any gaps between goals and achievements. The CAO needs to help deans work with department chairs and faculty to demonstrate how annual reports, assessment, strategic planning, and program review should all work together to both evaluate and promote quality.

Typical Descriptive Data Elements

- Enrollment Data: number of applicants, number admitted, number enrolled, enrollment trends, admissions requirements, and transfer credit policies
- Degree Programs: number of majors in each program and concentration, number of students completing each degree program by

concentration, placement of graduates, and enrollments and degree completion by program in off-campus locations

- Curriculum: five-year course history by section and enrollment, additions and deletions to the curriculum, changes in degree requirements by each degree and concentration, accreditation, course demand by other majors, and participation in internships

- Student Data: mean and range for undergraduate SAT scores; graduate GRE, GMAT or other exams; geographical distribution; gender and ethnicity; retention; and outflow to other majors

- Faculty Data: number of faculty by rank and tenure status, percent of credit hours taught by part-time faculty, changes in total full-time equivalent faculty over five years, teaching load for each faculty member by course and student credit hours (SCH), and allocation of faculty to undergraduate and graduate

- Other Personnel: clerical staff, specialized personnel (e.g., lab manager and technology support), and graduate assistants by work assignment

- Facilities for Exclusive Use of Program: office space as assigned, teaching space (e.g., classrooms, seminar rooms, and labs), research space, and technology resources

MAKING JUDGMENTS AND RECOMMENDATIONS

For program review to have credibility, faculty must be directly involved not just in designing the process or in the department self-study but also at subsequent stages when recommendations are made. Most campuses use a representative committee made up of administrators, faculty, and students to provide variety in perspectives and to balance competing political pressures. Some campuses use separate faculty panels for the initial review of each program. Large campuses often use committees within each college to make recommendations before the self-study goes to a central committee. Some campuses take advantage of already existing structures such as curriculum committees rather than establish separate committees. Whatever the structure, the membership, or the authority of the program review committee, the importance of informed judgments and the meaning of "recommendation" must be clear.

Critics of program review committees argue that vested interests will always be at play and question the degree to which faculty can be relied on for honest self-evaluation. Thus many campuses use external reviewers to increase the impartiality of the recommendations. External reviewers can also break through a good program's self-satisfaction and provide a fresh perspective. The campus may send the documentation to an external reviewer, invite an external reviewer to sit with the committee as it deliberates, or encourage the program to include observations from an external reviewer as part of their documentation. Each approach has a different purpose and value but must have the confidence of the faculty to be effective. Many campuses believe external reviews are particularly important for doctoral programs because the programs are expensive, departments rely on graduate students for undergraduate teaching, and there are concerns about overproduction of doctorates. If external reviewers are used, it is particularly important to orient them to the institution so that their recommendations and perspectives are meaningful, rather than reflect assumptions based on their home campus.

Typically, campuses involve some administrators on the review committee to provide institutional perspective. The chief academic officer may sit with the committee, at least in the final stage to hear the discussion, or receive only written recommendations. The specific role of the CAO is particularly important to clarify. The extent to which the CAO is bound by the committee recommendations or can exercise independent judgment must be understood.

No matter how clear the process and how much faculty have participated, evaluation always leads to tension. The chief academic officer needs to be especially careful about the tone and language of recommendations and correspondence with faculty to avoid an adversarial response due to these heightened sensitivities. To further minimize the inevitable tensions, members of the committees must be committed to understanding each program in several ways: on its own terms, as it is affected by the larger institutional planning and resource context, as the program impacts and is affected by its relationship to other programs such as general education or honors, and as the program functions in comparison to similar programs in the institution.

Program review recommendations should be of two types—those that are program specific and those that address broader institutional concerns. When the issues revealed by program review are a result of institutional challenges such as enrollment, it is unfair to hold a unit alone responsible for addressing the issue. To do so damages the credibility of the process. The program-specific recommendations serve as the basis for the departmental action plan for improvement and may or may not be shared with the full campus. In contrast, all institutional issues that are revealed through program review should be widely shared so that they can inform the planning, budget, and decision-making processes that affect the future of the campus.

Most models for program review leave the critical decisions about enhancement, continuation, or termination to the chief academic officer. Many campuses arrange for consultation between the program faculty and the review committee before their recommendations, with justifications, go to the chief academic officer. The CAO, in turn, may arrange to consult with the department before making final decisions. The time spent on such discussions is a far better investment than time spent on clearing up misunderstandings afterward. In all cases, actions based on recommendations should follow established governance processes and match the decision-making culture of the campus. For example, curricular revisions would go through all the appropriate curriculum committees. CAOs who unilaterally require changes or use a separate decision-making process will create faculty resistance.

Recommendations for program discontinuance are particularly difficult to make and are usually preceded with recommendations for reconfiguration or consolidation in an effort to see if incremental change will make a difference. Critics would argue that either step delays the inevitable and defeats one of the primary purposes of program review. Nevertheless, only after consultation with faculty, deans, the chief business officer, and the president should a chief academic officer take on the difficult issue of recommending program closure. Program termination must always follow campus policies for reassigning faculty and providing for program completion for students.

Invariably, despite efforts to make program review a collegial and positive experience, on many campuses faculty feel it is bureaucratic and unsympathetic to their interests. The psychology of evaluation is complex; the negatives are heard and remembered long after the praise is forgotten. The value of faculty involvement in program review is that they are sensitized to these psychological dimensions and also get a better sense of institutional priorities and limitations. They learn that from the outside a program can appear quite different from how it seems to the department, that there are no easy choices when faculty interests are at stake, that many problems are shared by others, that resources are limited, and that change is inevitable. They may also learn that too many programs can mean that all are underfunded. Because it does take adequate resources to make a quality program, in a zero-sum game priorities must be set. Nonetheless, most program review processes emphasize recommending areas for improvement and are silent on just how decisions for reducing or phasing out a program might be made. Even fewer recognize or reward exemplary programs in any significant way.

Table 1
Program Review Recommendations

Criteria to Be Used for Review	Maintain an Academic Program	Strengthen an Academic Program	Reduce or Phaseout an Academic Program
Importance of the program.	Central to the university's mission and strategic plan.	Central to the university's mission.	Not central to the university's mission.
Demand for the program.	Measures of demand are strong (e.g., program supports other majors, fills niche in region and strong placement of graduates).	Program's production and demand need to be strengthened (e.g., potential to increase enrollments, and redesign to meet employer needs).	Program's demand and production do not meet the university and/or state performance expectations (e.g., low enrollment, limited job opportunities).
Quality of the program.	Program's quality is substantial and notable (e.g., relationships and/or alliances with other academic units are strong, assessment data on student outcomes very positive and active faculty).	Program's quality could be strengthened through program reconfiguration, (e.g., needs substantial modification of the curriculum, deleting areas of concentration, and reorganization of the department faculty).	Program's quality and/or contribution to the institution is not substantial enough to justify its continuance (e.g., productivity of faculty inadequate and assessment of learning shows inadequacies.)
Costs of the program.	The data demonstrate that the program is cost-justified and efficient (e.g., appropriate income/expense ratio).	Efficiency could be increased (e.g., through relationships with other units and elimination of courses).	The program's reduction or phaseout would not adversely impact other units at the university.

ALTERNATIVE USES OF PROGRAM REVIEW

To maximize the advantages of any evaluation process, the process should be designed with the end in mind: What actions are to be taken? What information will help support those actions? This section addresses three quite different decisions based on program review—curriculum improvement, establishing selective excellence, and program termination. If evaluation is to be worth the effort, campuses must make difficult decisions about quality, determine what programs are worth investment, and be committed to reform as well as renewal.

Using Program Review for Curriculum Improvement

Many models of program review focus primarily on student credit hours and give little attention to close analysis of course offerings, course sequences, currency of content, or methods of evaluating learning. It is assumed that these matters are taken care of as part of the daily life of departments and that offerings are consistent with national norms. In reality, curriculum is designed a course at a time, reflects special interests of the faculty and trends of the discipline, and seldom receives scrutiny in its entirety by the program faculty. As a result, over time a program can become ungainly, have courses supported by a single faculty member, or have outdated program options with almost no enrollments. Reconfiguring the curriculum, refining the mission of the program, and adjusting course sequences so that they are relevant and offered regularly are all recommendations that a department should make on its own behalf and not leave to a program review committee. Yet with little pressure to review the overall curriculum and no leverage to handle special interests, such regular housecleaning does not get done.

A useful program review guide that focuses on curricular integrity, *Program Review and Educational Quality in the Major* (Association of American Colleges 1992), emphasizes attention to educational practices, faculty commitment to teaching and learning, and the structure of the program. The self-study would address critical questions, such as: What is the strategic environment in which the curriculum operates? How does each course contribute to student outcomes? How is the curriculum structured to move from introductory work to more advanced work? How is the curriculum in total assessed to ensure that students have the requisite knowledge and skills? How is this information used to improve the curriculum, concentrations, and courses? How are courses that meet general education requirements assessed and improved? What curriculum changes are anticipated in the next five years? In this way, the adequacy of the process for keeping the curriculum vital and the resulting curriculum are evaluated. Program review models that emphasize currency of the curriculum require a status report on the discipline, a trend analysis from the disciplinary society, course comparisons with institutions deemed to have strong programs, and evidence of ongoing curricular change.

Using Program Review to Establish Selective Excellence

Program review recommendations often suggest additional resources to remedy program deficiencies. The more controversial outcome of program review is the allocation of additional funds to an already strong department. Such efforts to designate "centers of excellence" are based on the premise that no institution is recognized for all its programs but rather for just a few truly outstanding programs. Administrators rightly claim there should be no tolerance for any weak programs and, moreover, find little evidence that adding additional resources to a weak program will do much more than make it average. In a highly competitive environment, there is no demonstrable value to making all programs average as the result would be a whole campus that is merely average. Consequently, in an effort to establish institutional distinctiveness, already strong programs are candidates for new funds to be invested in prominent senior faculty, endowed chairs, higher stipends to attract excellent graduate students, and reduced teaching loads to facilitate research—all strategies believed to further strengthen a good program.

The arguments for the strategy of selective excellence have become stronger as resources have tightened. Observers of higher education criticized the "upwardly mobile" focus of the 1980s, claiming that all institutions cannot expect to be outstanding but can aspire to selective excellence and should allocate resources for the best return (Hawkins 1998, 12). Selecting programs for investment can be based on carefully chosen actual as well as aspirational peer data to demonstrate a program's present strength and future potential. New resources are then directly related to a multiyear plan with clear goals and broad faculty commitment to achieving the measures of excellence. The assumption is that the faculty desire to achieve, which initially made the program strong, will continue and have even greater impact with additional resources.

Using Program Review for Program Termination

Politically, the most difficult program review recommendations are those that call for a significant change in a program or, at the extreme, its closure. If there are few enrollments or the program has temporary faculty, there may be little claim for continuing the program, but it is never that easy. The more difficult case is when a program meets societal need, has high student demand, and selective enrollments, yet does not have the resources to compete effectively for faculty or provide up-to-date facilities. Without other highly productive programs to subsidize the strong but underfunded program, the prudent administrator may well suggest its closing because the resources necessary to sustain quality simply will not be there in the future. In this case, program review reveals issues related to long-range viability.

Chief academic officers faced with continuing decreases in resources are beginning to fear that all programs will be starved into mediocrity. With few other choices, they may propose that eliminating several programs, departments, or maybe even colleges is essential pruning for survival. Because many program review processes are not explicit about the criteria for program closure, one study suggests that, in the end, the rational process of program review is not the sole basis. Administrators purport to make decisions based on program review information and have "to give the illusion of doing the right thing" but make the program closure decision that they can get faculty to accept (Eckel 2002, 238–40). Programs with weak leadership, no champions, no linkage to other programs, and few faculty and students are the most vulnerable.

Despite the difficulties and admonitions against "institutional cowardice," there are positive case studies of campuses using program review to effect change (Leslie and Fretwell Jr. 1996; Dickeson 1999). One particularly persuasive president challenged faculty to make all programs excellent within three years, and if they could not do so, to consider other ways to configure their curricular offerings or be phased out. As a result, many programs took systematic steps to become strong, some elected to be eliminated, and others joined efforts to develop innovative interdisciplinary programs. Such campus case studies can help CAOs identify incentives and strategies to encourage responsible faculty action on their own campuses. More important, these campus experiences clarify the need for strong leadership and careful selection of faculty leaders, and also confirm that major restructuring is possible.

Making Changes Based on Program Review

- How can unit-developed action plans improve quality? improve productivity?

- What incentives are there for faculty to willingly engage in curriculum revision?

- How can curriculum improvements be made without additional resources?

- If a program is out of step with trends in the discipline, what support will faculty need to revise it? What opportunities are there for interdisciplinary development?

- Should certain programs receive special treatment and be singled out as candidates for selective excellence?

- How will these programs enhance the overall image of the university?

- Should weak programs be strengthened or should resources be invested in programs with potential to become stronger?

- If programs are chronically weak, should they be terminated outright rather than be allowed to drift and be further weakened through reduced support?
- What would it take to increase the expectations for students and standards for programs throughout the institution?
- What institutional resources are needed to achieve higher levels of performance?

STRENGTHENING PROGRAM REVIEW

Program review can promote internal integrity of a program, provide guidance for improvement, and suggest viability in the future. However, for the "whole to be more than the sum of its parts" and advance the institution, program review must be directly linked to assessment, strategic planning, and budget. When these processes work in tandem, program review is the framework for assessment of student learning, an impetus for developing new programs to meet new student needs, and a realistic guide for funding priorities.

Linking Program Review and Assessment

Assessment is the natural follow-up to course design and instruction, providing useful data to improve an individual faculty member's teaching and document student learning by course or program. The challenge for any CAO is how to create a well-understood campuswide assessment program that evaluates the total student experience and supports institutional development. Faculty are increasingly well informed about assessment, and many campuses are allocating resources to help tailor assessment strategies to individual faculty, unit, and campus needs (Schilling and Schilling 1998). Extensive writing and national meetings on assessment offer good advice on how to plan assessments, the types of data-gathering methods, and varied uses of the findings (Erwin 1991; Banta 1993). Nonetheless, what is missing on many campuses is a way to coordinate the wide variety of assessment activities, learn from the results, and integrate assessment into institutional life rather than have it remain an add-on.

To achieve better results, many campuses use program review as the framework to promote continuous assessment, to ensure regular use of assessment findings, and to monitor the quality of the assessment program. The CAO can encourage faculty to be selective in what they choose to assess, gather data regularly, and document the steps they take to improve student learning based on the assessment findings. That information is then presented as part of the program quality measures, either in terms of value added or absolute outcomes of student success. When recommendations for improvement or program changes are made, the assessment strategies are also carefully designed and a timetable is established for monitoring effects.

Leaving assessment focused at the program level, however, will not address the significant challenge of setting high institutional expectations. The program review committee, in looking at a number of programs at the same time, should identify areas in all programs that need institutional attention, for example, communication skills, increasing student responsibility for learning, or greater engagement between faculty and students. When assessment strategies cross programmatic boundaries, program review leads to greater coherence for the student's total academic experience. Guided by the report *Greater Expectations: A New Vision for Learning as a Nation Goes to College*, all campuses are encouraged to use a "culture of evidence" and commit to raising standards for student achievement (Association of American Colleges and Universities 2002, 40).

Linking Program Review and Strategic Planning

When a campus has sufficient resources to support new ideas, proposals for new programs do not require complex analyses and assessment of student and faculty interest. In the current environment with little, if any, institutional risk capital available, chief academic officers often wonder how curricular renewal and new program development can be supported. Many campuses have found that one solution to the matter of stasis is to link strategic planning and program review to create an environment that expects innovation and redesign of the future of the campus through identification of new program opportunities, reconfiguration of programs, and elimination of programs no longer central to the mission of the institution.

When program review requires an environmental scan, a critical stage in the strategic planning process, the unit must take account of both what is happening in the discipline and what new societal demands are emerging. The environmental scan could also lead to investment in programs with high employer demand for graduates, such as information systems, or provide protection for programs that are not keeping up with national demand, such as education or nursing. In addition, such an analysis would reveal that the end of the Cold War has all but shut down Russian programs and Soviet Studies, yet world terrorism has created demand for expertise in intelligence work, security studies, and public health. Campuses with current strengths in related areas or fledgling programs in these areas can reallocate resources to do proactive program development.

Understandably, many faculty are not at all comfortable with the idea of creating new programs through elimination of others nor of developing the curriculum by substitution. At the same time, administrators are not comfortable with just maintaining the status quo as that feels as if the campus is stagnating. To stimulate curriculum development, many CAOs carve out incentive funding for new ideas. Another option that has proved successful in stimulating innovation is to give faculty who are likely to lose resources first right on developing new program ideas before the resources are reallocated to another unit.

For public institutions, in an era of limited resources, there is far less opportunity to develop new programs. However, a proposal based on an environmental scan could demonstrate that the proposed program will meet community needs. To make the case for the program, a model needs assessment would include the following: service area and selectivity of competing programs, enrollments and unmet need in competing programs, employment opportunities in the region to be served, and employer or federal and state incentive support for students. Documentation of resources for the program might include: faculty currently available, quality of faculty professional activities, description of unique facilities and equipment, opportunities for internships, program budget compared to comparable programs on campus and on other campuses, library resources, and financial aid to support students. The full budget would include the offset of expected tuition revenues, grants, and fund raising.

Some states have decentralized the authority for program approval to the campuses and substituted rigorous reviews after a three- to five-year period to replace the "promise" of quality with an emphasis on "actual" program quality. Documentation of program quality should address both processes and outcomes. A process analysis could include: evaluation of curricular sequences, availability of advisors and mentors, individual courses and teaching effectiveness, retention, and student satisfaction. Student and program outcomes assessment data could include: certifications, initial employment, employment five years out, average salary, graduate school placement, program revenues, and grants and sponsored activities. This model links systematic planning, assessment, program evaluation, and accountability.

Linking Program Review and Budgeting

As campuses have addressed budgetary concerns over the last 20 years, they often have turned to program review for guidance on internal reallocations. However, an extensive study of 750 public institutions noted that campuses found the process only somewhat helpful in making budget decisions. Program review was successful in identifying priorities and resource needs, but did not work well for allocation decisions because of "inadequate funds to meet too many needs, ineffective analysis, inadequate/ineffective follow up by leadership, and lack of experience in using program review" (Barak and Sweeney 1995, 12). Campuses committed to integrating budgeting and program review can overcome these shortcomings, except for the amount of funding, by requiring that the program review committee set priorities among their recommendations. The CAO can then present them to the planning and budget committee at the beginning of the budget development process.

Rather than set priorities for open discussion in designing the academic affairs budget, some campuses try to link resources directly to program review results by awarding points and dollar increments from a central pool of funds for good performance in program review. Other campuses have decided not to punish a program for poor performance but rather to provide additional resources to shore up the program. The first approach makes the "rich get richer" whereas the second is a disincentive for initiative. The CAO who wants program review to be strategic will work toward a multiyear adjustment of resources linked to the expected incremental changes in the programs as outlined in their action plans for future development.

Bringing the Parts Together

- What assessment efforts are already in place and how can they be linked to program review?

- To what extent can regular assessment be conducted within the unit under the guidance of the institutional research and assessment office?

- How can linkages be established between state performance measures, accreditation, and assessment requirements to document effectiveness to the institution's publics?

- How can budget decisions be used as incentives to improve programs and accomplish institutional goals?

- How can program review be used to increase efficient and effective use of institutional resources?

- If strategic initiatives based on institutional planning are funded, what role does program review play in documenting success?

- If institutional standards are set, should "bonuses" be given to programs that meet or exceed established standards? Will resources be removed if performance falls below expectations?

SUCCESSFUL PROGRAM REVIEW

Even after two decades of financial constraints, strategic planning efforts, and evidence of institutional change, too often both faculty and administrators appear to still favor program review primarily for improvement of current programs and are unprepared to use program review to systematically reshape institutions. They expect change to take place slowly and over time with all programs continuing indefinitely while new ones are added. To counter that inertia, the chief academic officer must mobilize faculty discussion about the current status of the campus, involve them in refining the institutional vision, and demonstrate the value of program review and assessment data in academic decision making. An effective program review process that is based on persuasive data, good communication, and regular follow-up will promote a culture that sets priorities, is responsive to change, and strives for high standards.

When program review is also linked to the aspirations of individual faculty and departments, not merely institutional goals, it has a greater chance of success. In that way it taps the energy and enthusiasm of faculty that is essential if they are to engage students and derive satisfaction from their work. Faculty can accept honest evaluations of their work and the success of their students, if they have been responsible for setting the goals, designing the programs, and choosing the evaluation measures. They will resist evaluation when the criteria do not appear valid for their program, the decision-making process appears heavy handed, and there is little provision for recommendations from faculty on how to improve.

A carefully designed program review process must be complemented by the leadership of a chief academic officer who is respectful, flexible, and open based on a genuine belief that faculty are ultimately the guardians of quality. Without a fundamental commitment to quality, faculty may protect self-interest, be complacent about being "good enough," and remain reluctant to expect higher standards of performance from students. The CAO must be prepared to provide support and encouragement for the hard work of the faculty. Ultimately, the effectiveness of program review depends upon the capacity of a campus to make the difficult but necessary decisions to relentlessly pursue academic quality.

CHAPTER

Continuous Improvement: Enhancing Value, Service, and Efficiency

ollege admissions materials heartily proclaim, "We are here for you." Orientation speeches emphasize that the campus is "student centered." Faculty are touted as "always available." Yet, too often, students complain about bad advice, lack of availability of courses, and poor coordination of services. Being given "the run around" is not only frustrating, they claim, but also creates barriers to academic success. Although many chief academic officers (CAOs) argue that no campus could provide service that meets student expectations for having it their way, they do concede that despite promises of responsiveness, academic support services and processes are, too often, bureaucratic, cumbersome, and difficult to understand.

In addition to high expectations for service, parents and students are careful consumers and expect value for their money. The investment in a college education is justified by the promise of higher lifetime earnings; however, with tuition and fees rising faster than the Consumer Price Index and student indebtedness reaching all time highs, colleges and universities are challenged to demonstrate that quality is also increasing (Lissner and Taylor, 1996; Manno 1998). With a declining economy and reductions in support for higher education, colleges and universities must be more efficient and maintain standards. To address these concerns, many campuses as well as entire state systems have adopted principles from the quality movement in business aimed at improving service, reducing costs, strengthening competitiveness, and being more accountable (Sallis 1996, 1–11; Freed, Klugman, and Fife 1997, 27–34).

Higher education has always been committed to excellence; however, studies of campuses adopting Total Quality Management or its variation Continuous Quality Improvement suggest that these systemic initiatives have been more easily sustained in business areas of the campus than in academic areas. After considerable interest during the 1990s resulting in some "show-case campuses" (Freed and Klugman 1997), quality initiatives appear to have flagged in academic affairs or have been narrowed in focus to merge with curriculum improvement and assessment initiatives. Academic quality initiatives emphasize the product of academic activities such as graduation rates, career placement, and national rankings, and to a lesser degree, the instructional processes. As important as a quality product is, however, it is equally important to apply quality principles to academic management, analyze how students' needs are being met, and use data to improve services. How students experience the campus on a daily basis is as much their measure of quality as the degree they earn.

Although some observers believe faculty are resistant to thinking of students as customers, campuses do use continuous improvement (CI) principles to improve teaching and learning. It is the broader application of CI to the academic environment that has been less effective as faculty are not sure how best to improve service. It also appears that on many campuses faculty are not so much resistant as they are apathetic (Roberts 1995, 12). Because faculty are busy and on most campuses were not involved at the outset when quality initiatives were introduced, they are uninterested in one more "good idea" from the administration (Freed, Klugman, and Fife 1997, 140). They may even question whether everything can be improved.

It is also likely that assessment of academic outcomes, where there are hard numbers, is easier to pursue than measurement of service and process, where quality is based on expectations and perceptions (Sallis 1996, 21–23). To some extent, the immediacy of service from ATM machines, drive-through fast-food restaurants, and on-line shopping has established expectations that are difficult for colleges and universities to match. Nevertheless, to begin to close the service gap requires understanding how parts of an institution form a system, setting realistic goals, reengineering hundreds of paper processes, and addressing attitudes about an overall service ethic for the campus.

Those who have worked intimately with efforts to transform campus cultures note that changing attitudes alone cannot overcome problems in the system such as limited understanding of goals or failures in analysis of data. In order to achieve the full promise of continuous improvement, all parts of the system—leadership, strategic planning, attention to stakeholder needs, information based decision making, investment in training faculty and staff, educational processes, and assessment of outcomes—must be strengthened (Bishop et al. 2000, 36–37). Tinkering with one or several parts of the system can bring improvement but will not achieve a true "culture of quality" (Freed, Klugman, and Fife 1997, 41–44).

If the chief academic officer is not in a position to introduce a comprehensive approach to quality management, at a minimum the CAO can provide leadership for examining some of the least effective services with the aim of using information as the basis for improvement. In addition, the CAO can demonstrate how bringing together separate improvement efforts spread over several divisions can begin to create an institutional approach to strengthening education. For example, linking recruitment, orientation, advising, counseling services, residential life, and faculty development can impact retention. Although these limited efforts will not transform the campus, they can create an environment more responsive to student needs and expectations.

The extensive interest by all of the regional accrediting bodies in applying quality ideas to institutional effectiveness can add credibility to the chief academic officer's efforts. For example, the Higher Learning Commission of the North Central Association of Colleges and Schools (NCA) has adapted the criteria from the Malcolm Baldridge National Quality Award Program to its Academic Quality Improvement Project (Commission on Institutions of Higher Education 2000). The Southern Association of Colleges and Schools (SACS) requires not just a self-study of the current status of a campus but also a forward-looking Quality Enhancement Plan to serve as the basis for the next review (Commission on Colleges 2001, 7). Under these new guidelines, reaccreditation is not an accomplishment or end point but rather the baseline for future progress through campuswide collaboration.

This chapter provides an overview of the rationale for continuous improvement and describes some of the analytic tools used for identifying areas for improvement. It calls for a shift in thinking from merely "what we do" to include "how we do it" and "how we need to change to do better." In addition to several other examples to illustrate the philosophy and the tools of CI, one major system, curriculum management, and one service area, the library, are discussed in some detail. They have been selected because they are functionally the responsibility of academic affairs but demonstrate the need to cross institutional boundaries and collaborate if students are to be served well. Particular attention is paid to the way in which time and cost savings can be achieved. While there are many good reasons to apply new thinking to serving students, given the continuing strain on resources, chief academic officers would be irresponsible if they did not work diligently to increase efficiency as well as quality.

APPROACHES TO PROBLEM SOLVING

One of the shared frustrations of chief academic officers is the way in which problems are delivered to their door to become their problem or they are asked to make decisions that could be handled by others. A central principle in quality focused management is delegation—not in the hierarchical sense of the administrator deciding what should be done and then delegating it to someone else to do, but rather delegating the decision making to those who are closest to the problem or the operation and thus should know the most about how to handle the situation (Freed, Klugman, and Fife 1997, 103–9). This calls for a shift in thinking from centralized CAO administrative authority to decentralized empowerment of deans, department chairs, faculty, and staff. Faculty already claim responsibility for many academic matters but are less often given the information and the tools to positively participate in improving management. To tap this resource, the CAO needs to create a culture that gives everyone in academic affairs permission to think proactively about how to improve the learning environment.

Whereas many academic administrators might argue that their staff or department chairs "know what to do" or "know what I expect," as if there were fixed decision rules to be invoked, problem solving and decision making in a continuous improvement environment do not rely on rigid adherence to rules. Instead, new thinking about old issues is encouraged as well as responsiveness to new situations in order to effect long-term improvements rather than aim merely for short-term troubleshooting. The assumption underlying problem solving is that there are choices about how to handle matters and the options need to be weighed by those who will be affected. After a careful analysis of alternatives, judgment is required to make a decision. In a quality management mode, chief academic officers invest their time in strengthening the judgment ability of their colleagues rather than in trying to make or control all decisions. To do so, they need to place their trust in others—a fundamental tenet in the quality movement.

Often chief academic officers are challenged with the observation, "If it's not broke, don't fix it!" Embracing the philosophy of continuous improvement means that something does not have to be broken to get attention. As chief academic officers spend a considerable amount of their time solving problems and trying to keep operations running smoothly (Mech 1997, 291), they are well aware of how "grit in the gears" can take time and energy from more important strategic issues. Learning how to solve the "root cause" of a problem rather than handling the same situation over and over is both effective and efficient (Tague 1995, 20). Learning how to redesign interconnected processes will produce a positive ripple effect throughout the institution.

At times, the sense of responsibility that the chief academic officer feels for the well-being of the institution and the quality of its performance can make it appear that everything needs to be fixed. To identify areas that need attention requires: looking at an issue and asking, "Is there a trend or a pattern?"; listening to a complaint but carefully questioning, "What else is at stake?"; rethinking an issue that seems to keep bouncing back by asking, "Is this a new problem or an old one in a slightly different form?" Without these analytic habits of mind, the CAO can be fully occupied in a reactive mode, handling the issues as they come and reviewing the work of others but not taking initiative and providing leadership for continuous improvement. Quality focused management requires proactive behavior focused on those issues that will have the greatest impact in improving institutional effectiveness and efficiency.

Approaches to Analyzing Problems

- Whose problem is it? Does it require central administration attention, or can it be handled at another level?

- How important is the matter to institutional performance? How is it related to goals?

- How would different individuals and constituencies define the problem or issue? What are the competing perspectives?

- Is the issue unique or recurrent? an exception or a systemic issue?

- What is the present situation in comparison to the desired situation?

- What information or data will verify or clarify the issue?

- Does the issue require a minor adjustment or a complete overhaul?

- Who should be involved in the generation of alternative solutions and deciding on a course of action?

- Have other institutions had the same problem? What solution did they find? Would the solution work for us?

- What are the measures of a "good decision" or a "good solution" (e.g. acceptability, permanence, timeliness, limited risk, feasibility, affordability, or consistency)?

- Under what circumstance should one seek the optimal (best) solution or merely the satisfactory (good enough) solution?

- How will the results of the decision be monitored and used for additional improvement?

TOOLS FOR CONTINUOUS IMPROVEMENT

Quality efforts on many campuses have bogged down under unfamiliar terminology, complicated diagrams, and abstract principles. When quality is defined simply as "meeting the needs and expectations of stakeholders," and continuous improvement means "making changes as those needs change," the terms are easier to understand. To lead an effort focused on quality requires engaging the campus in asking: What are we doing? Why are we doing it? How are we doing it? Could what we are doing be improved? Is there something else we should be doing? When "quality" is understood as "systematic problem solving" and a commitment to excellence, it becomes a way of thinking that permeates the institution (Seymour 1992, 20).

The use of quality tools can help address several conditions that are seen as barriers to the pursuit of quality. Typically, improvement efforts in academic matters address the parts, such as evaluation of individual courses and faculty, rather than the processes that undergird the activities, such as curriculum and faculty development. In addition, the decentralized nature of academic management inhibits administrators, faculty, staff, and students from working together to clarify goals and rethink the practices and relationships designed to achieve the goals. Furthermore, faculty and administrators usually assume improvements or new initiatives cannot be achieved without additional resources. Using the principles of quality management can bring academic systems into focus, overcome fragmentation in responsibility, and identify resource trade-offs.

Some amount of training for administrators, faculty, and staff is necessary to integrate continuous improvement efforts into the campus. The chief academic officer new to quality management ideas or interested in knowing more can find guidance on the theory and practice in the extensive literature that also includes campus case studies, lessons learned, and pitfalls (Chaffee and Sherr 1992; Teeter and Lozier 1993; Freed and

Klugman 1997; and Fife 2000). At the same time, academic administrators will want to weigh the validity of critical commentary that calls continuous quality improvement merely a "management fad" (Birnbaum 2000) and notes the distrust academics have for "corporate practices" put forth with "missionary zeal" (Ewell 1999, 11). Both the advocates and the critics do agree on the importance of shared commitment to goals and continuous measurement of progress toward them.

Whether a true believer in total quality management or merely interested in identifying a few campus systems to be made more effective and efficient, the chief academic officer will find useful the variety of analytic tools that are carefully catalogued in the literature (Lewis and Smith 1994, 157–79; Tague 1995). More important than knowing a tool, however, is understanding when to use it. *The Quality Toolbox* describes a variety of approaches, new ways to use them, and most important, a matrix of applications: "idea creation tools" (e.g., brainstorming and affinity diagrams), "process analysis tools" (e.g., flowcharts and work-flow diagrams), "cause analysis tools" (e.g., fishbone diagrams and Pareto charts), "planning tools" (e.g., force-field analyses and plan-do-check-act cycles), "evaluation tools" (e.g., matrix diagrams and plan-results matrices) and "data collection and analysis tools" (e.g., check sheets, graphs, and surveys) (Tague 1995, 2–4). Visual methods such as diagrams, flow charts, and force-field analyses are particularly useful as they succinctly convey relationships among many variables. The fundamental idea is to select methods that match the task and can provide the necessary information to systematically analyze and solve problems.

Benchmarking, an additional tool for continuous improvement, is based not only on studying how your own campus functions but also looking for "best practice" on other campuses (Alstete 1995). By identifying other campuses that have solved the problem or achieved the performance level sought, the chief academic officer can learn from their successful practices, set realistic standards for performance, and calculate comparative costs. As useful as benchmarking is, determining the process behind the result is often difficult (Epper, 1999). Through visiting other campuses, attending national meetings, reviewing accreditation self-studies, and seeking further information on effective practices, the chief academic officer can identify both practical and innovative ideas that improve campus operations.

A close look at the quality tools reveals that they are a prompt for thinking in a new way, seeing something from a new perspective, and making connections (Sallis 1996, 94–103; Ewell 1999, 14–15). Quality tools can also be combined with standard research and statistical tools, as well as many other data-gathering techniques such as suggestion boxes and focus groups. The institutional context that supports the use of these tools has already been noted throughout other chapters of this book that emphasize the importance of setting priorities, asking questions, gathering information, identifying barriers, building teamwork, being systematic, and committing to change. The chief academic officer is likely to find it far more difficult to make time for improvement projects than to identify the problems, questions, approaches, or tools for the projects.

Leadership for Continuous Improvement

- To what extent is there agreement on a student-centered vision of institutional quality?
- How might faculty and staff become interested in continuous improvement?
- How can the processes currently used to measure institutional effectiveness be linked more productively?
- In what ways can areas for improvement be identified?
- What training in the concepts and tools for continuous improvement is available?
- What level of "buy in" is necessary to get started? Is there a pilot project that could begin the process?
- How can a campus culture that rewards new ideas, innovation, and change be developed?
- What resources, if any, will be needed to implement new ideas and practices?
- What structures and individuals could support the continuous improvement initiatives?

INVOLVING OTHERS IN CONTINUOUS IMPROVEMENT

The importance of committed leadership and collaboration is well documented (Freed, Klugman, and Fife 1997, 123–36). Although the chief academic officer can make use of many ideas based on continuous improvement to do a better job of academic management and problem solving, without some degree of teamwork the impact of those efforts will be very limited. To interest colleagues at the vice president level, the chief academic officer might identify processes that have a significant impact on institutional effectiveness, touch upon the operations in all divisions, and take up a significant amount of everyone's time and trouble-shooting energy. Conversations about common concerns and hoped-for results can begin to generate interest and confidence that improvements are possible and worthy of collaborative attention.

Understanding activities as integrated systems that require shared responsibility at many levels to be effective is at the core of continuous improvement. Enrollment management is a good example of a system that has many stakeholders and broad institutional consequences. Consequently, it has been the focus of continuous improvement on many campuses. Initial efforts were limited to campus processes occurring once a student applied. For example, recognizing the drawbacks of lost paperwork in admissions, delayed financial aid packages, confusing bull-pen registration, and long lines to pay bills, campuses redesigned these processes. With improved service to students as the goal, admissions, financial aid, registration, student billing, and housing were integrated into a seamless one-stop center with cross-trained staff. Technology offered further improvements replacing the need for face-to-face interactions with many operations handled via the Web.

As the consequences of greater access, competitiveness, and student mobility have become clear, campuses have identified additional enrollment goals beyond efficient student services, including budget stability, campus reputation, and diversity. No longer willing to view enrollment as merely who shows up in the fall, campuses now take a more strategic approach and coordinate actions at many stages of the process. The enrollment management system has been expanded to include outreach and recruiting activities (e.g., letters, publications, videos, and articulation agreements), admissions processes (e.g., application and evaluation), enrollment activities (e.g., orientation and advising), retention activities (e.g., first-year programs and tutoring), and campus engagement (e.g., cocurricular activities and housing). To ensure integration of these parts of the system, many campuses choose centralized management, either through a division under a vice president for enrollment management or through matrix management by an associate vice president in the student affairs division who can ensure effective collaboration among the number of directors spread across campus (Dixon 1995, 8). An advisory team made up of vice presidents, deans, faculty, and students provides strategic systems-thinking to the planning and communicates the plans back to their constituencies.

Campuses interested in shaping their entering class with attention to ethnicity, gender, geographical distribution, and quality have become deliberate in their image development, outreach, and marketing strategies. Drawing upon the data tools of CI, campuses committed to retaining students have turned their attention to selectivity, predictive models, and student behavioral profiles to complement assessment information from summer orientation, transition programs, learning communities, and support programs. A whole field of consulting has developed to help campuses with sophisticated market research and modeling to provide data for decisions aimed at meeting or exceeding enrollment goals and retaining students.

The faculty hiring process provides another example of how continuous improvement is being used, not just to streamline activities for efficiency but also to be more effective. Hiring should be closely connected to strategic planning, workload analyses, resource allocation, enrollment projections, and curriculum development. Managed at the department level, the process is, too often, protracted, cumbersome, costly, and not strategic. To save time and money, campuses use standardized correspondence, place composite ads on behalf of the campus to reduce advertising costs, simplify processes for receiving applications and gathering Equal Employment Opportunity (EEO) statistics, conduct phone interviews to reduce the number of candidates brought to campus, check references only for finalists, manage the calendar to complete the process in a timely manner, and make all policies, benefits, and other human resources information available on-line to save on mailings. These common-sense changes save resources and reduce the burden on faculty search committees.

To impact the campus positively, the CAO needs to provide oversight and coordination with other strategies and decisions. Thus the more powerful application of continuous improvement is determining how changes in the hiring process can achieve, for example, the broader institutional goal of a more diverse faculty. Collaboration among human resources staff, the diversity committee, faculty, and administrators in analyzing where the system can be improved to increase diversity has led campuses to revamp the search process. To improve results at each stage, they appoint diverse search committees, openly discussing biases about perceptions of candidates that "fit" the campus before reviewing any applicants, target outreach to invite women and minority candidates, conduct research on availability of women and minorities by discipline, review the pools to be sure they include underrepresented populations consistent with availability before continuing the searches, and give the deans and department chairs responsibility for monitoring the process. In addition, they attend to the campus climate for diversity and mentor women and minority faculty to enhance success. When administrators and faculty work together on improvement efforts they commit to guiding principles—in this case, fairness, equal opportunity, and quality in the hiring process—as well as to actions to be taken.

Because collaboration is fundamental to the success of continuous improvement efforts, most campuses rely on task forces, work groups, or teams to study an issue or a process and recommend changes. The group may be cross-functional, cross-divisional, single task, temporary, or permanent. Many of the larger campuses rely on some sort of "quality council" to provide training, identify issues, set policy, and coordinate the improvement activities of the campus. Whether a formalized institutional change process or a single activity, the responsibilities of a quality workgroup are the same: define the problem, examine the problem, determine the causes of the problem, recommend actions to eliminate the main causes, study the results, communicate the changes through training, and prepare a statement about what was learned for future reference (Lewis and Smith 1994, 195). Even with presidential leadership, campuses often struggle to maintain momentum in their improvement initiatives, especially in academic areas (Ammons and Gilmour 1995, 58).

Using an Improvement Workgroup

- Does the workgroup have the authority to identify systems that need improvement?
- How do others on campus understand the role of the workgroup?
- How are the activities of the workgroup connected to other campus initiatives?
- What training have the members of the workgroup had in the principles of continuous improvement and tools of analysis?
- Who provides leadership on campus? in the workgroup?
- What strategies can the workgroup use to keep projects from getting bogged down?
- How can the workgroup and others access necessary data?
- How will those who will implement the recommended changes be trained?
- How will the workgroup monitor changes in the process and learn from the experience?

IMPROVING THE CURRICULUM MANAGEMENT SYSTEM

Paradoxically, the single largest process in any university—curriculum management—is the system least likely to receive collaborative attention for continuous improvement and increased efficiency. As presidents and business officers worry about the financial health of the institution and struggle to contain costs, they can outsource the bookstore, defer maintenance, streamline cleaning services, or introduce new technologies. What they cannot touch is the curriculum, which is directly linked to the largest single expense in the budget—faculty salaries. The authority for the curriculum is delegated to faculty. Even the chief academic officer must depend on the faculty to ensure that program priorities, resource allocations, and course offerings meet student needs. Program review may be relied on to promote curricular quality but it has little if any impact on the delivery of the curriculum. Faculty typically focus on effectiveness; they seldom share responsibility for efficiency.

An analysis of the full curriculum system on any campus will reveal opportunities to both better serve students and conserve resources. Among the many components of the curriculum management system are program and course development, credit/contact hour assignment, program and course approval, course scheduling, room assignments, advising, registration, and degree audits. Although students are the primary stakeholders, the staff in student affairs and business affairs as well as faculty and staff in academic affairs are also stakeholders with needs and expectations to be met. The operation of this system is critical, not just to student success but also to financial stability, faculty hiring and productivity, and efficient use of facilities.

Due to the distributed responsibility for decisions, unexamined assumptions, inconsistent communication, and unclear standards for quality and efficiency, the curriculum management system is vulnerable at many points. The decisions of many affect the system but no one person is seen as in charge of the system in its entirety. The policies and processes, to the extent that they are spelled out, are scattered through governance documents, office operations manuals, catalogs, and academic policy committee records. Consequently, an analysis of this complex system will reveal many opportunities for improvement.

In this discussion of improvement, the focus is primarily on service, efficiency, and financial issues rather than academic program quality issues that are discussed in the previous chapter. Readers interested in additional perspectives on applying principles of continuous improvement to course and program quality may want to consult other texts that focus on content, student learning, and assessment, such as *The Quest for Quality: The*

Challenge for Undergraduate Education in the 1990s (Mayhew, Ford, and Hubbard 1990), *Academic Initiatives in Total Quality for Higher Education* (Roberts 1995), and *Handbook of the Undergraduate Curriculum: A Comprehensive Guide to Purposes, Structures, Practices, and Change* (Gaff and Ratcliff 1997).

Program and Course Development

Program design and course development are the responsibility of faculty and subject to their initiative. On most campuses, suggestions about program development from an admissions counselor who knows that students are asking about programs in criminal justice or from the registrar who notes students are transferring because there is no program in physical therapy would receive a cool response from the faculty. Indeed, typically, the curriculum committee is limited to faculty, staffed by the registrar, and serves only to review proposals initiated by faculty and academic departments.

Continuous improvement requires a different role for the curriculum committee. New ideas could come from any quarter; indeed, members of the committee would be responsible for monitoring external sources for ideas. Curricular change would be proactive, strategic, and responsive to student and employer demand. Program ideas would be innovative and less dependent on the specialized interests of individual faculty members. The cross-divisional team would brainstorm new ideas for programs followed by a benefits/barriers/cost analysis based on mission, expected revenues, contributions to the community, availability of faculty, and costs for staff, equipment, and facilities. Such a feasibility analysis might reveal, for example, that an estimated $200,000 cost for additional faculty and a reorganization of course offerings makes criminal justice as a major serving many students possible, whereas the $2 million cost for faculty, facilities, and student support for a graduate program in physical therapy that would serve a small enrollment is beyond the means of the campus. In this new model, program development is linked with enrollment management processes, institutional research information, program review, and planning and budgeting in a systematic way.

Assignment of Credit/Contact Hours

All campuses rely on credit-hour/contact-hour equivalencies as the basis for scheduling courses and determining course and program requirements. The imperfections of the system have been revealed by a national study sponsored by the Institute for Higher Education Policy in Washington, D.C. Among the initial findings are several that impact curriculum management, including:

- The student credit hour has become the de facto measure of learning, but it is neither defined nor enforced and, therefore, not a substitute for learning goals or standards.

- The credit hour is applied inconsistently with considerable variation among institutions and disciplines and levels of instruction.

- Once credits are assigned to a course at the time it is first approved, there is no audit or process for later adjustment.

- Faculty workload policies, as well as budgetary decisions and allocations of resources, are often based on courses and credit hours (Wellman and Ehrlich 2001).

These findings should alert chief academic officers to the need to determine how the credit/contact hour system is used on their campus and whether changes could be made that would enhance quality and efficiency.

Such a study would likely reveal that faculty who assign credit hours and contact hours to courses seldom discuss the meaning of this system. As a result, they do not all apply the same rules; for example, in one department three fifty-minute hours of lecture might be given three credits, whereas in another, three fifty-minute hours of contact time is given four credits. Although the variations may have a rationale when linked to learning goals or difficulty of the course, since these credit/contact hour variations, in turn, influence faculty workload, student cost of education, coherence of the curriculum, and space utilization, the impact of individual faculty decisions has a ripple effect on the institution and should be studied.

Graphing all courses by credit/contact hours will show the extent of the variation. Tracing the ways in which the various credit/contact hour equivalencies create unique time blocks and idiosyncratic scheduling will reveal the impact on classroom use and time. Checking the effects of irregular blocks of time on student schedules could reveal how many students find it difficult to put together an efficient full-time schedule. Transcript analysis followed by focus groups could reveal whether students transfer or drop out because they cannot get the courses they need or, alternatively, show that many students fill the time and meet degree requirements with excessive credits. In either circumstance, there is a financial consequence for the campus.

Campuses that have studied the extent to which students are graduating with excess hours find hundreds of thousands of dollars wasted in faculty resources alone (Ferren and Slavings 2000). By analyzing registrations, the extent to which the credits are educationally intentional (e.g., intensive language instruction) and the extent to which they are enrichment (e.g., aerobics) is evident. Understanding the reasons why students take more courses than they need to graduate is particularly important for campuses with a full-time tuition rate for 12 to 21 credits that may encourage students to fill up their program in order to get their money's worth. Reducing some of the variation in credit/contact hour equivalencies may better serve both student and institutional needs.

Program and Course Approval

Course and program approval is a bottom-up process with successive reviews at the department, college, and chief academic officer levels to ensure the course or program meets academic standards and has a strong rationale. Year after year, more courses and programs are added to a campus portfolio of offerings than are dropped, a fact easily checked by reviewing the registrar's annual records of all course additions, deletions, and changes. Few campuses enforce rules about dropping infrequently offered courses and even fewer would argue that for every new course added, one needs to be eliminated. Curriculum "bloat" is very expensive for a campus as a high number of courses, when there is no significant increase in students, fragments enrollments and increases department demands for faculty positions to cover every specialization. The approval process on most campuses offers overkill on certifying individual course quality but is ineffective in ensuring overall curricular integrity or curbing costs.

Although faculty usually fill out the section of the course approval form stating "no additional faculty will be needed" and "no additional funds are required," micro-costing techniques show that everything has a cost. At a minimum, costs of faculty, library resources, equipment, and facilities, as well as impact on enrollments in other courses should be part of the analysis of the financial impact of the decision. Arguing that "total quality management equals total cost management," (Jenny 1996, 178) the National Association of College and University Business Officers has developed a variety of micro-costing techniques that include the full cost of a course based on elements such as the credits generated by the course, the net student revenue per credit hour, and the costs to produce the course (Jenny 1996, 91–127). To manage costs of the curriculum, the chief academic officer and faculty could work collaboratively with business officers to understand how to apply such cost/revenue analysis techniques before approving changes in the curriculum.

One improvement that faculty would easily support is a revision of the submission process. An unaccounted-for cost is the significant waste in faculty time for curriculum approval. Multiple sets of documents are prepared, studied by large representative committees, defended by department representatives before being passed on to other committees, and defended again. It often takes months, sometimes most of an academic year to get a major change approved and sometimes another year to get it into the catalog. Using flow-chart analysis, many campuses have streamlined the process with smaller committees, electronic posting for review by anyone on campus, only major actions reviewed in committee meetings, minor changes (e.g. title and prerequisites) made over the signature of the committee chair and the registrar, and catalog copy created from the electronic document. These improvement efforts are the result of bringing those who have been responsible for the process together to diagram all the steps and analyze how to streamline the process without compromising academic standards or faculty opportunities for involvement.

Course Scheduling

Faculty design and deliver the curriculum and assume that the scheduling works. Increasingly, both students and faculty question whether some of the practices that shape the course-scheduling system might be changed to enhance student learning. For example, despite significant changes in pedagogy, most campuses still use the traditional Monday-Wednesday-Friday 50-minute class period balanced with a Tuesday-Thursday 75-minute schedule. Both students and faculty prefer the longer class period believing it both more convenient and more productive. In addition, for convenience both faculty and students try to avoid early morning and late afternoon classes. As a result, a disproportionate number of classes are offered on the Tuesday-Thursday schedule and bunched toward the middle of the day. Using a matrix analysis would reveal that such a schedule has not only academic consequences but also direct resource consequences including underutilization of classroom space and decreased tuition revenues from working and adult students—both matters of concern for administrators.

When presidents and provosts realize that a compressed schedule leads to an almost empty campus on Monday and Friday, a possible erosion of commitment by both students and faculty to time on campus, or delayed progress toward graduation, they are alarmed. Their responses have ranged from speeches to the faculty exhorting them to change their ways to strong handed management of the curriculum with enforced decision rules for the percentage of classes to be offered at particular times of the day. With leadership attention focused on the perceived effects, rather than the cause, it is hard to bring about sustainable changes necessary to make the course-scheduling system address the varied student and faculty needs as well as institutional goals.

One campus trying to rationalize its scheduling identified several goals for the project, including increasing opportunities to get a full-time schedule, improving planning and course selection, enabling students to manage work and family responsibilities without interfering with their academic work, helping faculty balance their obligations to the institution, encouraging innovative teaching, and strengthening the academic community. Another campus turned to members of the business faculty to apply their knowledge of business process improvement to understand the possible relationship between the class schedule and poor retention rate and prolonged time to degree for their students. In both cases, with clear goals in mind, the systems analysis unearthed a variety of factors affecting scheduling in addition to faculty and student preference, for example, ad hoc credit arrangements, last minute changes in staffing, and innovations that led to offering courses at nonstandard times. Working through the causes allowed the institutions to see that a structured design that adheres to a limited number of conventions for delivery (e.g., three-credit courses offered two times a week for 75 minutes) and conforms to an established schedule is necessary to enable students to take courses offered by several departments. A rigid schedule with no extended time blocks, however, would not accommodate new understandings about how students learn.

The decade of research on student learning and the diversity of learners provides critical data to inform a study of class scheduling. Widespread interest in new approaches, such as learning communities, undergraduate research, and study in depth all suggest greater attention to student time on task and involvement in learning. The National Survey of Student Engagement is based on gap analysis and can provide data on the degree to which students experience activities that require more class time, for example, forms of active learning, including group projects, cooperative learning, debates, or case studies (Kuh 2001). Campuses can use national norms from similar colleges and universities to understand the profile of instructional activities on their campus. With some analysis, campuses might conclude that the 50-minute class period has outlived its usefulness.

To date, relatively few campuses have figured out how to schedule all five days of the week if classes only meet two times a week because they are still locked into the Monday-Wednesday-Friday and Tuesday-Thursday mindset. Use of idea-generation quality tools might suggest interesting alternatives including a Monday-Thursday and Tuesday-Friday schedule with Wednesday for labs, experiential learning, and one day a week classes. Alternatively, a rotating schedule for program-based combinations of Monday-Wednesday, Monday-Thursday, Tuesday-Thursday, Tuesday-Friday, and Wednesday-Friday could be designed. If scheduling is compounded by credit/contact hour irregularities, both matters need to be addressed at the same time.

Scheduling Rules

As the primary goal of scheduling is to make the maximum number of classes accessible to students given the classroom space available, most campuses have very specific rules to regularize their offerings and minimize overlap in times. To manage the delivery of thousands of courses to thousands of students requires rules about the percentage of classes offered on particular days, percentage of classes offered during peak times, and percentage of a department's offerings that can be scheduled in any one time slot. In addition, departments are expected to set their own internal rules about frequency of offering and class limits, but even those might be reviewed in a curriculum management study to determine whether efficiencies would result from less-frequent offerings that reduce the number of small sections in subsequent semesters.

Campuses rely on the registrar to manage course scheduling. That authority to reject schedules that do not conform to scheduling rules must be supported by the chief academic officer as both department chairs and individual faculty often try to negotiate incremental changes to meet their own needs. The cumulative effect of small departures can produce a schedule that does not meet student needs. The question most commonly asked on campuses that enforce scheduling rules is, "If our department abides by the principles, what assurance can you give me that all others will?" This question is particularly relevant when there is a culture of backroom negotiations. Such departures are understandable because the appreciation of a department chair or a reduction in faculty complaints is a more immediate incentive for the staff member than accommodating the needs of faceless students. Application of one of the cause analysis tools or flow charting could reveal the prevalence of these informal negotiations and course-by-course adjustments.

Because schedules attempt to match supply of courses with student demand, to improve efficiency in course scheduling several standard reports should be generated by the registrar's office and provided to department chairs for their use. The reports might include, for example, a five-year history of enrollments by sections, times, days; course add-drops before the census data; number of students seeking a course who were closed out; patterns of adding students over the enrollment limits; underenrolled sections dropped from the schedule; and categories of petitions for exceptions to requirements. This kind of hard data encourages better planning at the department level, which then reduces problem solving at the registration and advising stages.

Although department chairs could use a data warehouse and run their own queries, effective curriculum management is facilitated when regular reports based on the same variables are available to all who make decisions in scheduling courses. Department-based scheduling programs should allow chairs to plan course offerings two to three years in advance and take into consideration both student and faculty needs. Even with technology, many chairs still schedule by hand working off the last year's schedule. In this way, inadequate planning is built in year after year. For example, incremental declines in enrollment are hard to spot. If the average class size in a multisection course is 28 students, the next year 25 students, and the next year 21 students, the number of sections should have been adjusted to match supply and demand. An analysis of under-enrolled sections of multisection courses could reveal thousands of dollars wasted in faculty resources (Ferren and Slavings 2000). Poor scheduling also impacts the efficiency of other departments.

Assignment of Rooms

Another step in the curriculum management process is determining classroom assignments based on time of day, seating capacity, and specialized equipment. Many factors keep this stage of the curriculum system from being efficient. On some campuses, room assignments are still made by hand and adjusted by special pleadings, such as a classroom near the faculty member's office. Adding to the scheduling challenge is the long-standing habit of adding students over the pre-established limit. When overenrolling is analyzed, faculty report they "save a few spots for students they really want in the class" and "there are hard-luck stories to be responded to." If class limits exceed actual seating capacity and result in last-minute room changes, a domino effect through room assignments is set off. When limits are enforced, standard scheduling software can save staff time and optimize space utilization.

A continuous improvement project team would need to persuasively demonstrate the institutional benefits from changes in individual behavior and habits. On some campuses, staff in the registrar's office resist taking the time to learn new technology. On other campuses, because faculty are not informed about the advantages of electronic scheduling, they complain that a faceless scheduler kept them from getting a preferred classroom or otherwise prevented them from managing the room selection system for their benefit. Because the scheduling software can be partitioned and rooms assigned to departments or kept out of the general schedule, such as multimedia rooms, most campuses find the program flexible enough to be tailored to staff, faculty, student, and institutional needs.

Advising Support to Improve Student Academic Planning

The best curriculum or course-offering pattern cannot compensate for inadequate guidance to students in planning their program of study. Although academic advising on many campuses is criticized by students, both faculty and advisors argue they can only do so much and that students must take more responsibility for their own planning. An activity analysis would reveal that students primarily see their advisor when they need a signature to register or after they have a problem. Increased use of technology can provide students with information and advice even when they do not seek it, such as the degree audit, which flags students well before graduation if they have not met all requirements.

To determine the quality of advising, the continuous improvement team might begin with a satisfaction survey. However, a satisfaction study alone does not give sufficient data to understand how the advising processes are linked to quality outcomes. For a more thorough understanding, analyses of petitions, advising sheets, and summer school enrollments can provide hard data to indicate whether students are taking courses they do not need, making up courses they should have had, or finding the frequency of offerings does not match their needs. Creating a collaborative group with representatives from the registrar's office, the academic departments, and the advisors to analyze the data can reveal options for improvement, including enforcing prerequisites, indicating in the catalog the semester a course is offered, and strengthening faculty understanding of curriculum coherence and their role in advising. One process improvement strategy with good potential is having students file a plan of study electronically so that course demand can be captured and used as a basis for scheduling courses.

Campuses are experimenting with initiatives designed to increase student responsibility for academic planning such as special program support for freshmen, intrusive initial transfer advising, and college- and program-based peer advising. Tracking the impact on retention on one campus showed clearly that such initiatives, although having a cost, result in savings, increased revenue, and increased student success (Ferren and Slavings 2000). As budget pressures force some campuses to reduce support staff and give up advisors to protect faculty positions, the improvement team might need to determine how best to protect the campus from negative impacts on persistence, retention, and overall student satisfaction.

Registration and Degree Audit

Technology has completely changed the way in which students review the course schedule and their requirements. Sophisticated systems allow students to search for any class at 10 A.M. on Tuesday. Although this may not be the best way to put together a schedule, it does match student needs. Technology also allows campuses to enter the course equivalencies for all institutions from which students transfer so that students can do a quick review of what they need to take to complete the degree. At least one state has an accessible system that lets a student from the community college or any other institution check the requirements at all the four-year institutions to determine where they will receive the most transfer credit in the program of their choice. The value of these technology applications is that they improve transfer articulation, student responsibility for completing degree requirements, and advising support for students who want to change majors.

Systematic Review of the Curriculum Management System

To identify areas that need improvement the continuous improvement team should do a complete review of all parts of the curriculum management system. Before making any changes, they need to consider how a change in one part of the system may affect another part of the system and how best to integrate the improvement plans to produce the desired results. The CAO can identify areas where improvement is called for by auditing the curriculum management system and asking to what extent such statements as expressed in Figure 1 describe the institution.

PROMOTING IMPROVEMENT AND CHANGE IN LIBRARY SERVICES

Continuous improvement is based on the premise that needs and expectations of stakeholders change over time and that the institution should be responsive to those changes. However, the principles of CI can also be used to promote change. The rate of change in information technologies makes libraries an interesting case study in how continuous improvement efforts can be both responsive to stakeholder needs and lead them to higher service expectations.

At one time seen as repositories of information and guardians of materials, libraries have been transformed by technology to be the gateway to information and librarians have become the guides. On-line card catalogues, electronic data bases, e-books, full-text document delivery services, and statewide networked systems are just a few of the changes that have increased the capacity of libraries to serve the needs of faculty and students. At the same time capacity has increased, funding for libraries has been flat, collection budgets have eroded through inflation, electronic materials costs have increased, and increased service demands have not been matched by increases in staff. In this dynamic but challenging environment, libraries are transforming themselves by integrating their strategic plan with the institutional plan and implementing continuous improvement efforts to increase effectiveness and efficiency. On many campuses the library is a campus leader in change.

Responding to Customer/Stakeholder Needs

Central to the quality principles is understanding the needs of the customer. The library presents an unusual situation in that the patrons are unaware of all that is possible and, consequently, understate their needs. Typical sources of information such as suggestion boxes, analyses of customer complaints, and patron surveys can be reviewed by a continuous improvement team aimed at improving quality of services and perceptions of responsiveness. With a focus on satisfaction, improvement is possible but will not be up to the pace of the rapid change in the information

Figure 1
Reviewing the Curriculum Management System

Program and Course Development
- The curriculum is competitive with other campuses.
- The programs and courses students demand are available.
- Innovation and creativity are encouraged, and duplication is discouraged.
- Demand data are used as a basis for new program development.

Assignment of Credit/Contact Hours
- Credit/contact hour rules are used consistently across the curriculum.
- Credit/contact hour equivalencies are appropriate to course requirements.
- Courses with variable credits are not difficult to schedule.
- Students can meet degree requirements without taking excess credits.

Program and Course Approval
- Process for approving programs and courses is efficient.
- Both quality and cost of the program are reviewed.
- All proposals are costed out for both direct and indirect costs.
- Control over the total number of programs and courses is exercised.

Course Scheduling Process
- Frequency of offerings and times are matched to student needs.
- Departments monitor student demand and course histories.
- Required courses are scheduled to meet student needs.
- Class sizes are set realistically and based on pedagogy.
- Students have no difficulty in putting together an efficient schedule.

Rules for Scheduling
- Courses are arrayed throughout the day to meet student needs.
- All majors are available both during the day and the evening.
- All class periods are used once before the second round of courses is scheduled.
- At least 30 percent of courses are offered before 9 a.m. Or after 3 p.m.

Assignment of Rooms
- All rooms are reviewed regularly for suitability and upgraded as needed.
- Classrooms with special facilities are matched to faculty needs.
- Faculty have few complaints about the size, location, comfort of the rooms.
- Classroom utilization reports are used to manage facilities efficiently.

Advising Support
- Students can plan their program based on a two year schedule.
- Students have access to advisors and faculty to plan their program.
- Offerings are consistent from semester to semester and year to year.
- Patterns of problems with course availability are identified and corrected.

Registration
- Students have easy access to telephone or on-line registration.
- Course closeouts and waiting lists are maintained.
- Priority registration matches student needs.

Degree Audit
- Transfer students can review requirements on-line and determine which majors would be most efficient for finishing their degree.
- Students can access their records at any time.
- Students are advised of deficiencies that would delay graduation.

environment. It takes a significant reorientation of patrons, continuous training of library staff, and opportunities to introduce new services for users to take greater advantage of the resources. Continuous improvement, in this instance, will be based on identifying the gap between "stated" customer needs and "potential" customer needs.

Almost every campus has a library advisory committee made up of faculty and students and used as a sounding board for ideas. A more proactive approach to guiding future developments in a library would be to invest in that advisory committee, provide training in all the information technologies, set an aggressive schedule of meetings, and create a team with the library staff in envisioning the library of the future. Starting with the usual quality questions such as "What do our patrons come for" and "how can we do what we do better" will result in such efficiency aids as library maps, signage, on-line tutorials, easier checkout procedures, on-line renewal, and more convenient return receptacles. More strategic questions, including "How can we do what we do differently?" and "What new services should be provided?" might result in quality-focused suggestions such as a multimedia training center, student research support center, coffee shop, or lecture series.

Information Retrieval Instruction

The continuous expansion of electronic and print materials creates needs for more guidance in accessing these materials. Library faculty have increased the amount of bibliographic instruction, established on-line tutorials, and increased both print and Web-based services. Information literacy is a high priority and faculty and library staff are working together to provide students with the information access skills essential for their education. Where once reference librarians were occupied at a desk surrounded by reference materials finding answers for patrons, they are now on the floor helping students at terminals and are on-line guiding faculty who want to access materials in the classroom to teach new search strategies and standards for evaluating sources. On many campuses, information literacy is integrated into courses and team-taught by faculty and library faculty.

Quantity, quality, and time have become critical variables in accessing information. Browsing in the library is not the same as browsing on-line, and many patrons report being led astray or overwhelmed with too much information. The continuous improvement team focused on leading, not just responding to patrons, will need sophisticated data-gathering tech-

niques to understand the thinking processes related to accessing information. Focus groups can help librarians understand the issues so that
they can provide the in-depth information necessary to show that the
logic for accessing print materials may not work for electronic materials.
Library home pages caution students against reliance on "first found, first
used" research and explain more appropriate strategies as well as the challenges and limitations of electronic searching. Although students use such
on-line assistance, they still prefer face-to-face contact, which presents a
challenge to libraries to provide sufficient personalized services (Online
Computer Library Center 2002).

Work Flow Efficiencies

Library work has always been labor intensive, often relying on students
for the tedious tasks of reshelving books and handling checkouts and
returns. One continuous improvement project, focused on backlogs in
shelving, discovered that when students worked alone they felt isolated
and if they had a question they set the book aside. Working in teams was
more motivating, efficient, and effective as they could get help from each
other, send someone to track down the answer rather than put the material in a corner, and cover larger sections of the library. Other analyses
suggest ways that staffing patterns for professional staff can be changed;
for example, when staff are cross-trained they can work together to even
out the peaks and valleys of production work. Time savings have already
been achieved as activities once done by hand have been replaced by
electronic cataloging and barcodes. Despite conscientious improvement
efforts, the savings in both dollars and time for most libraries still has not
kept pace with enrollment increases or service demands.

Integrating New Services

Increased capacity that is unused is neither effective nor efficient. If one
begins with the principle that there is always something new at the library,
then time must be allocated to publicize new resources and services, provide workshops, and conduct training. One campus adopted "just in time
training" and made use of the 4:45–5:00 P.M. staff time to teach new
skills. Students and faculty could drop in during early morning hours or
over lunch to get a 15-minute introduction to new resources. These need-
to-know activities replaced the scheduled workshops, staff development
days, and broadcast activities that produced far fewer participants. In

short, choosing improvement strategies that match the culture of the campus is important.

Reshaping the Library Facility

As fewer and fewer students come to the library to do their initial research, libraries are asked to justify their space and staffing. Whereas once library staff could monitor the gate to determine usage of the library, electronic access requires different methods to gather data and understand the usage patterns. In many cases, students are coming to the library to find a quiet place to study or to do group work. The model of no talking is giving way to group study rooms, soft seating, and coffee shops. Changes in behavior call for new services and new amenities as well as a different metric for library performance. One campus built a new student center that integrates a food court, facilities for commuting students, and activity spaces with open stacks of library materials and study spaces on the upper floors. Another library opted for a separate coffee shop at the entrance to the library and eventually relaxed their rules about taking materials from the library to the coffee shop once a student pointed out that larger tables would provide enough space to work and safely drink coffee. Usage analyses show that such changes keep students and faculty in the library when they otherwise would take a break for refreshment and leave. Applying continuous improvement to all aspects of library services results in wholly new concepts about learning, the boundaries of the library, the role of library faculty, and how to bring services to students. Innovative campuses create new forms such as an "Information Arcade," a "Media Union," or an "Undergraduate Academic Center" (Klumpp 1997).

Collection Development Processes

Collection development based on department or individual faculty requests has given way to new approaches, including subscription services, monitoring of collections based on electronic comparisons with other institutions, determining gaps in the collection, and proactively developing collections in new fields. Applying cost-benefit analyses can help target the library budget for the materials that must be on hand rather than borrowed through interlibrary loan or made available through library consortia. A typical analysis is a journal survey to determine which journals have high usage and are important to campus programs. Many libraries find a journal once thought to be critical can now be replaced or the funds saved altogether.

Conducting a Review of Journals to Improve Quality and Cut Cost

- Identify the Problem: (e.g., very few new periodicals can be ordered because of the limited materials budget)
- Gather Data: (e.g., survey faculty asking them to rank order the list of periodicals essential for undergraduate, graduate, and faculty needs)
- Analyze Data: (e.g., using the survey results, usage data from previous years, information on the availability of electronic versions, and the cost of the subscription, identify periodicals as candidates for cancellation)
- Develop Actions: (e.g., review proposals with faculty and then discontinue periodicals that can be accessed electronically or are no longer necessary)
- Implement Improvement: (e.g., allocate some portion of the cost savings to new periodical subscriptions based on faculty requests)

SUCCESSFUL CONTINUOUS IMPROVEMENT

At least a decade of writing has outlined new options for structuring relationships between faculty and students, delivering courses, and improving service without additional resources. Yet the most common faculty response is "How can we be expected to do more with less?" Clearly, if campuses try to continue to do the same with fewer resources, quality is at risk. Institutions that will thrive in this tough environment will shift their thinking to ask, "What can we stop doing?" and "What should we do differently that will increase quality and efficiency?" Perhaps the strongest argument for thinking differently is that the resources most stretched on campuses—the people—are surely reaching their limit. Frustration, low morale, turnover, anti-administration feelings, and complaints that people do not feel in charge of their lives impact daily campus life.

Learning more about continuous improvement, its philosophy, the tools involved, and the leadership required, can help administrators, faculty, and staff restructure the environment to produce the levels of service, education outcomes, and quality of life reflected in their goals and aspirations. If the core activities of teaching, research, and work with students can be more productive, they will also be more rewarding. If processes can be streamlined, the energy spent on complaining and maintaining cumbersome systems can be redirected to activities with a higher payoff. The chief academic officer is in the unique position of having both the institutional perspective to identify problems and the authority and influence to seek improvement.

Faculty or staff skeptical about continuous improvement may demand evidence that the change effort is worth it. The chief academic officer must be prepared with hard data showing that quality can be improved and costs contained. Every effort to eliminate waste, consider different levels of service, use technology, restructure to improve productivity, and train faculty and staff will fall short without new thinking and measurable results. Resistance fades when change leads to increased retention and revenues, for example. If higher education is to continue to meet the high expectations held for it, not just good management but creative management is essential.

CHAPTER 9

Faculty Workload:
Understanding Productivity
and Equity

Many faculty members believe that initial interest in faculty workload from those outside of higher education was prompted by a legislator observing a faculty member cutting his grass in the middle of the day and concluding that he should have been "at work." The grass cutting story may well be apocryphal, but there is no question that external constituencies are concerned about what faculty do and the results of their activities. Despite campus efforts to provide data on faculty contributions and publicity about its merits, there is still a nagging feeling among many governing board members, business leaders, legislators, and taxpayers that some of what faculty do is unsupervised, unclear, and unproductive. Prompted by these concerns as well as constrained resources, both public and private institutions conduct workload studies with an eye toward increasing productivity, containing costs, and documenting how well faculty fulfill their obligations to students and to society.

Understandably, faculty resent any implication that they do not work hard or cannot be trusted as professionals to balance their individual career goals with their obligations to the institution and larger community. They argue that a standard 9-to-5 workday and five-day workweek does not fit faculty whose early morning class preparation, midday committee meetings, late-night grading, and weekend research are not apparent to observers who choose, instead, to note only the few required class hours and nine-month schedule. Faculty increasingly express concern about quality of work life and the growing demands on their time.

To many faculty, it appears that no matter how hard they work, neither pay nor appreciation measure up.

Chief academic officers (CAOs) understand that how faculty time and energy are deployed is critical to an institution's ability to fulfill its mission and attain quality. Further, they agree that workload is a legitimate concern as increasing costs and erosion in funding require greater productivity from all resources and a closer match of human resources to academic priorities. However, rather than treat faculty work with suspicion, thoughtful CAOs recognize that faculty are their most important asset. They understand that if work assignments are not perceived to be fair, manageable, or rewarded, faculty performance is affected. Faced with the nexus of good human resource management, accountability, and cost-effectiveness, CAOs need comprehensive and accurate methods to assess faculty resources and workload.

At the same time CAOs are striving to manage for greater efficiency, they also are reexamining the meaning of faculty productivity. Workload analyses are a useful tool for understanding allocation of resources, but they are not very useful for measuring the quality of work or encouraging faculty to align their activities with institutional goals. To better understand faculty effectiveness, many campuses are redefining the traditional tripartite model of faculty work—teaching, research, and service—and questioning whether the model is inclusive enough to match the growing expectations for higher education. Further, they doubt whether the "one size fits all" approach is realistic given the varying strengths of individual faculty and the varying needs of programs. In addition, they are reconsidering the degree of autonomy faculty have in choosing how to allocate their time. Finally, many CAOs are collaborating with faculty in rethinking how incentives and investments in faculty are related to faculty performance and institutional effectiveness.

This chapter addresses how the chief academic officer can analyze the two intertwined issues of workload (what faculty do) and productivity (what faculty achieve) to respond to concerns of external stakeholders, the needs of the institution, and the interests of faculty. The tools and data described can support academic planning and guide resource allocations to promote institutional quality. The questions and information can support better decisions about how to align faculty activities with the mission and the strategic priorities of the institution. In addition, the chapter describes the value of linking analyses of faculty resources, effort, and outcomes with curriculum, student needs, faculty development, and new community roles for higher education so that faculty are recognized for what they accomplish. Ultimately, what society needs to know about higher education is not how hard faculty work but whether the benefits to individuals and society are a good return on tuition and tax dollars.

MEETING EXTERNAL EXPECTATIONS ABOUT FACULTY WORK

Although the questions, "How hard do faculty work?" and "What do faculty do?" may have been initially motivated by campus and state needs to control costs, the questions now are part of the general public concern about the quality and affordability of higher education. Concerned about rising costs, greater access, and competing demands on public resources, a majority of states have instructional workload policies that specify the full-time faculty teaching load in credit hours, require regular reports as part of the documentation for faculty salary appropriations, or set maximum employment levels based on enrollment. In addition, states that have adopted performance funding require documentation of productivity consistent with the institutional mission. Neither these policy initiatives nor the evidence of faculty productivity appear to be sufficient to fully allay public concerns.

Recognizing that formal class meetings represent only a fraction of faculty work, many workload studies document how many hours faculty work spread across broad categories of activity. These studies show faculty work steadily increasing, now well above 50 hours a week on average, with over half the time spent on teaching activities (Rees and Smith 1991, 54–59; Middaugh 2001, 12–18). Nonetheless, skeptics paint a picture of faculty life as an easy job with few pressures, considerable discretionary time, summers off, and job security. Some of these perceptions are understandable as many academic activities are hard to quantify and do not have meaning to those outside the academy such as "keeping up with the field" and "contemplation" (Miller 1994, 11).

Given the growing number of students going to college and the need to retrain workers for a knowledge economy, states legitimately are concerned about the proportion of precious faculty resources allocated to teaching. At the same time, these external stakeholders need to recognize that faculty priorities should be aligned with the institution's mission. Data from the National Study of Postsecondary Faculty sponsored by the National Center of Education Statistics in 1997 does show that, appropriately, faculty in public research institutions gave 40.4 percent of their time to teaching while faculty at private liberal arts colleges gave 63.5

percent of their time to teaching (Middaugh 2001, 15). Measuring faculty work in this way demonstrates that, in the aggregate, faculty activity is shaped by the priorities and the reward structure of the campus.

Even recognizing the legitimacy of institutional differences, many stakeholders continue to question whether faculty are committed enough to teaching. Faculty have been described as not caring about teaching undergraduates, spending less time on individual student learning, focusing on graduate students who help them with their research, preferring to teach special seminars rather than offering the courses students need to graduate on time, and generally putting their own interests ahead of student needs (Jordan 1994, 15; Middaugh 2001, 1–4). An analysis of changes in faculty time allocation over a 20-year period reveals that, contrary to the popular view, full-time faculty are actually spending more time on both teaching and research (Milem, Berger, and Dey 2000, 471). However, as faculty time is limited, the researchers were curious about what was suffering and discovered it was counseling and advising students. These findings confirm the perception among many CAOs that faculty are spending less time on campus in informal interactions with both students and colleagues.

Clearly, the goal of all this scrutiny of faculty work is not merely to increase the amount of time faculty spend on teaching but to improve student learning (Fairweather and Beach 2002, 98). When workload studies connect faculty time to outcomes, they are more appropriately called productivity studies. Unfortunately, too often the studies for external stakeholders are limited to a quantitative emphasis and make little use of multiple measures. For example, because of the ease of measurement, many studies translate faculty work outcomes into credit hours produced, degrees granted, and numbers of students holding jobs in their chosen field. State reporting requirements that simply use these instruction-based measures as the stand-in for total faculty productivity give no credit for research and service, even though those activities are the basis for individual evaluation and salary decisions and are recognized responsibilities of the academy. Another shortcoming of many productivity studies is their focus on short-term results, whereas faculty believe they are producing lifelong learners whose contributions to society cannot be measured immediately.

To some extent, colleges and universities are responsible for this lack of understanding as they fail to effectively explain their multiple purposes that go well beyond undergraduate instruction. As a result, there is little public recognition for contributions in areas as diverse as health care services, biotechnology research, continuing education, and small business development. Investments in these activities, especially for public institutions, are significant. Based on an analysis of the portion of faculty time devoted to nonsponsored research activity, one state estimated it annually spent 200 million in salary dollars subsidizing research (Miller 1994, 10). Clearly, CAOs have a responsibility to help the public relations staff share the work of the faculty and publicize their contributions.

Campuses note the limitations of studies that focus just on whether faculty are spending enough time on the right activities and do not document the quality of those hours and the results of the efforts. To overcome that weakness, workload reports are coupled with reports on key performance indicators and assessment of student learning. Using additional performance measures, such as dollar value of sponsored programs, impact of continuing education on job creation, number of new inventions, and number of nationally recognized awards to faculty, gives a fuller picture of both faculty productivity and how well an institution is performing. Whether public or private, external mandate or not, more and more institutions respond to stakeholder interests and issue public relations materials and marketing messages that describe student success and institutional contributions to the community in an effort to demonstrate their solid commitment to academic quality, fiscal integrity, and societal well-being.

Explaining Faculty Work to External Stakeholders

- What distribution of faculty time on teaching, research, and institutional, professional, and community service is appropriate for the institution?

- What evidence demonstrates the priority the campus gives to undergraduate education?

- How is the quality of faculty activity in each area measured and documented?

- How do institutional expenditures of both time and money reflect the priorities of the campus and faculty?

- How does information on student satisfaction, standardized test performance, degree completion or other performance measures influence how faculty set their priorities?

> • Through what mediums does the institution explain faculty work and
> its outcomes to its stakeholders?

MEETING INSTITUTIONAL EXPECTATIONS ABOUT FACULTY WORK

State policies, faculty handbooks, or collective bargaining agreements specify minimum instructional workload requirements, such as 12 credit hours a semester. However, classroom instruction is just one of many faculty responsibilities that include, for example, advising, directing theses, developing curricula, undertaking research, and participating in institutional decision making. Thus some campuses concerned about managing workload and ensuring equity have developed elaborate systems based on "work unit" equivalencies that go well beyond the course to include, for example, six work units for the first offering of a three-credit distance-education course or two units for directing a theatrical production. Some workload systems also provide for adjustments in subsequent semesters if faculty fail to accomplish the professional development or service for which they were given work unit credit. Such a system recognizes that no single institutional workload standard based on a certain number of classes, minimum enrollments, service activity, and research production fits the needs of all programs nor all faculty. The system also gives credit for many necessary but previously unrecognized activities.

Although all campuses maintain the individual as the primary unit of analysis for salary or promotion, an increasing number find that the department or program is the better unit of analysis for workload. In those cases where faculty workload is described in credit hours, the interpretation is that this means "on average" for the unit. The department is assigned an expected credit-hour production and the department chair is responsible for work assignments that accommodate individual interests and strengths while meeting the expected department workload. The dean approves policies on equivalencies for nonstandard instruction, such as for lab courses, private music lessons, on-line instruction, and supervision of internships. The unit-based policies may also include formulas for how much reassigned time is available to the unit to be distributed to cover administrative duties, curriculum development, or research. In this way campuses establish workable metrics for equity in assignments, meet all obligations within the resources of the campus, and still retain enough flexibility to meet the needs of faculty.

The CAO who begins to gather data to understand work assignments that reflect campus policy, custom, or individual negotiations often finds that the very terms "workload study" and "productivity analysis" produce negative faculty responses and charges of administrative micromanagement. Learning from the experience of others, CAOs recognize that for campus-based workload studies to be useful for resource management, deans, department chairs, and faculty must have a shared understanding of the purpose and context in which data will be interpreted. If analyses are to successfully encourage individual reallocations of time and improve alignment of resources with priorities, faculty must be directly involved in reviewing data from the studies. When faculty are not involved, the information has little impact on persuading faculty to be good citizens of the community, thoughtful stewards of scarce resources, and realistic about how best to achieve the mission of the institution.

Chief academic officers often take advantage of new conditions and new pressures as the rationale for institutional attention to workload. First, as expectations of higher education change, they suggest that the measures of and rewards for faculty work should change to match the emerging priorities. Second, as states reduce the percentage of their funding or provide funding based on calculations of resource requirements, campuses have no choice but to be more efficient. Third, since faculty salaries account for 80 percent or more of the academic affairs budget, CAOs want to be sure that human resources are used optimally. Finally, because many faculty feel overworked, CAOs want to compare faculty work among units and to other campuses to understand this perception and establish an appropriate standard for the campus.

Although CAOs may emphasize budget and planning concerns, they must also be interested in matters of job satisfaction and how alternative formats and innovative pedagogy can increase student learning. When a task force of faculty and administrators begins analyzing faculty work, they soon discover that there are no easy answers to questions such as: Should faculty time be measured by contact hours or credit hours? Should faculty be expected to "give" their time to student affairs as club sponsors or freshman recruiters? Should faculty receive course release for accreditation studies or chairing the faculty senate? Should faculty be able to "bank" courses and self-fund release time in future semesters? How much time should faculty spend on campus? If faculty consult, is this a meaningful contribution to their teaching and research? Such questions show just how multifaceted faculty work is and how many institutional, professional, and personal demands there are on faculty time. Questions like these must be answered by each campus in order to determine what data to gather and how to make the information meaningful to faculty and useful to campus decision makers.

Analyses of faculty work by institutional type and field, based on extensive research, can provide perspective to campus studies (Middaugh 2001). The findings confirm that faculty distribute their time in a way that is consistent with the mission of the university and norms of their discipline, not merely their own preferences. Further, the studies show that even when there is a prescribed standard course load, there is variability in student credit-hour production per faculty member among programs within a single institution as well as from institution to institution. CAOs who want to understand the complicated internal cross subsidies of their campus need workload reports that document credit-hour production by individual faculty, departments, and colleges and separated by lower-level and upper-level undergraduate and graduate courses.

Despite the shortcomings of workload analyses and the difficulty of linking activity to goals and results, the information is useful for planning and budgeting when coupled with other data such as assessment and program review. Before using workload studies as the basis for decisions about cost containment or resource allocation, CAOs should first clarify priorities about the kind of education they want to provide. Recognizing the differences in teaching capacity, for example, between nursing programs with clinical responsibilities and psychology departments where there are economies of scale, can move the discussion from assuming that "one size fits all" to one that measures how faculty resources are aligned with expected results.

Ultimately, questions of cost cannot be avoided, as faculty salaries account for the largest portion of the academic affairs budget. Further, the pressure for both greater efficiency and greater effectiveness requires CAOs, deans, department chairs and faculty to think carefully about how best to array faculty resources to accomplish academic goals. If the negative factors driving up personnel costs, such as course proliferation, underenrolled classes, and poorly designed curricula, can be managed, the CAO can make positive recommendations that improve both the use of faculty resources and student learning.

Managing Factors that Drive up Personnel Costs

- What strategies can offset the expense of a high number of faculty at the highest rank and salary?

- How might the variety of courses and class size be matched to educational goals yet be managed to control personnel costs?

- How might the structure of the curriculum (e.g., general education and major requirements) or policies on transfer credit be modified to reduce personnel costs?

- How do pressures for reduced teaching loads based on specialized accreditation standards or graduate instruction impact standards for all units?

- What impact do off-campus programs and distance education have on staffing needs?

- How has increasing the number of students doing experiential work that requires individual supervision and faculty travel time (e.g., internships, music lessons, student teaching, and clinical placements) added to personnel costs?

- How do various pedagogical and curricular innovations impact the cost of instruction?

UNDERSTANDING FACULTY PERSPECTIVES ON WORK

No matter how well communicated the value of workload analyses nor how well developed the model, faculty instinctively resist what they believe is unwarranted reporting and institutional pressure. Faculty cynically muse about whether the concern is about "what we actually do," "what we should do," "whether we are doing enough," "how well we are doing it," "what else we are doing," or all of the above? For faculty to find workload studies an acceptable academic planning and management tool, they need to believe their perceptions about equity and amount of work are understood and respected. For workload studies to reshape time commitments, faculty need to have a say about meaningful incentives to support their efforts to change. In the current environment of budget cuts and reductions in full-time faculty positions, the chief academic officer especially needs to help colleagues in other divisions understand that faculty time is neither a "free good" nor an infinitely "elastic" resource.

In general, faculty perceptions about their work suggest a continuously changing profession with significant stresses affecting quality of life (Finkelstein, Seal, and Schuster 1998; Lindholm et al. 2002). One study of hundreds of new faculty noted that they feel "under siege" and criticized for not working hard enough; their main complaint is "lack of time" (Rice 1996, 2). Indeed, by some measures, faculty work all the time

including when they are listening to a student's personal problem, reading a new book, or advising a community agency. Concerned about
constant "add-ons," such as uncompensated internship development,
faculty try to overlap activities. They may argue that not only are they
allowed a day a week to consult, but if they take a student with them,
it also should count as teaching or supervision of a practicum. As many
activities and functions are interrelated and open-ended, faculty feel
constantly busy with little discretionary or personal time.

Some studies suggest that faculty frustration is the result of juggling
so many different activities, lack of clarity about how important some
of them are, an academic calendar filled with constant deadlines, and
long lapses between actions and results especially with regard to research
and publication (Lawrence 1994). Consequently, if faculty feel out of
sorts and unsure of what they should be doing, they are ready to suspect
that many administrators' expectations are unreasonable. Even at the
end of successful careers, senior faculty claim they received little guidance or support from colleagues or the institution as they struggled to
figure out how to create a rewarding career (Ferren 1998). Those faculty
who are able to develop a productive rhythm to their life, establish
meaningful goals, and see their ambitions being fulfilled, do not feel as
pressed. Clearly, for workload studies to be meaningful to faculty, the
studies need to focus not just on how many hours faculty work, but how
rewarding that work is.

There are two types of faculty work overload. Quantitative overload
is simply too much to do, whereas qualitative overload is having to do
things that make one feel incompetent such as teaching several new
courses or chairing a university-wide task force for the first time (Lawrence 1994, 36). Many faculty wonder how they will find the time and
the energy to learn new technologies, try new pedagogies, and keep up
with changes in their field. One result of workload analyses could be to
discover what type and amount of activity faculty deem appropriate at
various stages in their academic careers. Another result could be to recognize the impact raising children, caring for aging parents, or commuting has on productivity. Chief academic officers, sensitive to faculty
productivity over a lifetime, must think carefully about just how much
pressure to put on faculty to continuously "produce" and weigh new
initiatives against the tradeoffs in effectiveness, efficiency, and morale.

CAOs must also interpret faculty work to others on campus and be
advocates for reasonable and rewarding work. To do so, they need to be
sensitive to the realities of faculty work life and the impact of rising
expectations. For example, a nonacademic administrator may question

the legitimacy of a two day a week teaching schedule without considering whether, in fact, the uninterrupted blocks of time for research, course development, or preparing grant proposals make the faculty member more efficient and productive in these other areas of responsibility. The business officer may welcome the flexibility and cost-effectiveness of temporary and part-time faculty without taking into account the impact this lack of stability has on institutional effectiveness, full-time faculty productivity, and continuity in service to students. The chief academic officer, in dialogue with colleagues, must overcome these divergent perceptions and develop accepted institutional measures of faculty workload and productivity that are consistent with the realities of faculty life and the financial resources of the campus.

Because of variations in personal productivity, disciplinary standards, and department requirements, prescriptive standards for individual faculty work are not realistic. In the end, some faculty work harder, regardless of institutional or departmental expectations. Some faculty are more productive than others, regardless of institutional rewards. Some faculty do only the bare minimum. Although poor performance can be accounted for in individual evaluations, it is not financially realistic, nor is it good management, to allow any faculty member to coast. Department chairs, even with no backup from a campus policy, often try to increase the work demands on those faculty who do not take initiative on their own. Campuses that endorse differential workloads do so based on the assumption that individuals may make different contributions but all should make comparable contributions to the collective effort of the unit.

For department-based productivity standards to work well, the department chair and faculty need a shared understanding of the meaning of the assignments. For example, untenured faculty need to have the opportunity to do the kind of work necessary to develop a tenurable record, rather than be assigned "housekeeping" chores. Case studies of several campuses using differential teaching loads revealed that on one campus, faculty "believe that some 'nonproductive' researchers were 'made' to teach more to ensure equity in overall productivity," whereas on another campus, faculty believed their colleagues "were encouraged to follow their strengths and focus exclusively on teaching if they chose" (Fairweather and Beach 2002, 112). Ultimately, the CAO's task is to shape an environment that positively endorses individual flexibility, has a reward system that accommodates differences yet aligns faculty work with institutional priorities, and ensures that collective efforts accomplish institutional goals.

Common Faculty Queries about Workload

- How many different preparations should a faculty member have per semester?

- How should class size be weighted when measuring workload?

- How might differences in curriculum lead to different workload measures?

- How does the availability of graduate students to help with teaching and research affect the measure of workload?

- If a faculty member is teaching a graduate seminar focused on his or her research, is this an easier or a more difficult assignment than teaching an introductory survey course?

- If faculty can receive reassigned time to do research, can they receive reassigned time to develop their teaching or design a new course?

- Is service a personal choice or a requirement of campus citizenship?

- How should out-of-class student contact be accounted for?

- How congruent is what the administration says is valued with what is actually rewarded?

INTEGRATING MEASURES OF QUANTITY AND QUALITY

Much of the recent conversation about faculty productivity has been shaped by the national movement to review "faculty roles and rewards." The focus of that decade-long effort, initiated by the American Association for Higher Education, is to encourage more significant institutional rewards for the quality of what faculty do and to direct attention to the need to reshape faculty behavior to meet new challenges in higher education (Rice 1996). The underlying premise is that what is valued is measured and what is measured is what faculty attend to. New definitions of scholarship have been debated (Boyer 1990), and new concepts of faculty service beyond the campus have been recommended (Elman and Smock 1985; Driscoll and Lynton 1999). As a result, quantity such as student credit-hour production or number of publications, while still considered necessary measures, are no longer considered sufficient measures of faculty productivity and performance.

CAOs must be able to integrate the focus on quantity with that of quality at both the individual and the institutional level. The American

Association of University Professors (AAUP) notes "traditional workload formulations are at odds with significant current developments in education emphasizing independent study, the use of new materials and media, extracurricular and off-campus educational experiences, and interdisciplinary approaches to problems in contemporary society" and they suggest campuses develop "more sophisticated discrimination and weighting of educational activities" (American Association of University Professors 2001, 153). No matter how carefully measures are developed, they will never account for the time faculty spend on letters of recommendations, e-mails from students, creating course Web sites, or mentoring of doctoral students nor the subtleties of those contributions.

On most campuses, for purposes of promotion, tenure, and merit pay, quality measures and weighting systems have been fairly well worked out. Only recently has such work on appropriate qualitative measures and group incentives for departments been developed, and campuses are still unclear exactly how differential work should be appropriately rewarded (Wergin and Swingen 2000, 7). Since both units and individuals are responsible for high performance in teaching, research, and service, CAOs need to work with departments to develop appropriate methods for support, incentives, assessment, and rewards so that both individual and institutional productivity increases. Adaptations of faculty annual reports and work plans can be used to integrate individual goals with unit goals and to develop the work plan for the unit that must also be congruent with the strategic plan. In this way, individual faculty understand that their work will be weighted and measured as it contributes to the unit and the institution. The fundamental principle behind this new approach is to preserve faculty autonomy while promoting collective responsibility (Wergin 1994, 1).

The first step in any study of workload and productivity is defining and prioritizing the faculty activities the institution values. In *Assessing Faculty Work*, Braskamp and Ory pull together commonly held definitions of activities related to each category of faculty work (1994). The "Work of Teaching" is defined in terms such as grading, advising, designing courses, developing teaching materials, conducting classroom research, and attending faculty development programs (39–41). The "Work of Research and Creative Activity" is defined in terms such as writing books, presenting papers, writing plays, editing journals, writing proposals, and managing funded research (41–43). The "Work of Citizenship," often called campus service, is defined in terms such as serving on campus committees, mentoring other faculty, serving on accreditation teams, and providing leadership to the profession (48–50).

Added to this traditional tripartite definition is a fourth area, an elaboration of service, to include the emerging role of extension, outreach, and application of knowledge to solving societal problems. This "Work of Practice and Professional Service" is described as including, for example, conducting applied research, consulting, participating in economic development activities, and performing clinical service (42–48). Far more demanding than campus-based service and somewhat different from traditional research and scholarly activity, this area takes into account the increasing demand on higher education to participate more fully in communities and contribute to the common good.

Whether using these categories or others, each campus must elaborate on those activities that are counted as faculty work, identify the relevant activities for units, and establish weightings that are aligned with institutional priorities. There must also be agreement on the decisions that will be based on the data, for example, improvement in performance, matching strengths with assignments, accountability for advancing the strategic plan, compliance with minimum workload standards, or rewards for high performing units.

The next step in analyzing work is to arrive at standards for measuring quality and giving credit for the activities that distinguish between workload (what faculty do) and productivity (what faculty achieve). For any measure of productivity to be useful, it must possess certain characteristics: identifiable (we must know that it is a measure of productivity when we see it), understandable (everyone would agree that the measure has validity), directly linked with desired outcomes (the clear linkages ensure that those being assessed will see the point of the measure), measurable (if a metric cannot be applied, the results will appear fuzzy/challengeable), substantive (trivial measures that do not significantly impact faculty time should be avoided), accessible (the data must be reasonably attainable), and comparable (the measure must be applicable to all faculty). Ideally there should be multiple indicators of productivity, the indicators should cross-validate each other, and they should be able to be aggregated to produce a result. For example, individual teaching performance might be measured by the cluster of credit-hour production, teaching evaluations, peer-visit reports, and external review of the syllabi. At the program level, the cluster of indicators might be external ranking of the program, aggregate teaching evaluations compared to institutional evaluations, average credit hours compared to state funding formula, comparison of curriculum with peer institutions, and findings from program review or external accreditation.

Campuses appear relatively comfortable with establishing criteria and identifying the documentation or relevant evidence to show the degree to which the criterion is being met; for example, student evaluations of teaching are used as one measure of quality of instruction. The more difficult step is setting a standard for performance, that is, how high must the teaching evaluations be to qualify as meeting or exceeding expectations. Establishing meaning is especially difficult if, for example, 80 percent of the students rank all faculty in the top two categories. It is even more difficult to establish sufficiency, that is, how much or how consistent should the performance be. How many faculty members must use technology and for how many courses for the department to be deemed innovative? What level of student approval is sufficient to show that the technology innovation supported their learning? What learning outcomes are necessary for the innovation to be deemed successful? No matter how much effort is made to clarify the meaning of workload and productivity in the context of a single campus, setting standards and drawing conclusions based on information still requires judgment.

Hoping to find a formula that does not rely on judgment, too often campuses merely add up the number of publications rather than assess their quality through citations and journal reputation or they take the total extramural funding without regard to the significance of the research. Although faculty agree that mere counts provide insufficient information, they are drawn to simplicity and would rather require a research standard of two articles in three years than be faced with judging the quality or importance to the field. Departments may even resist judgment, claiming, "Evaluation is divisive to our sense of community." Unfortunately, such avoidance attracts external criticism that faculty are unwilling to commit to high standards.

The chief academic officer must be a resource to any task force charged with studying faculty work, as few department chairs or faculty have an overview of the entire campus, understand differences in disciplines, recognize variations based on accreditation requirements, or are aware of the role of faculty involvement in some community-based programs. Without taking variations into account, decisions about new faculty positions, course sizes, reassigned time, or credit for service will not be defensible. For example, an accredited business school is expected to have a low enough teaching load to support an active research agenda. Faculty in education are expected to provide hours of field-based service where the results are hard to measure, yet the involvement is critical to curricular integrity and good relations with the community. Each of these requirements affects the weightings of different elements, the standards for performance, and the context in which to interpret performance.

When equity and appropriateness are the goal, quantitative measures such as number of students taught, credit hours generated, expected number of office hours, contact hours for clinical practice, and the like will be debated. For public institutions, where funding may be calculated by formulas based on credit-hour production by discipline, the chief academic officer will want to use the state formulas for guidance but supplement them with internal heuristics that better match program needs, student demand, and faculty availability. For example, the state formula may group all humanities disciplines together, yet the curricular requirements of the campus make calculating English with the foreign language courses more appropriate. Small residential campuses interested in promoting greater faculty engagement with students may include quantity formulas related to the number of advisees or enrollment in first-year seminars. Whatever the work expectations are, both individual and unit reward systems must match.

If the goal is excellence, not equity, selecting the most salient measures of quality is critical. Appropriate comparisons, both within an institution and across institutions, can provide context. Many campuses rely on national rankings of programs, research productivity ratings, and the citation index to verify quality of faculty efforts. The increased emphasis on student learning, however, has placed greater emphasis on activities that go well beyond traditional classroom instruction to include activities such as mentoring, collaborative consulting, connecting co-curricular experiences with the classroom, and undergraduate research. Active engagement with students, contributions to the intellectual and cultural life of the campus, and support of colleagues are seen as essential investments in the campus quality of life. As program review relies on measures of quality as well as efficiency, much of this documentation of faculty work and productivity will be included in the program self-study.

Measuring Faculty Productivity

- What is the appropriate unit of analysis—the individual, the program, or the unit?
- If activities are weighted, are the variations based on the individual, the program, or the unit?
- What kind of qualitative and quantitative data represents teaching productivity?
- What kind of qualitative and quantitative data represents research and keeping up in one's field?

- What kind of qualitative and quantitative data represents contributions to the campus, the profession, and the community?

- How will qualitative data as well as quantitative data be used for decisions such as program review and resource allocation?

USING WORKLOAD INFORMATION FOR MANAGEMENT DECISIONS

Workload analyses only have value if there is agreement among deans, department chairs, and faculty about the kinds of decisions the information can support. The chief academic officer will want to focus on those decisions that are most important to the institution's well-being. Among the most common management decisions the CAO faces where workload information is useful are monitoring equity, authorizing positions, containing salary costs, and improving curricular efficiency.

Monitoring Fairness in Workload

Faculty have a refined sense of equity and want an overall sense of fairness in assignment of work. If teaching loads are onerous, if class sizes are mandated, if small classes are cut at the last minute, or if faculty sense they are carrying more than their fair share of the departmental load, faculty morale is sure to slip. On many campuses, CAOs are concerned about the heavy load for assistant professors who teach the larger lower-level classes, and data from numerous studies confirm "an inverse relationship between rank and teaching load" (Layzell, Lovell, and Gill 1996). Unfortunately, tradition on many campuses supports such inequities, not just in teaching but also in committee assignments, curriculum development, and other duties. If full professors teach only small seminars while the junior professors carry large introductory classes or if full professors have few preparations while junior faculty teach several different courses each semester, the junior faculty may not only suffer from overload but also feel a lack of support from the department. To overcome such patterns, CAOs can introduce new ideas about collective responsibility and the faculty work culture of the department.

Rather than be prescriptive in redressing inequities, many department chairs and deans effectively use workload data to support open conversations about expectations of what an individual's fair share of responsibility is for total departmental output. Even the AAUP, serving as the watchdog of faculty rights and responsibilities, has taken a nonprescriptive position on appropriate workload and merely calls attention to some of the common causes of inequity, including failure to recognize differences in difficulty of teaching a course, number of different course preparations, time required to develop and teach a new course, class size, expectations for original research, and assignments for advising or service to the institution (American Association of University Professors 2001, 153–59). Nowhere does the AAUP endorse lighter workloads based on rank or seniority.

Using departmental profiles, the chairs and dean can review not only the assignments of individuals but also department loads. When they do, they will see that some programs subsidize others. In many cases, sharing workload information encourages faculty to cooperatively reallocate their assignments and rethink program requirements for a more realistic match with faculty resources. Campuses that focus on institutional productivity within resource constraints may try to address the burden of the general education program on certain faculty or departments by providing resources for part-time faculty to give some relief. Both department chairs and deans share responsibility for overseeing workload and for helping faculty understand that equity and fairness are not the same thing. Reductions in one activity might be made up in another area of responsibility with the focus on comparable levels of effort that are consistent with both the program and the broader college or university needs. Ultimately, although distributing work equitably is a goal, assigning work to support optimal performance of individual faculty is equally important to institutional effectiveness.

Authorizing Faculty Positions

Typically, when a faculty position comes open due to retirement, resignation, or failure to reappoint, the department assumes the position is still theirs. Given the importance of aligning limited resources with priorities, many CAOs reclaim centrally all open positions for reauthorization or reallocation, although some assure a unit that if the faculty make a hard tenure decision, they will not lose the position. Without agreed-upon guidelines, however, faculty may claim that the process is more political than rational. On many campuses, faculty allocation models are simplistic and count all classes, regardless of enrollment, of equal value. Other campuses use multipliers to accommodate variations in class size, such as a class of 100 counts as 1.5. Other models are outcomes based and try to establish the number of courses and faculty required to produce a specific result.

To integrate principles of equity and adequacy, the chief academic officer needs both accurate workload information and a good sense of how workload relates to faculty productivity and institutional quality. Many CAOs rely on a representative task force to establish criteria for authorizing positions. Typically, the task force will give priority to criteria such as student enrollments, accreditation requirements, optimum class size per discipline, the availability of alternative faculty including graduate students and part-time faculty, and special needs such as doctoral instruction. The criteria are usually a mix of quantitative and qualitative measures. Recognizing different needs reduces the reliance on credit-hour production as the basis for position allocations and leads to recognition of other resource needs. For example, a unit with high credit production needs faculty, whereas a unit with a high number of majors needs advisors and staff.

Once decisions are made, deans and department chairs find it easier to explain position authorizations to their faculty when they have both the guidelines and up-to-date information on faculty staffing for all of the units. Workload data helps faculty understand the link between institutional priorities and overall staffing patterns, faculty assignments across levels of the curriculum, and the percentage of credit hours handled by nontenure-track faculty. Nonetheless, even though faculty may say they are committed to fairness and rationality, departments will still be disappointed if they do not get approval for their requests. Faculty become more realistic when they understand the limits on institutional resources that require difficult choices.

Managing the Proportion of the Budget That Is Allocated to Faculty Salaries

Academic affairs is a labor-intensive unit and salaries can account for 80 to 90 percent of the operating budget. When budgets are constrained or must be reduced as has been the case in many public institutions, the logical place to look for resources is in positions and salary increases. Several states have not authorized faculty salary increases for several years in a row. Faculty may understand that the national economy affects all employment, yet CAOs recognize the long-term effect of managing the budget by capping salaries. With both faculty morale and competition in a tight labor market as concerns, chief academic officers need to consider what the appropriate salary levels are for the campus while at the same time try to keep the academic affairs budget from being almost completely locked into salaries.

There are only two ways to accomplish increased salaries without increasing the percentage of the budget in salaries—new money or fewer faculty. When faculty are directly asked whether they would rather have fewer faculty who are better paid, they always say no, even though they do not always know what the optimal size of the faculty should be to accomplish institutional goals. Comprehensive workload studies can show positions that do not need to be replaced. Administrators and faculty alike know there is a point of diminishing returns, however, when the workload would be too much for faculty to manage if instead of replacing faculty members, the salary from open positions was redistributed to those remaining.

Increasingly, campuses are hiring part-time and temporary faculty to replace tenure-track faculty. With limited resources, it is prudent to take advantage of lower-cost labor in order to continue to give raises and not increase the proportion of the budget allocated to faculty salaries. However, the remaining tenure-track faculty must either pick up more of the responsibility for advising, committee work, administrative tasks, and curricular planning or let things go. As there is a limit to stretching full-time faculty resources further and further, CAOs must consider other ways to reduce the pressure on the budget in order to protect faculty and student learning. The most promising options are to identify program areas that can be phased out and to intentionally restructure the work of the campus to eliminate low-priority activities.

Increasing Curricular Efficiency

Another approach to managing instructional costs is to use workload analyses in reviewing curricular efficiency and productivity. Analyses will reveal the potential for reducing costs through alternative ways to deliver services, including greater use of technology, larger class sizes, more credits earned through internships and other off-campus experiences, and reductions in overly specialized courses. Workload analyses linked with curricular analyses can reveal where to make reductions that do not eliminate all the richness of the curriculum nor threaten student learning success. With the faculty member as the unit of analysis, the data would show that small classes can be subsidized by the very same faculty member teaching several other large classes. If the course is the unit of analysis, modeling would show that some courses can be offered less frequently, combined, or section sizes increased incrementally to increase efficiency of faculty resources.

Additional analyses of this type show that faculty productivity also increases when student learning increases (Ferren and Slavings 2000). Reducing the number of course failures and withdrawals and increasing student success in upper-level courses are other ways to make faculty resources more productive without adding to workload as it eliminates repeated classes. Technology especially holds promise for improving learning productivity. By substituting capital for labor, especially in large introductory classes, and tailoring the instruction to student needs, both the unit cost of instruction and faculty workload can be reduced (Twigg 1999).

Another option introduced on some campuses is to turn the traditional three-credit course into a four-credit course. Faculty teaching loads are effectively reduced when they teach three, four-credit courses instead of four, three-credit courses because they have one less preparation and fewer students to know and interact with. Students also benefit as they take fewer courses and study a subject in more depth. In addition, the fourth credit can be met in many ways, not only through contact time. Faculty may have students undertake laboratory work or go off campus for service learning. Some faculty choose to add group projects. Others require more individualized work. The transition to such a model requires careful assessment to be sure that both the goals for improved student learning and reduced faculty workload are achieved.

Managing Faculty Resources

- What data should be included in faculty position tracking systems to help in assessment of resource needs?
- How can faculty participation in determining work assignments address issues of equity and comparable contributions?
- How can a fair workload be established for all departmental faculty regardless of rank, tenure, and years of service?
- What are the resource implications and quality implications when vacant faculty positions in low productivity areas are reallocated to other programs?
- What incentives are there for departments to seek curricular efficiency? Should they be the beneficiaries of the savings or lose a faculty position?

USING PRODUCTIVITY MEASURES TO IMPROVE QUALITY

Not only do chief academic officers want to use information on faculty work to improve efficiency but they also want to find ways to improve quality as increased productivity pays off for both the institution and the individual faculty member. CAOs who view faculty as a critical and renewable institutional resource shift their focus from "purchasing the services" of the faculty to "investing in capacity" (Layzell, Lovell, and Gill 1996). Campus workload projects interested in better management of assets focus on the importance of differential work models, the value of matching individual interests to institutional needs, and the importance of strengthening the relationships between faculty and their institutions. The recommendations from these projects address such issues as support for new faculty, faculty development, succession planning to ensure program support, and changing views of faculty roles.

Supporting Career Development of Junior Faculty

When chief academic officers view faculty as an asset that must be taken care of, workload studies become relevant to decisions about how to support, invest in, and reward faculty rather than how to demand more of them. Investing in junior faculty is particularly important as their level of productivity sets the stage for the rest of their career. In the initial years, junior faculty report spending long hours on course preparation and struggling to find time to begin a research program. For that reason, many campuses give faculty a reduced load in their first year or two and factor that reduction into their analyses of departmental productivity. Since time costs money, yet that is what faculty say they need, administrators can also consider inexpensive strategies to give time such as limiting the number of different course preparations, giving relief from committee assignments, and ensuring a teaching schedule that provides blocks of time or full days for research activities. At a minimum, giving faculty control of their schedule can help them feel less overcommitted and more able to match their activities to campus productivity expectations.

At the same time junior faculty are establishing the foundation for their career, they also have child care obligations, need to make friends in a new community, and want to connect with colleagues on campus. Time overload is a concern as well as "work-life spillover" where there are few boundaries to work time (Sorcinelli and Near 1989). Faculty read in their field while on vacations, add a day to conference travel and call it time off, and work over dinner as they socialize with department colleagues. As a result, work seems omnipresent. Academic couples are even more challenged, and, increasingly, campuses are asked to make accommodations such as job sharing, help in finding a position, or creating a position to help reduce the stress of commuting (Wolf-Wendel, Twombly, and Rice 2000). Modeling the cost of investing in junior faculty compared to the cost of losing faculty members can help CAOs make decisions about scheduling, support services, and policies.

Cynical faculty believe campus administrators worry more about wear and tear and deferred maintenance of buildings than about wear and tear and deferred maintenance of human capital. In that regard, many campuses have made it easier to receive leave, including instituting a leave after the first three years in order to help junior faculty develop the record necessary for tenure. Some campuses expect senior faculty who have already achieved a level of competence and security in their teaching, research, and scholarship to take responsibility for coaching and assisting junior faculty in advancing their careers. Time reassigned to mentoring can be accounted for in the workload of a professor and the departmental analysis. Being recognized in the role of "senior statesman," both in the unit and on the campus, is important as there is considerable evidence that senior faculty feel a kind of disappointment that, after having achieved the highest rank, there is nothing more to achieve (Ferren 1998; Bland and Bergquist 1997).

Stimulating Faculty Career Development

All CAOs recognize that the vitality of institutions is directly related to faculty remaining energized and excited about their careers. Faculty shape their choice of activities to be both personally and institutionally rewarding and often change their priorities over the course of their careers. Research on faculty careers suggests that flexibility in work assignments, peer support, and new opportunities stimulate faculty and keep them fresh and enthusiastic about being academics (Bland and Bergquist 1997, 91–102). Thus chief academic officers need to be sensitive to how adjustments in workload can allow faculty the opportunity to reshape what they do. To do otherwise and adhere to strict guidelines for absolute equity and the same load year after year would inhibit opportunities to promote faculty renewal.

Department chairs have the authority, within agreed upon guidelines, to adjust teaching and committee assignments to match faculty interests, strengths, and needs, and the CAO should encourage tailoring work as-signments to support development. The chair can provide reassigned time from teaching so that a faculty member can develop a new program, initiate a new line of research, or participate in an institutional priority. Alternatively, some campuses require faculty to earn reassigned time. For example, rather than be given time to do research, a faculty member would get a course release after writing a book. Campuses concerned about the overall productivity of faculty are making greater use of institutional incentives such as small grants, although almost all faculty note that it is time, not additional resources, that they need. Equally important, CAOs must make sure that department chairs promote a supportive environment.

Comprehensive research on faculty work suggests that how faculty shape their work choices is far more complex than just time or context; there are real differences in faculty interests, commitments, and oppor-tunities (Blackburn and Lawrence 1995). Those differences have both institutional and personal consequences. Those that spend more time on teaching do less research. Those that publish more generally have higher salaries (Meyer 1998, 14). Some CAOs are increasingly sensitive to the research on faculty activity that suggests that gender and race are not neutral factors and have an impact on the faculty member's career op-portunities and choices (Tack and Pattitu 1992). Chief academic officers must provide oversight so that work assignments are appropriate and sup-ported so that faculty can reap the institutional rewards. Otherwise they risk watching certain faculty members fall behind on salary and rank.

Managing Succession Planning for Stability in Programs

As faculty turnover from resignations and retirements increases, so does the concern about how to plan for and compete for replacements. Pre-dictions on the number of faculty available to replace the large number of faculty currently in the 55 to 65 age range suggests an increasingly competitive job market. The age profile for a department can reveal how many faculty would potentially retire within the same time frame and create either a crisis or an opportunity, depending upon other factors such as institutional program priorities. If linked with strategic planning and program review, this data can call attention to faculty needs with enough time to stabilize a strong program and, similarly, might suggest an oppor-tunity to redesign or phase out a program.

One alternative, when unsure about authorizing a tenure track position, is to authorize a multiyear term appointment that allows the holder to be a candidate should a tenure-track position be authorized. To model several scenarios, the CAO needs a database with every position's history, when the position was authorized, who has held the position, as well as comparative data for all units including student/faculty ratios, type of appointment, and age of all current faculty. A long-term staffing plan, as part of program review and the planning and budget processes, can ensure necessary resources are available or positions are reallocated as appropriate.

Workload analyses can also play a part in making projections about replacement needs in order to stabilize faculty resources as programs evolve and change over time. Before mandatory retirement was uncapped for faculty in 1994, institutions expressed concern that faculty would not retire and would stay on despite declining productivity. However, studies show that the vast majority of faculty continue to retire in their sixties and there is little or no relationship between age and productivity (Hammond and Morgan 1991; Bland and Bergquist 1997). Demographic studies, surveys, and personal interviews support the fact that retirement is not simply an age or productivity-related decision, but is also influenced by health, financial well-being, family status, and other interests (Lozier and Dooris 1991, 28–31; Ferren 1998).

Believing faculty turnover to be beneficial as a way to make room for "new blood" and to provide flexibility to manage enrollment shifts or budget constraints, many campuses have established retirement incentive plans, including phased retirement. From time to time, the pressure to retire is so intense on some campuses that faculty report equal pressure not to retire from their colleagues who fear the department will lose the position. Under ideal circumstances, retirement would be not just an individual decision but also an institutionally supported decision. To be effective, for both the individual and the institution, retirement incentive plans need to be costed out, linked to faculty staffing priorities, and accompanied by counseling focused on adjusting faculty work throughout a career and not just in the period prior to retirement.

Severe budget crises make a retirement incentive program an important aspect of budget management as it encourages highly paid faculty to take advantage of enhanced retirement benefits and reduces the salary commitment for the campus in the future. State systems with defined benefit programs often require the campus to pay into the retirement system for the years of service credited toward the "early out," which leaves the academic affairs budget with short-term debt to achieve a long-term budget reduction. Too many retirements in one unit can threaten the viability of a program and the budget of academic affairs; thus the chief academic officer must reserve the right to approve each applicant.

Workload analyses can help the CAO determine whether the campus can afford to support every faculty member eligible to retire during the proposed window. A more manageable model, usually on campuses with defined contribution retirement programs, also limits participation when it is critical to a program but aims to make the program self funding. During the period of the pay-out or terminal sabbatical, the department cannot replace the position, as the salary is committed. Although there is a short-term burden on the members of the unit who pick up the extra workload, the program can be financially sustained indefinitely.

Integrating Public Service with Institutional Service

Most workload studies do not try to quantify faculty service nor community activities. Faculty annual reports do include such service, but faculty would feel it intrusive to have too many questions asked about the worth of their participation. Because there are mixed views about the value of committee work, professional involvement, and outreach, yet an increasing call for campuses to contribute to their communities, new ideas about how to document such activity have been developed with an emphasis on "impact" (Driscoll and Lynton 1999). Whether such activity is discretionary needs to be addressed at the campus level.

Most CAOs agree that for professional service to be included in workload studies it cannot be just a matter of good citizenship, but rather should meet rigorous standards and be related to the university function of creation, dissemination, and application of knowledge. Credit should be given for public service when it is an intellectual activity that "draws upon one's professional expertise and is an outgrowth of one's academic discipline" and not just time put in (Elman and Smock 1985, 12). This kind of outreach is distinguished from campus or professional service and from traditional forms of research and scholarship and includes, for example, technical assistance, applied research, or clinical work. If done under the auspices of the university, it is not consulting even if the faculty member is paid.

Campuses recognize that such faculty involvement is both cost-effective and academically important as the faculty member often provides internships, career counseling, and employment contacts well beyond what the campus career center can provide. Similarly, campuses place a high value on positive publicity about faculty and students participating in community service or offering clinical services. Such publicity is more effective and less costly than a full-page ad about the campus. There is some evidence that connecting with the community and making it possible for faculty to have visibility also makes it easier to retain them. Engineering schools, for example, would rather the faculty members supplement their academic salary through outreach to the community and consulting than lose them to industry. Campuses that view outreach as an obligation to society and an important value of higher education also need to recognize the activity as part of faculty work.

Reshaping Faculty Performance with Incentives

- What incentives are meaningful to faculty at varying stages in their careers?
- What should the balance be between time and money in supporting faculty development?
- How might performance contracts be used to help a faculty member develop over a period of time?
- What role does the department play in the development and support of faculty colleagues?
- How might special administrative assignments in other areas such as student affairs, institutional research, or development refresh a faculty member?

SUCCESSFUL MANAGEMENT OF FACULTY RESOURCES

The previous discussion implies that the management of faculty resources is easily amenable to rational processes when, in fact, the issue can create ill will because decisions have such an immediate effect on individuals. The dilemma academic decision makers face is that perceptions about workload often overwhelm reality. Despite a CAO's best efforts, not all faculty change their perceptions based on information, comparative trends, open communication, and clear policies. Old histories are never forgotten. One CAO tells the story of a meeting with department members during her first year on campus in which they claimed they were short five positions. When asked when they had full staffing, the reply was "1977." All the changes on the campus, in the curriculum, or in enrollments over 20 years had not affected the department's perception that they were "owed" positions.

As faculty workload studies take on greater prominence in higher education, CAOs, deans, and department chairs must do a better job of explaining to faculty the rationale behind such studies. When linked with discussions of limited resources, faculty recognize that workload and productivity must be an ongoing rather than a one-time discussion. Having accurate information set in context helps faculty understand that hard work is not enough and that their efforts must be aligned with strategic priorities. Results, not mere activity, are the measure of productivity. CAOs recognize that human resources are the foundation of the university and must be invested to support institutional effectiveness. Consequently, any efforts to reshape faculty workload must be directly related to improving learning, supporting professional development of faculty, and encouraging a collaborative culture in departments and across campus.

Faculty workload is not just an academic affairs issue. All divisions of the institution must recognize the broad institutional contributions that faculty make to all divisions ranging from serving in judicial affairs and recruiting students to writing grants and participating in alumni activities. Bringing rationality to human resource planning can impact faculty productivity and satisfaction. However, showing greater appreciation of the work of faculty is an investment in the future of the institution. Meaningful rewards are the responsibility of the CAO. Thus, workload issues must be systematically and intentionally moved by the CAO into the mainstream of operational and strategic planning both within academic affairs and within the institution. To do so, the CAO must collaborate extensively with faculty, with academic administrators, and administrators in other divisions in moving beyond measuring faculty work to creating strategies for investing in, caring for, and allocating this invaluable resource.

CHAPTER

Faculty Compensation: Applying Equity, Market, and Merit

Few issues are as sensitive for faculty as compensation. Claims of gender inequity, salary compression, age discrimination, and lack of market competitiveness affect both an institution's ability to recruit and retain quality faculty as well as its ability to foster commitment and productivity. Campuses that provide across-the-board increases and fixed salary ranges are perceived as fair but often have difficulty hiring new faculty in competitive fields and retaining highly productive faculty. Campuses that set starting salaries according to the market remain competitive in hiring but may then face complaints about salary compression from current faculty. Campuses that base raises solely on merit are challenged to have appropriate criteria applied equitably. Finding the right principles as well as sufficient money to sustain an effective compensation system is a central issue for chief academic officers (CAOs) in strategic planning, budget development, and human resource management.

Chief academic officers on the front line, dealing with faculty morale and efforts to hire top quality faculty, are spending an increasing amount of their time on compensation issues. Not only concerned about appropriate and equitable faculty salaries and benefits, they also recognize that compensation is complex and includes nonsalary factors. Candidates in hiring interviews ask about start-up funds for research programs, moving expenses, and reduced teaching loads. Current faculty press for student assistants to help with teaching and additional equipment and supplies. Inevitably, when budgets are tight, in order to preserve base salaries, many of these other forms of faculty compensation are cut.

Higher education is no different from other employers who are challenged to provide competitive compensation; however, employment security, individual autonomy, special benefits, and opportunities for extra earnings distinguish faculty from many other professionals. Although faculty tend to focus just on their salary, over a quarter of compensation is in the form of benefits, for example, retirement contributions, medical insurance, and long-term disability, that are often "more generous than those offered in the for-profit sector" (Baum 2001, 45). Many faculty also take advantage of valuable tuition benefits, sabbaticals, and professional travel support—benefits not available in other professions. Faculty can also supplement their base salaries with additional compensation such as for summer teaching or administrative duties. Furthermore, on most campuses faculty have the right to one day a week for consulting or other external professional activities. All of these factors contribute to an individual's overall earnings and standard of living.

Nonetheless, chief academic officers know that perceptions about compensation are as important to faculty morale and institutional competitiveness as reality. Any review of faculty compensation, therefore, must focus on how compensation, strategic priorities, fiscal responsibility, faculty confidence, and quality are linked. This chapter discusses factors that affect compensation, the importance of both good policies and good procedures, methods for ensuring equity and responding to market competition, the role of merit in determining individual salary increments, and the importance of conducting systematic salary reviews. In collaboration with the president, chief financial officer (CFO), and the institutional research office, the chief academic officer must manage faculty compensation with consistency as well as advocate for fair salaries within the resource capacity of the institution. Institutional effectiveness depends upon appropriate faculty rewards aligned with individual productivity and institutional goals.

LINKING COMPENSATION AND INSTITUTIONAL QUALITY

The first issue a chief academic officer needs to address is whether the overall level of compensation is appropriate as both "the absolute and relative levels of faculty compensation have an impact on faculty behavior" (Sutton and Bergerson 2001, 6). Analyses of faculty salaries in constant dollars confirm the faculty perception of only moderate progress since the 1980s compared to the cost of living (Sutton and Bergerson

2001, 12). In addition, salary studies show academics have fallen behind comparable professionals in certain fields (Hammermesh 2002, 27). Many faculty also believe that as a group they are underpaid compared to their worth to the institution. Whether higher salaries in nonacademic positions would compensate for the lack of security and autonomy, whether compensation affects who chooses to be an academic, or whether faculty leave higher education because of salary is not as clear.

Chief academic officers intuitively understand how their own institution's salaries measure up by tracking turnover, resignations at upper ranks, and ease of hiring their first-choice candidate. When the CAO needs to explain to faculty and administrative colleagues the degree to which the institution's salaries are competitive, the question is: Competitive by what standard? Faculty often cite salaries at top research institutions when arguing for increased faculty salaries. *U.S. News and World Report* uses faculty salary level as one measure of institutional quality (Ehrenberg 2003, 151). The chief academic officer, however, must be realistic and make three types of relevant institutional comparisons: peer institutions, "aspirational" institutions, and specific institutions with which the campus directly competes in hiring faculty.

Peer institutions are those that have similar characteristics, such as mission, enrollment, quality of students, range of programs, and percentage of faculty with the terminal degree. Some states, concerned about overall competitiveness of the system, select peer groups for each campus and set targets for faculty salary averages as a basis for appropriations. Internal salary allocations are left to the institution. Chief academic officers argue that state goals are often too low to effectively compete for and retain first rate faculty. For example, setting the goal for the salary average at the 60th percentile of peers will not make the institution very attractive. In addition, even though the selection of peer institutions is based on careful methodology, CAOs know that a peer institution in rural Iowa has little to do with the appropriate faculty salaries for a peer institution in suburban Baltimore because of the significant differences in cost of living and availability of other job opportunities.

Alternatively, focusing less on comparability and more on quality, the CAO could argue for setting comparisons with aspirational institutions, the group of institutions the university emulates. Most state governing boards and funding authorities do not recognize aspirational institutions when allocating salary funds, but some major public institutions have been able to present a compelling case that their becoming nationally or internationally known in research and knowledge transfer benefits the state. As a result, they have been able to change their peers and thus the basis for budget appropriations. Presidents and CFOs of private institutions, with a close eye on competitiveness, are more easily persuaded to use a mix of peers and aspirational institutions to set strategic targets for salary levels as an investment in institutional quality. To a large degree, however, compensation is governed by total institutional resources.

Another basis for determining competitiveness is by comparing salaries to those at institutions with which a campus directly competes for faculty. Often this is a mix of types of institutions in a region recognizing that faculty may choose a place where they would like to live and then look for employment at all institutions in that area. In other cases, campuses are nationally competitive and measure their salaries against a core group of institutions, for example, all major public research universities. To fully understand competitiveness, the CAO needs not just salary data but also information on what perquisites are being offered, both monetary and nonmonetary. Some campuses provide joint appointments in interdisciplinary programs and research centers to assure young faculty that they will be able to keep up their specialized interests while also serving the general departmental curriculum. Other campuses use reduced teaching load, pretenure leave, or summer research salary to attract new hires.

Working only with the overall salary average for a given year, however, will not give the CAO an accurate picture of competitiveness nor institutional quality. The mix of salaries is always changing as high-paid faculty retire and lower-paid new assistant professors are hired, thus decreasing the campus salary average. Indeed, this has been the basis of considerable misunderstanding on some public campuses where the actual salary average is lower than the authorized salary average because of early retirement programs aimed at reducing state personnel costs. The fact that some high-paid faculty have retired and the average has declined does not mean that all the remaining faculty suddenly have inadequate salaries.

The more accurate basis for reviewing competitiveness is to look at salary averages and salary ranges at the rank and discipline level. Because the data are easily accessible, faculty often look at the data collected by the American Association of University Professors (AAUP) that is reported in four salary groupings. For example, being in group 3 for doctoral institutions means the salaries fall between the 40th and 60th percentile of all doctoral institutions. The CAO should check the grouping for each of the ranks. An uneven distribution, for example, assistant professors at group 2 and professors at group 3, would suggest that salary distribution in recent years has favored new hires. The AAUP data also can be helpful to CAOs who want to know whether their campus salaries are increasing at the same rate as other institutions.

Deciding to raise the overall salary grouping for all ranks in order to be more competitive could be daunting. To gain ground would require annual increases above the average increases given by other institutions each year for several years. To calculate the cost, the CAO can take the difference between the salary average at each rank for the campus and the salary average at each rank in the desired grouping times the number of faculty at each rank, and then take into account the anticipated average annual salary increase. One campus that had raised admissions standards, revised curricula, and held faculty to higher standards for research and teaching excellence, also made raising faculty salaries part of their strategic effort. The CAO believed that faculty compensation should parallel the overall improvement in institutional quality. Another campus, concerned about losing full professors, gave increments for that rank each year for three years to make up for the cumulative effect of their low starting salaries, established 20 years earlier when the campus was not as competitive and did not have the resources.

Yet another way to understand whether faculty salaries are competitive is to take into consideration the comparative cost of living. For example, to be equivalent, an $81,000 salary in Atlanta would need to be $165,000 in San Francisco and only $58,000 in Evansville, Indiana. Salaries that are appropriate to the region must stay competitive. When state budget crises freeze faculty salaries, public institutions become vulnerable to "raiding by better financed private institutions in the area" (Upham 2002, 11). The only option for public institutions when no additional salary funds have been appropriated is to reallocate funds from other priorities to maintain annual salary increases.

Finally, competitiveness must be considered in terms of supply and demand for faculty, both in particular disciplines and overall as the labor market is affected by enrollment increases, retirements, and the declining number of potential faculty (Finkelstein, Seal, and Schuster 1998). Although there are many who argue that all faculty should be paid roughly the same as they all carry similar responsibilities, only a minority of campuses are that egalitarian. The majority accept the reality that they are competing with other employers outside of higher education, which bids up the salaries for accounting, marketing, and engineering professors. The CAO can order College and University Professional Association for Human Resources (CUPA-HR) salary data for peer institutions or any selected group of institutions, reported by discipline and rank, to get a comparative perspective on whether the institution's salaries by discipline are market competitive.

Ultimately, although influenced by type of institution, geographical area, and supply and demand, compensation is the link between institutional resource capacity and expected levels of institutional productivity and faculty performance. The best option for CAOs faced with depressed faculty salaries across the board, within disciplines, at certain ranks, or some combination is to advocate for additional funding as internal reallocations risk quality in other areas. CAOs faced with constrained resources, yet committed to institutional change and quality, must keep faculty compensation a high priority. They need to help the president and chief financial officer understand the importance of new revenues for salaries to strengthen the relationship between faculty and institutional effectiveness. In the long run, faculty compensation can only be competitive if it is an institutional priority to which all administrators are committed.

Promoting Institutional Goals through Compensation

- To what extent is faculty compensation a priority in the strategic planning and resource allocation processes for the institution?
- How congruent is compensation with expected levels of faculty performance?
- How often are faculty salaries adjusted to keep up with cost of living, comparable professionals in the community, and comparable institutions?
- How is compensation adjusted to reflect the market for faculty in specific disciplines?
- How has the level of total compensation affected recruitment and retention of quality faculty?
- What are appropriate comparisons to determine annual salary increments?

LINKING COMPENSATION AND INDIVIDUAL QUALITY

Making the compensation system understandable, fair, and reflective of institutional and faculty values is a challenge to every CAO. If compensation is set by a collective bargaining agreement or a salary schedule with steps, the CAO's role is considerably different—primarily limited to making sure faculty start at the right step in the matrix. However, as more campuses add merit increases to their salary schedule or give up across-the-board increases altogether and focus on pay for performance, CAOs find that they must guide the collaborative development of compensation policies and procedures. Those policies will differ by campus and reflect fundamental values such as the egalitarian culture of a small liberal arts college that eschews a merit system or the highly competitive stance of a major research institution willing to buy talent. CAOs must be skilled translators between the different perspectives of the faculty and the president and board.

The principles that underlie compensation are merit, market, and equity. At a minimum, faculty expect to receive annual increments to their salaries in recognition of their performance and as an incentive for future performance. Should the campus be unable to give increases, careful attention must be given in later years to addressing the impact of skipped years. If not, salary compression will disadvantage high-performing faculty. Faculty also expect salary levels to correlate with length of continuous service; thus there need to be policies about eligibility for annual increases, including during leaves. The annual increase is not merely a reward for service but also is assumed to reflect the additional expertise and knowledge developed over the years.

The foundation of the compensation system is that faculty are rewarded commensurate with their contributions to the institution's strategic direction. That reward system should be established through the evaluation, tenure, and promotion criteria and should be carefully followed as the basis for compensation. Despite increased attention to resolving the unnecessary tension between teaching and research, many CAOs find that even when the central administration stresses the importance of teaching and campus citizenship, departments often continue to reward faculty primarily for their research productivity consistent with disciplinary norms (Austin 1996). Those campuses that allow individual weighting of areas of faculty performance, within institutionally specified ranges, are better able to reflect both institutional needs and faculty strengths and, thereby, align rewards with institutional priorities (Diamond 1999, 6–8). Chief academic officers should be able to trust that if institutional priorities are clear, departments and faculty will do what is rewarded.

Faculty must be confident that all faculty are treated equitably. When faculty believe their compensation is unfair, it reduces their commitment to an institution and they often look elsewhere for rewards. Equity means comparable pay for comparable responsibilities, but it is not the only factor in setting salary (Moore and Amey 1993, 71–73). Nondiscrimination does not disregard performance or length of service and thus cannot be interpreted to mean that all faculty should receive the same salary or that salary averages should be equal. Comparing average salaries for women and men without regard to rank, time in rank, discipline, or length of service can be very misleading. Some argue that past practices that limited opportunities for women and minority faculty should be made up for by more generous compensation for current faculty or that underrepresented classes of faculty should be hired at premium salaries to meet diversity goals. Such practices, however, would constitute reverse discrimination.

Faculty also expect to see reasonable differentials between the salary averages at the different ranks. Promotion is based on both quality of performance and length of service, both of which faculty expect to be reflected in their salary. The rough spread on a campus with moderate salaries might be average salaries of $37,000 for assistant professors, $49,000 for associate professors, and $61,000 for professors. Without knowing the quality of performance, length of service, or length of service at a particular rank of the individuals in that grouping, a CAO who relies on merely scanning the dispersion of salaries in a department to determine whether they are appropriate would be misled. Using the rank-ratio method and applying the multiplier, reported by the AAUP, of 1.65 times the assistant professor average to get the relative full professor average can serve as a guide but may not fit the demographics of a particular campus (Hammermesh 2002, 25).

Although faculty are concerned about wide variations in salaries, faculty do expect to see the spread of salaries reflect the market for disciplines and specializations. Faculty in engineering will be paid more than faculty in philosophy because of competition with positions outside of higher education. Even specializations within a department may be affected by the market. For example, the educational leadership program faculty will be paid more than the teacher training faculty, mirroring the same compensation pattern in elementary and secondary schools. Because of the mix of faculty in each department and the mix of disciplines on the campus, merely using comparisons of departmental salary averages to review a campus compensation program for equity is also misleading.

Because quality depends upon each individual's continuous performance, yet compensation is not a motivator, CAOs are justifiably concerned about how to sustain individual performance and avoid plateaus. There is some evidence of reduction in effort and productivity once a faculty member is tenured or has been promoted to professor (Rees and

Smith 1991, 53–78). However, it may be that faculty see little at stake to justify increased effort when percentage increments are as low as two percent. Similarly, if increases are automatic for satisfactory performance, it requires internal motivation, rather than external incentives, to cause faculty to exceed that standard. Some faculty deliberately avoid new courses or new pedagogy as they are afraid it will affect their evaluations and salary. To link compensation with individual productivity requires both an effective faculty evaluation process and adequate resources. Failing that, length of service, rather than productivity, will be the best predictor of salary.

Even under the best circumstances, the chief academic officer will find that the different considerations that affect individual salary decisions are not easily reconciled. Rewarding merit to motivate faculty may turn off less-productive faculty or cause others to choose to do consulting, which takes less time and earns them more than the annual salary increment for time-consuming research and publication. Distributing salary dollars equally to units will not reward the high-performing units. Basing raises on individual performance will inhibit collective efforts to meet institutional goals. Setting faculty compensation levels to recruit new faculty may create inversions and appear to disadvantage current faculty, although the qualifications of new hires may be quite different. Allocating faculty salary adjustments to meet market levels may inadvertently create a perception of gender inequity because there are fewer women, especially at the professor rank, in some of the highly paid fields such as engineering and accounting.

In short, no matter how carefully designed the compensation program is, the resulting variability in faculty salaries raises the question: Are the factors that affect each individual's salary appropriate and understood? Making public the basis for allocations, monitoring the overall distribution of salaries, and maintaining a longitudinal perspective makes it easier for the CAO to correct misperceptions and address any inadvertent inequities.

Promoting and Rewarding Faculty Quality

- How can the compensation system promote individual faculty commitment and productivity?
- How can the compensation system promote faculty cooperation and collective effort toward institutional goals?

- How can the compensation system encourage faculty to be innovative, take risks, and try new activities that support institutional change?

- How can the compensation system have an effective impact on faculty performance that does not meet standards?

FOUNDATIONS OF AN EFFECTIVE COMPENSATION SYSTEM

Compensation systems aim to strike a balance among the faculty members' personal and professional needs; an institution's mission, vision, and goals; and planned or expected resource availability. To be effective, every compensation system must be based on clear guiding principles, governed by agreed upon policies; and administered through rational and well-founded procedures. Most campuses arrive at these principles, policies, and procedures through a collaborative process. All campuses try to document them in the collective bargaining agreement or the faculty handbook. However, as varying degrees of discretion are granted to department chairs and deans, without meaning to depart from agreed upon compensation principles, some of their informal practices in evaluation and setting salaries can undermine the system. Consequently, chief academic officers must regularly monitor the compensation system to be sure that it is founded on shared values, administered consistently, protects against arbitrary decisions, and has the confidence of the faculty.

Although no two institutions are quite the same nor will they have the same compensation system, certain guiding principles appear to be common as reflected in institutional compensation study documents and memoranda to faculty. First, compensation must be a priority when budgets are developed. Taking into account the strategic plan, sufficient resources to maintain the quality of the faculty and institutional effectiveness should be calculated by the president, CFO, and CAO early in the budget process. Many campuses use a faculty advisory committee to make recommendations on salary and benefits. Second, faculty salaries should be at an appropriate level to compete effectively with other opportunities a new faculty member may have. Failing to invest in competitive salaries can lead to poor hiring and high turnover and weaken the campus over time. Third, compensation for faculty in similar departments or disciplines with comparable rank, accomplishments, and contributions should be comparable. Fourth, if faculty are performing satisfactorily, compensation should keep up with the cost of living. Finally, to provide faculty with a more accurate picture of total compensation, the value of salary and benefits should be reported and reviewed annually.

The policies that govern compensation must be outlined in writing and accessible. Compensation is governed by federal nondiscrimination policies and must be reaffirmed in institutional policies. When salaries are based on performance, the criteria and how they are to be applied must be documented. Most campuses provide for the criteria to be tailored to different colleges or disciplines while maintaining that the standards for achievement are expected to be comparable. Providing documentation on the activities of the previous year to support the merit review is the responsibility of the individual faculty member. On some campuses, if faculty members fail to turn in an annual report or conduct evaluations of teaching, they are ineligible for any salary increase. In the same way that faculty have a right to request a review of their performance for tenure and promotion and appeal an evaluation, they should have the right to a review of the salary recommendation. Finally, the responsibility and authority for reviewing all salary recommendations rests with deans and the CAO before they are recommended to the president and the board for final approval. The reasons for salary recommendations that show little differentiation or that fall above or below the range recommended by the CAO should be explained in writing.

The most vulnerable part of most faculty compensation systems is in how the principles and policies are applied; thus the CAO needs to make sure all procedures are documented and understood. The procedures by which merit assessments are made should be in writing and identify those parties who contribute to the recommendations as well as those officially responsible for final decisions. Written annual evaluations should be structured around the departmental and institutional criteria and include recommendations for improvement, if warranted. Performance must be reviewed according to the same criteria as those used for reappointment, tenure, and promotion or risk a disconnect between performance and salary. Although some campuses rely solely on the department chair's evaluation, many more make use of peer review by the department personnel committee or a three to five person evaluation committee. Peer committees are sometimes elected and review all faculty. Others are made up for each faculty member. Peer review ensures that any individual concerns or biases are balanced by the broader perspective and information from other faculty. A single peer review committee will ensure that all faculty are evaluated by the same criteria.

How faculty evaluations are converted to salary recommendations must also be well understood. Some campuses allow department chairs to use qualitative standards balancing many factors while others use quantitative models such as a strict formula of evaluation points for dollars. As both models have inherent biases, the deans and the CAO need to know what methods are being used and review the results. On one campus, the CAO asked that evaluations be submitted with the salary recommendations and noted that faculty receiving high evaluations did not always receive concomitant increases. When the department formula, designed over a decade before during a time of low increases, was reviewed, it was clear that it had been developed to advantage young professors by giving flat dollar increases rather than using percentages. Such a formula causes salary compression within a department. At regular intervals, CAOs should encourage deans and department chairs to discuss their practices to protect against unintended biases in the formulas used.

On some campuses, once the dollars have been allocated by the department chair based on the evaluations, the personnel committee reviews all compensation decisions for accuracy and fairness prior to the decision being communicated to individual faculty. On some campuses, the dean reviews all individual salary recommendations with the department chair. Although unit administrators must have discretion to make compensation decisions that recognize the subtlety of faculty contributions, these decision makers must be unquestionably fair and consistent in the application of their discretion. Having to explain salary recommendations ensures that those responsible are conscientious and consistent. All faculty members are entitled to a meaningful explanation of disparities between their compensation and the overall salary structure of the department or college.

Because compensation programs "reflect the essential mission and philosophy of each institution through what it rewards, whom it rewards, and how it treats its most important human resource" (Moore and Amey 1993, iii), CAOs cannot take the compensation program for granted and only review it if there are complaints. Under pressure, they may take an ad hoc approach to addressing concerns, rather than a systematic approach. To protect the integrity of the system, many campuses have a faculty welfare committee that regularly reviews salary, benefits, retirement programs, standards and processes for tenure and promotion, and meets with the administration, as appropriate, in an advisory capacity.

When serious concerns emerge, although CAOs can defend the compensation program by demonstrating that salaries are not based on favoritism or individual negotiation, it is far better to involve faculty in a systematic review than try to turn around faculty dissatisfaction by explanations from the administration.

Effective Compensation Principles, Policies, and Procedures

- How objective and fair are the compensation policies that guide salary allocations?

- To what extent do faculty trust the procedures for determining annual salary increases?

- How are faculty helped to understand that the salary variations among faculty are based on appropriate and equitable factors?

- To what extent is the rationale behind merit pay endorsed by faculty?

- How well does the compensation system reflect the relative value the institution places on teaching, research, and service?

- What oversight or review is provided for salary recommendations?

- What provisions are there for reviewing individual salaries as well as the compensation program?

SPECIFIC SALARY POLICIES

The clearer the formal policies and procedures are, the less time the CAO will spend on managing compensation. For tenure-track faculty the decisions include initial appointment salary, annual increases, and increments for degree completion and promotion in rank. In addition, most campuses have standard compensation policies and procedures for part-time and continuing-contract faculty. Studies of shortcomings in compensation programs or sources of inequity reveal the importance of understanding how each element affects an individual's compensation and how a decision, such as an inappropriate starting salary or failure to recognize degree completion with a salary adjustment, can compound over many years and create inequity.

Starting Salaries for Full-Time Faculty

In order to maintain consistency with the overall compensation levels of the institution, the CAO, rather than the department chair or dean, should authorize initial salaries of new faculty based on analysis of relevant data. CUPA-HR provides information from comparison group institutions on previous year new hire salaries, as well as current salaries by rank and sorted by discipline. Data from more than one source will vary, yet be helpful in setting a range and explaining the salary offer to a candidate who may have offers from several institutions. For instance, to set the starting salary in marketing, the business dean would review CUPA-HR data at national, competing, and peer institutions as well as The Association to Advance Collegiate Schools of Business (AACSB) The International Association for Management Education data. The national CUPA-HR data would show a starting salary for a new Ph.D. of $79,100, the peer school data might project $78,300, and the competing school data project a salary of $82,000. National AACSB salary data might project a salary of $89,500, while a marketing list serve projects a salary of $83,300. Through a final check based on cost of living as well as current salaries in the department, the CAO could confirm that a starting salary of $80,000 is appropriate for the institution.

The same type of analysis should also guide setting the initial salary for a hire above the assistant professor level. Although some individuals on the job market in selective fields think they can "drive a hard bargain" or are looking for a high salary offer to take back to their own campus as leverage, basing salaries on individual negotiation will quickly get a compensation system out of line. If the established salary is insufficient to make a hire, the department chair or dean should consult with the CAO, but bending to individual demands always has negative effects in the long run as any overpayment compounds and the lack of consistency undermines faculty confidence in the compensation program. Similarly, CAOs need to set policies on whether or not to match external offers in order to keep faculty. Many believe that institutions should not match offers because giving an individual special treatment distorts the compensation system. Similarly, it is generally advisable to resist salary compression or inversion to avoid creating morale problems. However, in some cases faculty recognize the need for higher salaries to attract quality hires or retain faculty "stars" and are willing to bear an overlap in salaries.

Recognizing Degree Completion and Promotion in Rank

When faculty are hired at the instructor level before completing the terminal degree, the salary is set with the expectation of an adjustment when the degree is completed. To some extent, trying to finish the degree and start a new job is risky as the faculty member may be unable to develop the publication record necessary for tenure or performance may be depressed such that it results in lower annual salary increments during the pretenure years. On campuses with no written policy, the greater risk is that the faculty member is given a lower salary and after a few years, when the degree is completed, the department chair, dean, or CAO has moved on and there is no record that a salary adjustment is in order. To protect both the institution and the faculty member, the initial letter of hire should indicate the date by which the degree is to be conferred in order to continue on a tenure track and the salary adjustment when the degree is completed. It is also important that the appointment letter for a faculty member who expects to complete the degree before beginning indicates the salary if completed and the salary if not completed, often a difference of $1,000 to $2,500 depending upon the discipline.

Typically, promotion is accompanied by a one-time increase in the base-salary portion of a faculty member's compensation according to a standard schedule. Most campuses use a set dollar increment, for example $1,500 for an assistant professor, $2,000 for an associate professor, and $2,500 for a professor. Many campuses have not adjusted these increments for years and thus they represent a smaller relative value each year. Alternatively, some campuses use a fixed percentage of salary at all ranks, and some campuses use either a percentage or a fixed dollar amount, whichever is greater. The percentage approach allows market and productivity to be reflected in the promotion increment. These increments are in addition to the annual salary increase based on performance and, if a percentage, calculated on the previous year's base.

Although some campuses fund promotional increases from the chief academic officer's budget, more typically the dean must hold back enough funds from the annual salary monies allocated to the college to cover all promotions. When funded in this way, merit increases for other faculty are decreased and can cause resentment and inequities over time. On some campuses the salary increases are deferred until January to be confident of fall enrollment. With a midyear adjustment, the decisions on promotions usually have not yet been acted upon; thus the CAO needs to cover the cost of promotion increases effective the next September. To have sufficient funds, the CAO counts on retirements and resignations to produce salary savings.

Annual Salary Increases

Annual salary increments may be based on a fixed dollar amount, a percentage of base salary, or some combination of the two. Campuses that use a service-based salary schedule automatically move faculty to the next step. Campuses that provide a set merit increment, for example, $1,000 for satisfactory performance, $2,000 for above average performance, and $3,000 for outstanding performance, may not be giving a significant enough increase to serve as much of an incentive for faculty with high salaries. In addition, by giving fixed dollar amounts the institution creates salary compression as a low-paid faculty member could receive a 10 percent salary increase on a $30,000 salary base, and a faculty member with an $80,000 base would receive only a 3.75 percent increase, even though both are considered outstanding.

Campuses that provide a set percentage across the board with the rest for merit, such as 2 percent for everyone and an additional 2 percent for all those recommended for a merit increase, have no way of knowing at budget development time how many faculty will qualify for the 2 percent merit increase. However, if the campus establishes a 4 percent pool, with one half distributed for cost of living and the other half for merit, the CAO can establish a workable budget but cannot guarantee the amount each faculty member will receive. Some faculty argue that the cost of living increase should be variable and greater for those at the lower salary levels, as a larger percentage of a low income goes to basics rather than to discretionary spending. Campuses are more likely to respond by adjusting benefit costs than salary for those at the lower income levels. Clearly, CAOs need to both work out the principles that guide annual increases as well as understand whether the increases, as distributed, accomplish institutional goals.

Many campuses struggle with issues related to the evaluation system that is the basis for merit recommendations, including how merit will be defined, what information is pertinent and reliable, and how the information will be used to make a merit increase decision. Common issues include how often evaluations should be conducted for tenured faculty and how many years a particular activity can be counted. Many campuses do not allow a cumulative effect, thus a faculty member may be better off writing short pieces such as journal articles to maintain a consistent record of publishing rather than write a book that may be counted in only a single year. On campuses where tenured faculty are evaluated only every three years and the evaluation is used as the basis for the merit increment for the next two years as well, there is some evidence that faculty go through a burst of energy and productivity in that year of evaluation and then coast in the off years.

A few campuses, aiming to use salary increases as a direct incentive for improvement, allow faculty to contract for a salary increase rather than base merit on comparative productivity. All faculty members that meet the goals in their approved plan receive the merit increment. Other campuses ask faculty to submit an annual plan and designate in advance their priorities for the year as the basis for evaluation. However, in practice, department chairs often weight the factors after the year is over, placing emphasis where there was success, in order to maximize scores. Serving neither as an incentive for established goals nor as a way to discriminate among performance, the maximized scores also lead to salary compression. Some campuses freeze a faculty member in step if they fail to be promoted from associate professor. Each of these practices has an impact on faculty perceptions about the institution's values.

Merit-based salary increases typically come from recommendations by department chairs based on their annual evaluations of faculty. Evaluation ratings may be quantitative, but they are far from standardized and result in marked differences from one department to another (Ferren and Aylesworth 2001). For example, in a desire to boost faculty morale, a department chair may give evaluation ratings of "outstanding" to almost all faculty within that department, making only small distinctions between faculty within the "outstanding" range, and leaving the "real" evaluation to the salary recommendations. Another chair may make more significant distinctions in faculty evaluation ratings based on very similar faculty data. Such differences—even when salary increase funds are allocated proportionally to departments based on current salaries—lead to faculty questions and even distrust in the procedures. For example, faculty in the department where all received an evaluation of "outstanding" will get only an average increase of say 3.5 percent yet learn that faculty in the other department with an "outstanding" rating will receive an above average increase of 5 percent.

The chief academic officer faced with trying to ensure fairness in compensation is also challenged to support high-performing departments. If all faculty actually are doing an outstanding job there is no way for them to get an above average raise if the pool of funds is the same percentage for all departments. At the same time, a department where few faculty are performing well will still receive merit monies. To address compression among departments and even colleges, many CAOs hold back a percentage of the salary monies. Reallocations to units, not individuals, are based on recommendations from the dean. If the discrepancy is between colleges rather than departments within the college, the CAO needs to make the allocations.

Part-Time Faculty Salaries

Part-time salaries are usually based on a per credit or per course schedule with little differentiation for class size or quality of performance. A single salary schedule for all undergraduate and all graduate courses or one with rates equivalent to three ranks is far easier to administer than one that calculates a different salary for each individual based on qualifications, experience, length of service, and performance. Some campuses provide an increment for longevity, for example, a $100 increase for every six semesters of service with good evaluations. Some campuses have different department or college rates that reflect market; for example, business faculty get paid more than humanities faculty. There is no standard salary for all campuses. Indeed, the CAO needs to set salaries to be comparable to those of local competitors. As the market for part-time faculty is local, competition pushes part-time salaries up in rural areas due to low supply, exactly the opposite of full-time salaries.

Whatever the policies and the rate, many believe part-time faculty are underpaid and suggest the salary be prorated on the base of a full-time faculty member. The counter argument is that part-time faculty have no research or service obligations; thus, they do not really do comparable work. The general presumption that part-time faculty believe they are not treated fairly is not borne out by research, although CAOs should conduct their own campus-based study if they rely heavily on part-time faculty. There is no evidence "that full time or part time faculty experience different levels of satisfaction with their workloads, job security, opportunities for advancement, pay, or benefits" (Antony and Valadez 2002, 46). Even so, those part-time faculty who try to piece together the equivalent of a full-time position through teaching at several campuses will feel disadvantaged if they have no access to benefits.

Increasingly, CAOs are calculating the cost to the institution of part-time faculty participation in health insurance, retirement, disability, and life insurance programs as opposed to a salary increase. The part-time faculty member is often willing to pay much of the cost in order to benefit from the group rate. Access to these and other benefits such as tuition, child care, or parking on a prorated basis may be more cost effective than raising salaries. Some campuses give the part-time faculty member an additional increment and leave the choice to pay for benefits up to the individual. CAOs find standard policies are easier to fund and administer. Nonmonetary benefits such as library privileges, office space, and Internet services must be available to all part-time faculty as these benefits are fundamental to their work performance.

Faculty Reassigned to Administrative Positions

When a faculty member is reassigned from the faculty to a full-time administrative position some campuses add two-ninths salary, some annualize the teaching salary, and some pay a flat stipend. How the salary is then converted back when the faculty member returns to the faculty should be a matter of policy so that such faculty do not end up with inflated salaries because of the time spent as an administrator. To address this issue, a campus may restrict annual increases to the nine-month portion of the salary to the same percentage and criteria as for the teaching faculty. However, some CAOs believe that time as an administrator ends up depressing later performance in research and teaching, which may not be made up for awhile. Thus the resulting faculty annual increase, often well below the average, is balanced by the higher salary increases while serving as an administrator.

CAOs who fail to establish terms in writing at the outset, when faced with wanting to terminate an administrator, sometimes find they are forced to negotiate a high salary as a condition of return to the faculty. An additional problem develops if the department has not maintained the base for the vacated position. Several years of salary increases could have been distributed to others in the department because the vacant position was filled on a temporary basis. Highly structured compensation programs reduce some of these pressures on the CAO.

Establishing Base Salaries

- What standards are used for setting initial salaries and regularly adjusting them?
- What kind of discretion, if any, should deans or department chairs have in salary offers?
- Are the increments for promotion applied consistently and reviewed regularly?

- How competitive are the salaries and benefits for temporary and part-time faculty? Are they related to both market and amount of work expected?
- Are part-time and temporary faculty eligible for merit increases? cost of living increases?
- What terms are in place with regard to salaries for teaching faculty assigned to administrative positions?

STANDARDS FOR ADDITIONAL COMPENSATION

Most campuses have policies covering the types of institutional activities for which faculty can receive extra compensation that is not included with the base salary, such as summer assignments and overload teaching. Some campuses specify the amount for such activities to eliminate time spent on individual negotiations and to ensure equity. For example, half-time release from teaching and a $5,000 summer stipend might be the compensation for directing any special program such as general education, honors, or study abroad. Campuses set a limit on earnings from all institutional sources, ranging from 20 percent to 33 percent of the academic year base salary. Policies differ on how much of that can be earned during the academic year.

Department Chair Compensation

Compensation for department chairs is handled in a variety of ways including 9-, 10-, 11-, and 12-month contracts, stipends or reassigned time, or some combination. The terms of appointment as well as compensation need to be clear as it is not unusual for longtime chairs to expect to keep their stipend when they return to the faculty or for chairs hired externally to believe that the salary as chair will be their faculty salary if they step down. Half of all campuses have standardized chair compensation, whereas the other half allow individually negotiated compensation (College and University Professional Association 2002, 13). One CAO new to a campus found that each dean had a different arrangement for compensating chairs, including individual negotiations. One gave only a flat stipend regardless of responsibility, another gave stipends based on a percentage of salary, another gave full release time rather than any stipend, and another paid a stipend equivalent to the overload policy. In one case, a chair received full release time and a stipend with the expectation that the chair would do some of the work of the dean's office. A task force of department chairs took only six weeks to make a proposal that all supported as appropriate to their differential workloads. The proposal provided a standard combination of limited reassigned time and stipends based on grouping departments in three categories according to the number of students, number of faculty, and number of programs and teaching sites. It took $50,000 from the CAO's budget to effect the schedule and solve a problem that had caused hard feelings for a long time.

University Sponsored Extra Employment

Not all variations in faculty responsibilities are compensated with additional funds. Campuses increasingly recognize that the work of the institution includes a mix of teaching, research, and service with increasing attention given to continuing education, public service, economic development, and commercial ventures as part of each faculty member's responsibilities. As many as possible of these activities are handled by adjusting the individual faculty member's other responsibilities through work unit equivalents, rather than through extra pay. Many faculty would like to earn overload pay, but CAOs understand that additional duties increase total workload and have a negative impact on core activities. Further, it is difficult to justify overload teaching when faculty also claim they need reduced teaching loads. Collective bargaining agreements also endorse this idea of incorporating diverse activities into the standard workload of faculty but do not exclude the possibility of additional compensation.

Typically, additional compensation requires prior approval and is based on a set standard, either a percentage or a flat fee. For example, coordinators of off-campus programs would be compensated at $1,500 a semester or the overload teaching rate for advising and recruiting activities. When budgets are tight and annual salary increments are low, there is increased pressure for additional pay, to count stipends in the base, and/or to convert duties to full-time administrative positions. Most CAOs are reluctant to handle academic responsibilities through creation of an administrative position, such as director of the honors program, as it is far more expensive and reduces faculty confidence in the position. They also are reluctant to set a precedent such that faculty expect additional pay for any activity new to the faculty member. Keeping up with the field and new course development, for example, should be seen as a regular part of a faculty member's professional responsibilities.

Distance Education

In an effort to promote distance education, campuses provide incentives such as stipends to cover development and conduct of these courses. Some campuses grant the equivalent of teaching a course for the development of an on-line course and pay the department an adjunct salary to replace the course the faulty member was scheduled to teach. Others encourage development as a summer activity compensated at the same rate as summer teaching. Some allow faculty members to develop and teach the course as an overload and earn additional pay during the year. Some allow for revenue return to the department, after paying the costs for developing, teaching, and supporting the offering, as an incentive for departments to encourage faculty involvement and to cover course losses internally. Each option has strengths and weaknesses and the CAO needs to evaluate both the costs and the benefits to the individual and the institution. For example, the individual faculty member must be fairly compensated for specialized training but should not expect to be paid a "development" fee long after the course has been developed. CAOs are willing to invest in these incentives to increase future revenues.

Continuing Education

Continuing education is usually compensated on the same scale as overload teaching and governed by the same total salary limitations. Some faculty are much in demand for continuing education and training activities as they are in high profile fields and have the potential to bring in significant income to the campus. One CAO, with no policies to prevent it, discovered that a new assistant professor made almost as much in the College of Continuing Education as in her home department and, while conducting no research, claimed the training and workshops as scholarly activities. A more appropriate model would hire the faculty member during the summer, limit the total earnings, and distribute the responsibilities to other faculty and external trainers.

Payment for Summer School

Summer salary for 84 percent of all campuses is based on a percentage of the faculty member's academic base salary, sometimes with a minimum and maximum salary range (College and University Professional Association 2002, 5). For ease of management, some campuses use a set stipend per credit and compensate part-time faculty on the same basis. Flat fees disadvantage professors and often give junior faculty a greater chance of teaching in the summer. Chief academic officers are often asked how to handle situations such as pay for a newly hired faculty member in the summer before they begin and many do so at the full-time faculty rate. Recurring matters of this type should be covered by policies, rather than negotiated, to avoid charges of inequity.

Summer school policies should also cover how many courses can be taught in a term as well as over the entire summer. At times CAOs feel as if they are providing a summer job program for faculty rather than a student focused curriculum. Indeed, summer school policies often include various restrictive policies because faculty try to take advantage of what they see as a less supervised activity. Department chairs sometimes cause hard feelings as they claim a right to summer teaching so that, with their summer stipend and teaching, they earn the equivalent of a 12-month salary. To ensure equity, many departments develop formulas to prioritize who will teach in the summer. The chief academic officer needs to review such practices and be sure that summer school is managed with a firm hand as faculty mistakenly believe they only have to bring in enough tuition to cover their salary and fail to understand all the attendant costs for summer school.

External Employment Policies

All campuses have the expectation that faculty members give full time and attention to their university positions. Few campuses have found any way to control a full-time faculty member's outside earnings and few want to, although teaching for another college or university is usually prohibited. Many faculty handbooks outline the policies on extra employment to reduce the potential of a negative impact on the institution or the individual's productivity. Policies cover such aspects as avoidance of conflict of interest and no use of university resources. Some only require reporting if the employment exceeds a set amount, for example $1,000, on the grounds that many faculty do workshops, speeches, and training sessions from time to time that do not constitute significant outside employment. Many require full disclosure in writing to the department chair, with the form forwarded to the dean and the CAO. Notification rather than approval is the standard, and most CAOs believe consulting and applied research promote faculty development.

Campuses with faculty who have the potential for significant external employment such as dentists, architects, and engineers typically have carefully designed practice agreements and research partnerships to facilitate this work and ensure that some benefits accrue to the campus.

Many campuses believe the opportunity for supplemental income is cost effective for the campus as it allows the institution to have a quality of faculty that would be too expensive to support on their own. All policies on additional work should aim to facilitate professional development, reward faculty contributions fairly, and align their activities to also benefit the institution.

Managing Additional Compensation

- Are the activities that are compensated congruent with the academic goals and priorities of the institution?
- To what extent do standards for compensation match the additional responsibility?
- Is compensation sufficient to serve as an incentive for institutional activities?
- What are the limits on compensation earned through the institution?
- What policies appropriately protect the interests of the institution and the interests of faculty with high potential for external earnings?

POTENTIAL SOURCES OF SALARY INEQUITY

Chief academic officers often share their concerns about how best to handle the perception, and sometimes the reality, of salary inequities. Particular concerns are failure to apply the same performance standards, salary compression, salary inversion, and lack of comparability for faculty doing the same work. Without close scrutiny by the CAO, even small issues can contribute to faculty frustration, faculty disengagement, reduced institutional productivity, lowered faculty morale, and litigation. From time to time there are specialized individual cases that need the CAO's attention; however, they are best handled through a systematic review of all faculty salaries.

Nondiscrimination in Compensation

Pay-equity studies examining salaries of women and minorities have been conducted since the 1970s and reveal disparities that cannot be fully explained by rank, years of service, or performance (Barbezat 2002). Although there are many explanations for the pay gap, efforts to address inequities are not optional because nondiscrimination is mandated by federal laws and state statutes. Because the issues are complex, CAOs must be familiar with the literature in this area, for example, Robert K. Toutkoushian's *Conducting Salary-Equity Studies: Alternative Approaches to Research* (2002). The CAO's concern must be equity in both salaries and the general climate for women and minorities on the campus. One campus recently acknowledged that not only do their female faculty earn less salary but "inequitable distributions were found involving space, amount of nine-month salary paid from individual research grants, teaching assignments, awards and distinctions, inclusion on important committees and assignments within the department" (MIT 1999, 7). Even if unintended, subtle forms of discrimination can result in salary disparities when they limit opportunities for faculty that then impact their ability to publish, their access to research support, and the rate at which they are promoted.

Although findings of discrimination focus attention on addressing the class of individuals rather than single cases, gender inequity is not the only concern for the campus and discrimination is not the cause of many inequities. One CAO, studying the individual cases of both men and women flagged by regression analysis as below the expected salary, found several common causes: faculty hired at a salary lower than others, failure to adjust salary upon degree completion, failure to give a raise based on a sabbatical year, and failure to credit professional experience at the time of hiring. Department chairs and deans had received little guidance over the years. In short, inequities can also develop due to inattention.

Salary Compression

Salaries within ranks should be highly correlated with years of service and past performance (Snyder, McLaughlin, and Montgomery 1992, 113). When the salary differential between junior and senior faculty, either between ranks or within ranks, is smaller than it should be based on rank and time in rank it is considered compression. On campuses with merit salary systems, salary compression will develop if some faculty receive less than the average merit increase and others in the same rank receive a greater than average increase because of their outstanding performance. In that case, salary compression is not an inequity and need not be corrected. To moderate the effect of a single year's performance, most campuses try to look at a multiyear average.

Market imbalances can also lead to compression. In several disciplines, including nursing and computer science, the availability of high salaried positions in industry have caused many qualified faculty members to choose nonacademic careers. Limited supply and high demand lead to either unfilled faculty positions or the need to offer higher starting salaries than would otherwise be expected. With limited funds and growing enrollments, CAOs often have to make the difficult decision to use funds to hire new faculty rather than supplement the funds for faculty salary increases. In some cases, the newly trained faculty, although lacking experience, do bring skills and levels of productivity that warrant higher compensation. Compression caused by the market needs to be addressed with additional resources for continuing faculty, if warranted, and not by hiring less qualified faculty. CAOs can expect salary compression due to supply and demand to worsen as the projected shortage of new faculty coincides with an expected increase in faculty retirements (Finkelstein, Seal, and Schuster 1998).

Limited or reduced institutional resources and significant immobility of senior faculty can also cause compression. In recent years many public colleges and universities have experienced either flat or reduced appropriations. In constrained fiscal times, merit increases do not adequately differentiate the contributions of individual faculty as merit increases for "adequate" performers are just a few tenths of a percentage less than those for "outstanding performers" (Singleton 1990, 34). Limited resources throughout higher education also contribute to salary compression at the senior faculty level due to decreased mobility (Twigg, Valentine, and Elias 2002, 83). Whereas once professors could move to another institution, they now have fewer opportunities as campuses are unable to meet market salaries at the professor rank. Because salary compression is not the same as salary inequity and there is no universally accepted differential heuristic, compression can be diagnosed by comparison with peer institutions as well as through internal consistency across departments.

Salary Inversion

Salary inversion occurs when junior faculty salaries are greater than those of senior faculty. Just as with salary compression, salary inversion can occur between ranks as well as within ranks. Salary inversion can occur when a new faculty member is hired at a salary that exceeds that of a current faculty member of the same or higher rank or when merit increases move a faculty member past colleagues with more years of service but lower performance. Inversion due to hiring in a competitive market cannot easily be corrected without additional funds. When monies are available for market adjustments for an entire group of faculty, the CAO will want to be sure that the same relative positions related to performance are maintained. For example, the faculty member who received the higher salary when hired may not be eligible for the later market adjustment for all other faculty.

Inversions based on rewarding performance should not be corrected as the low performing faculty member has not earned the increments and slowly falls behind colleagues. Some campuses have a system of increments for longevity that does not allow inversion to happen and thus do not have a true merit system. However, if the inversion has been caused by several years without salary increments, the CAO will want to determine the fairest way to distribute merit monies to make up for that deficit and not treat all faculty the same. For that reason, many campuses, even when there are no salary monies, still conduct the annual evaluation as the basis for a salary recommendation so that the data is available when the funds become available.

Unique Situations that Create Inequities

Infrequently a unique situation will be reflected in a faculty member's salary and require the CAO's attention in consultation with the dean and department chair. For example, a faculty member whose work was ahead of the field had difficulty getting published. As a result, she received low merit increases and was held in rank at associate professor. Eventually the field caught up with her and she had three books published in one year. She was then promoted to full professor and her salary adjusted to bring it more in line with full professors of equal length of service and productivity. Even so, she would never make up the differential in retirement contributions as a participant in a defined contribution program. CAOs are obligated to review serious anomalies and must do the necessary research to be sure that any salary adjustment is appropriate. Regular salary studies provide the opportunity to address compensation issues on behalf of all faculty and the institution.

Dealing with Inequities

- What evidence is there that factors of age, academic rank, experience, and productivity have the equivalent impact on salaries of men, women, and minority faculty members?

- Are more recently hired women and minority faculty receiving more equitable treatment than their older counterparts?

- Do the current institutional evaluation policies and reward structures put women and minority faculty members at a disadvantage as they progress within rank?

- What salary models and statistical techniques will reveal the true effect of gender and ethnicity on academic salaries?

SUCCESSFUL COMPENSATION MANAGEMENT

To administer a compensation program, CAOs must understand the principles underlying the system and the sources of variation in faculty salaries. The variations that are to be expected when comparing salary rates include: differences due to type of institution, differences across disciplines, differences due to faculty rank, differences due to years of service, differences due to individual faculty performance, and differences due to institutional expenditures for salary increases. It is the last source of differences that faculty usually question when making interinstitutional comparisons and can only be understood in the context of competing demands for resources (Ferren and Aylesworth 2001).

When salary variations cannot be explained by these standard factors, CAOs must conduct salary studies and be prepared to redress any inequities. To do so, institutions need a formal policy on salary equity adjustments that includes regular review, how faculty will be identified for review, the statistical methodology for analyzing all salaries, and, if inequities are revealed, how they will be handled. Salary equity adjustments cannot be made piecemeal or by individual comparisons. When the principles, policies, procedures, and practices that affect the compensation program are carefully designed and continuously reviewed, the compensation program will be fair and consistent with faculty perceptions of their worth.

As campuses face limited resources and competing priorities, maintaining the competitive level of compensation is critical to institutional quality. CAOs must be advocates for the priority of attracting and retaining excellent faculty and make faculty compensation a priority in the strategic advancement of the institution. Appropriately rewarding faculty for their contributions is essential to keep higher education an appealing and energized profession.

CHAPTER 11

Improving Academic Decisions:
Using Institutional Research

Due to the changing fiscal and technological environment of higher education, the increasingly competitive markets for both faculty and students, and higher expectations for institutional performance, chief academic officers (CAOs) need accurate, reliable, and timely information for understanding their institution and making decisions. CAOs must be able to answer with confidence such questions as: How effectively is the institution meeting the needs of students and employers? Which institutional factors have the greatest impact on student learning? What is the true cost of instruction? What is the appropriate size of the faculty? How is technology changing productivity? Data alone will not ensure that CAOs provide effective leadership; however, without information, their judgment, experience, and good will are of limited value.

At times, CAOs are hampered in getting timely access to critical information because of limitations in the institutional information system, reporting lines, and actual or perceived ownership of the data. To some extent, the problem is not lack of data, but rather too much data with too little analysis. CAOs need accessible reports that get behind the numbers, make sense of the data, and address the most important issue they face. To avoid being inundated with pages of printouts and charts, CAOs must work closely with the institutional research (IR) staff to frame the necessary studies to support data informed decisions. To meet the needs of users and understand how administrators actually make decisions, IR staff must be at the table for institutional planning and collaborate with those making the decisions as well as those responsible for the outcomes of the decisions.

Many campuses are rethinking the role of IR and strengthening their technology support to enable IR staff to respond to diverse internal and external demands. Governing boards and legislators expect reports on institutional performance measures to guide budget priorities and appropriations decisions. Deans need information on individual and departmental workloads to guide position allocations. Department chairs want comparative information to support program review. Business officers need data on competitive tuition and financial aid policies. Given the many pressures on the IR staff, CAOs must be realistic in their expectations. At the same time, the IR staff must recognize how important it is for CAOs to have their support for collaborative, informed, and open decision making.

This chapter addresses the partnership between the CAO and the office of institutional research, the kinds of routine academic reports that should be available, and how customized studies can help the CAO address complex issues that go well beyond day-to-day management of academic affairs. For example, increasing institutional effectiveness depends upon tracking success of the strategic plan, understanding budget adequacy, and restructuring to preserve quality with limited resources. Strengthening student learning depends upon understanding how students engage with the institution, setting high standards, and assessing student success. Effective human resource management requires data on adequate faculty staffing, competitive compensation, and salary equity. When CAOs are backed by institutional research, they are better able to understand the complex relationships among priorities, processes, resources, and outcomes and guide their institutions with confidence.

COLLABORATING WITH INSTITUTIONAL RESEARCH

In an effort to make institutional data readily available, institutional research offices produce an annual fact book of statistical data, including enrollments, majors, and faculty profiles, that can be used to answer some of the more commonly asked questions. The fact book has been a data resource for institutional decision making for more than half a century, and "the data it reports are reliable, consistent, uniform, comparable, and conform to generally accepted institutional or regional and national data definitions" (Jones 1996, 17). The recent development of shared databases, institutional data warehouses, and electronic fact books not only enables CAOs, deans, department chairs, and faculty to access relevant data to answer their questions but also to conduct analyses to support their planning and decision making.

For the most part, fact book data are merely descriptive, often just a one-year snapshot of the campus, and do not provide the interpretation necessary to support decisions. Unfamiliar with how to put data into context, users of the fact book often bring their own perspectives and biases to the "meaning" of the data. Faculty committees and department chairs prepare reports stating "our classes are too large" and "our salaries are too low." While these assertions may be based on facts provided by IR, they are not always founded on complete information or purposeful analyses. Consequently, many deans and CAOs who are usually strong proponents of open information find themselves challenging the conclusions of such "unofficial" reports and trying to explain that the selected information does not really mean what the user thinks it does. Because perceptions are difficult to change, campuses need not more facts but more accessible analyses.

Preparing and updating the fact book is just one of the many IR functions central to the efficient operation of the institution. Data-gathering functions typically include providing a single point of contact and coordinating responses to external inquiries for university-related information, overseeing institutional participation in national surveys, coordinating accreditation reviews, maintaining shared databases or a data warehouse for users throughout the university, and being the official source of information to the university community. Analytic functions can include providing analytical support for university planning, policy making, management, and assessment activities; interpreting data on institutional performance; interpreting data about the environment of the institution; analyzing the economic impact of the institution on the community; and preparing customized studies to support decisions. As the demands on higher education increase, the demands on institutional research increase.

Offices of institutional research are further stretched by requests for countless ad hoc reports from both internal and external stakeholders. They serve as consultants on design, data gathering, and interpretation for specific projects. When their clients do not have well-articulated research questions, it takes additional IR time. Being responsive can mean that one ad hoc report leads to another until the small institutional research staff is exhausted and decides to provide only essential reports to designated administrators. However, if IR does not help design the study or others manipulate the data, the conclusions may not be based on appropriate assumptions or a sound framework for analysis. Increasingly, CAOs find they need staff skilled in data analysis housed in their own offices in order to respond to the many questions they face on a daily basis and to help deans, department chairs, and faculty access and make good use of data.

In collaboration with the many users, IR staff can determine what kinds of standard reports can help inform decisions throughout the campus. Typically, administrators need enrollment progression reports detailing the retention and graduation rates at all levels (university, college, and discipline) for graduates, undergraduates, freshmen to seniors, transfers, and all race/ethnic groups. CAOs also rely on facilities planning statistics on the need for student classroom space, faculty and staff offices, and laboratories and reports on classroom utilization by days of the week, hours of the day, level of instruction, and discipline. In addition, CAOs need faculty workload studies, compensation reports, and revenue and expenditure reports by college and program. Although data needs to be captured regularly to support such studies, analyses need not be fully developed and broadly shared unless actions are to be taken. At times, however, CAOs need information just so that they can take time to reflect on academic matters.

If IR does not report to academic affairs, the CAO must seek agreement among administrative colleagues and the president about the focus for the institutional research office and its range of services. Support for academic affairs needs to go beyond maintaining the basic fact book and institutional data warehouse to also include participation in important national studies, such as the UCLA Higher Education Research Institute (HERI) faculty survey, the Cooperative Institutional Research Program (CIRP) freshman survey, and the National Survey of Student Engagement (NSSE). The CAO may need specialized studies, often obtained by IR participating in data-sharing consortia, in order to link the institution to the larger issues facing higher education such as the increase in contingent faculty and distance education.

To facilitate better use of limited IR resources and develop a more focused capability, all administrators need to be selective in what they want to know and screen access to institutional research resources. To reduce faculty requests for special studies, yet reassure them that they can still have access to information, CAOs need to work with faculty in setting the agenda for institutional research to address key academic concerns by asking: Which questions are critical to understanding our current situation? What information will improve our planning efforts and our actions? and How will we use the information to improve or redesign our curricula, services, and environment? Collaboration in improving the institution also depends upon faculty turning some of their research skills to the task, helping academic administrators ask the right questions, and diligently using study results to strengthen both individual and program effectiveness.

Support Role of Institutional Research

- What decision areas are most important for the CAO, deans, and department chairs?

- What data are needed for effective academic decision making?

- To what extent is there a consistent set of data across the institution, permitting reports to be built on the same data definitions?

- How can faculty be included in developing and designing studies most relevant to their activities (e.g., workload studies, program effectiveness, and assessment of student learning)?

- How can greater use be made of the results of national surveys to improve institutional performance?

- How can peer comparison data help the institution understand how well it is performing?

- What initiative should institutional research take in suggesting appropriate studies and helping to train others in basic research and analysis skills?

MAKING DATA ACCESSIBLE

Getting the right data to the right decision maker, in a user-friendly form, and in a timely manner, challenges most colleges and universities. Too often, reports require that CAOs, deans, department chairs, and IR staff locate the source of data and request the data from the person maintaining it, which often means using programming resources to extract the needed data. The data must then be moved from raw form (generally referred to as a "flat file") to the format needed for integration, analysis, interpretation, and report generation. Because of the ad hoc nature of the process, the ability to track trends is limited and the data and analyses for the same decision may differ from year to year. Consequently, deans and department chairs may end up keeping their own separate records on course enrollments, faculty workloads, credit hours generated, or use of adjunct faculty and trust their numbers more than those from IR. Squabbles over data differences can undermine thoughtful academic administration.

Institutional data are typically captured and maintained by offices crossing all administrative divisions. On many campuses, the registrar's office, human resource office, computing services, and IR all have related data but are not set up to be able to provide timely information for analytic purposes. These "transactional" systems have been built to perform specific functions and store detailed data needed to support the operations of the unit. If the data needed by the CAO, deans, or department chairs have not been historically collected, managed, or archived by any single office it is difficult, if not impossible, to merge the existing data into a larger database to facilitate more complete and meaningful analysis. Data integration is also difficult because different databases capture data at different points in time or may not save data beyond some established date, frustrating the attempt to perform trend analyses. When CAOs anticipate the kinds of decisions to be made, they can be knowledgeable partners with IR and information technology (IT) professionals in the design of appropriate databases.

A single accessible data warehouse, with the capability to transform data into useful formats to assist decision making throughout the institution, solves many of these problems. Data captured and recorded in many institutional offices as diverse as student accounts, sponsored programs, and facilities management are combined into one data warehouse that provides a central source of data that have been screened, edited, standardized, and integrated so they can be effectively used. While no single person is responsible for inputting the data, all data are consistently gathered with agreed upon definitions and submission dates, for example, at the census date of the semester. The data warehouse is typically designed and managed by IR as these data are used for external as well as internal reports. With desktop access to data, the CAO, deans, and department chairs familiar with basic research methods, electronic searching, and spreadsheet software can organize information to support the operation of academic affairs.

To establish realistic expectations about information access and use, the CAO must work collaboratively with deans, department chairs, the faculty senate, the planning and budget advisory committee, the program review committee, and other internal governance committees to understand what data would inform their deliberations and what special analyses are needed, for example, to support proposed changes in the general education requirements or admissions standards. IR must let the decision areas drive data acquisition and archiving, rather than collect data for the sake of collection and then ask how the available data could be used.

The data in the data warehouse must be secure in regard to "change" or "write" privileges, but once established and secure, "read access" should be as broad as possible.

Typical elements in a data warehouse include financial data (e.g., operational budgets and year-to-date analyses), student information (e.g., demographics and consumption analyses), enrollment (e.g., targets by major and trends), performance measures (e.g., retention and graduation rates), human resource information (e.g., faculty data and workload records), and environmental information (e.g., economic trends and employer data). The data from several sources can be accessed, combined, and analyzed for a variety of purposes. For example, to understand faculty resource allocation, relevant data would be selected from a variety of sources, including the Integrated Postsecondary Education Data Systems curriculum codes from the office of institutional research; new freshmen and declared majors from the office of admissions; student specific course information, number of students taught, credit hours generated, and number of graduates from the office of the registrar; faculty rank, highest degree, tenure status, years of service, position tracking, and salary from the office of human resources; committee assignments from the faculty senate; program costs from the budget office; number of advisees, reassigned time, number of course preparations, and departmental committees from the department chair; and the number of refereed publications, community projects, and faculty awards from the faculty member. Some campuses require faculty to directly input their activities each semester, for example, entering the course number, credit hours, contact hours; research assignment, expected outcome, completion date, funding source; service assignment (e.g., program coordinator or math lab coordinator) and completion date. These work assignments are then verified by the department chair.

The design of any study determines which data elements are selected. For example, in the case of faculty resources, CAOs are particularly interested in trends, such as how the workload for each program has changed over time or whether the student/faculty ratios reflect changes in state appropriations. Department chairs note that if the percentage of credit hours taught by part-time faculty is increasing, it could justify additional full-time faculty. Deans care about tracking the declared majors for incoming freshmen as that suggests future program demand whereas tracking the programs from which they graduate reveals internal flow and program attrition, which might reflect program quality. Good research always starts with good questions. The rest of this chapter describes how to use data in responding to several of the most difficult questions CAOs currently face.

Developing the Data Warehouse

- Who should be involved in data warehouse development both within academic affairs and across the other divisions?
- Does the data warehouse support many levels of decision makers within the institution?
- How flexible is the structure of the data warehouse (i.e., is it able to handle a variety of queries or has it been designed to handle only specific questions)?
- Does the data warehouse permit users to generate complex queries that access large amounts of data?
- Can the data be provided in both detail or summary form; in narrative, numerical, tabular, graphic, or interpretative form; and in a variety of media including paper, electronic, or other forms?
- To what extent has the data warehouse lessened the burden on IR to provide ad hoc reports?
- What training is necessary to enable deans and department chairs to be effective users of the data warehouse?
- Is the data warehouse linked to and compatible with regional, state, and national databases?

IS THE INSTITUTION ACCOMPLISHING ITS GOALS?

CAOs have a high stake in the success of their institution's strategic plan as it aims to align the institution with environmental realities and serve as the framework for change. Recognizing the impact of competition and resource constraints, many campuses are streamlining and focusing their activities in an effort to stop "trying to be all things to all people." More future-oriented campuses are redesigning instruction and services, redefining their student base, and envisioning a new form for the institution that takes into account the changed technological and economic environment. Whether incremental or bold change is sought, the only way the CAO can know whether the campus is making progress in its change efforts is if specific process and outcome measures linked to the goals have been established and the milestones are regularly documented. With the responsibility for progress distributed throughout the institution, the

CAO must oversee implementation of action plans at all levels and depend upon IR to gather, analyze, and present the performance data.

Higher education has been criticized for relying on strategic planning with its linear approach because many believe that greater flexibility and innovation are necessary to respond to dramatic environmental forces and realign institutions with fiscal realities. It is not strategic planning that has failed higher education, but rather the process is impotent when campuses fail to make strategic investments and track results. Intentional tracking of key performance measures is necessary to assess both the effectiveness of the plan and its alignment with the environment. When data and analyses are readily available in an understandable form, attention can be directed toward making timely adjustments in strategies and actions to improve institutional performance.

The IR staff must first mark the starting point with appropriate data elements. For example, if the goal is "to increase the size, diversity, and quality of the entering class," the data at the point the plan is initiated will include number of applications, acceptance as a percentage of applicants, and matriculants by both in-state and out-of-state as well as, by gender, ethnicity, average GPA, average SAT scores, and test score range. This descriptive information is tracked for each year of the plan. The more difficult task is determining which specific recruitment strategies are linked to positive changes.

To fully understand enrollment processes, IR needs to design qualitative studies focusing on student satisfaction with the admissions process; the factors that affect the decision to apply; and the role of guidance counselors, parents, faculty, and other students in the decision to attend. Additional studies could focus on the impact on acceptance of financial aid, availability of specific programs, and perceptions about the academic reputation of the institution. Without these additional analyses, the units responsible for the processes do not know how to modify their efforts to improve results.

In addition to helping to improve the processes behind the strategic plan, the IR office serves as the point for collecting all outcome data. For this example, the data related to the quality and diversity of the class will include career placement of graduates and graduate school attendance, analyzed by gender, ethnicity, and region. As some of the data will be used for other purposes, the IR staff must array the relevant information so that it is useful to the continuous strategic planning effort. Toward that end, many IR offices include in the fact book the charts showing trends and outcomes for each of the critical issues in the strategic plan coupled with narratives based on the results of special studies. It is not unusual to see a mixed record of progress. Rather than hide the facts, IR and the CAO, in collaboration with the rest of the administration and faculty, need to determine how best to overcome the barriers to accomplishing the goals.

A full list of performance indicators for institutional effectiveness, including input, process, and outcome measures, and covering all aspects of the institution, would be far more extensive than needed (Bottrill and Borden 1994). Thus another critical role for IR is to guide the campus in selecting the most salient measures, limited to those directly linked to the strategic goals. Input measures alone, such as increase enrollment by 10 percent or raise the SAT average, do not help the campus understand how those factors might affect learning outcomes, retention, or alumni giving, all aspects of overall institutional effectiveness stated in other strategic goals. For example, as campuses well know, the SAT average can be raised by accepting students with very high test scores but poor performance in high school. However, the result will be a negative impact on retention and tuition revenues unless learning support programs are in place. Thus the CAO and IR staff must not only choose the appropriate measures but also understand how specific strategies impact other measures and costs. It is this continuous analytic and interpretive role for IR that is most important in making strategic planning an effective framework for change.

Monitoring Institutional Change

- How can IR increase the power of the strategic plan through the selected measures?

- How can unit action plan measures be integrated with institutional measures to show unit contributions to the overall result?

- What format is appropriate to show progress on strategic plan measures (e.g., trends, gap analysis, or single point data)?

- When results lag behind expectations, how can IR help the CAO audit the processes and determine the reasons?

- How can IR provide context for data to help the institution understand how well it is doing (e.g., predicted retention based on student profile and alumni giving compared to peers)?

- How often should IR conduct an environmental scan? Should annual scanning reshape the strategic plan?

ARE BUDGET AND STAFFING ADEQUATE AND APPROPRIATELY ALLOCATED?

Although most CAOs and faculty believe their institution has insufficient funds, few could explain what specific activities are currently underfunded, what budget would be adequate, or how resources should be arrayed. To establish a rational basis for determining resources tailored to mission, programs, and support needs, the CAO should start with a clean slate and current goals, rather than rely on past patterns of faculty and budget allocations. Institutional resources are typically distributed across five broad categories: instruction (e.g., faculty salaries and academic department operations), academic support (e.g., administration, libraries, and academic computing), student services (e.g., admissions, counseling, and student activities), institutional support (e.g., executive management, public relations, and campus security), and plant maintenance (e.g., buildings and grounds, utility costs, and maintenance). IR can help the CAO compare allocations to peer institutions to understand whether funds are arrayed as they are on other campuses with similar missions, activities, and resources. That comparison will reveal what higher education *currently is* rather than *what it could be*. Therefore, the CAO could consider with administrative colleagues whether resources are arrayed optimally or whether there could be alternative ways to structure and fund institutional activities.

To determine funding needs for the instructional area, the analysis is based on desired student/faculty ratios by discipline (e.g., business, psychology, and health professions) and level (e.g., lower division, upper division, masters, and doctoral). One state-funding study, for example, using actual ratios from many states as well as recommendations from campus administrators, established student/faculty ratios such as 24:1 for lower-level social science courses, 18:1 for upper-level social science courses, and 5:1 for doctoral programs in health professions (MGT of America 2001, 25–28). The CAO can establish program groupings based on data collected by IR from peer institutions, accreditation requirements, or faculty recommendations that recognize similarities and differences among disciplines. The number of discipline groups should be limited from three to six, depending upon the number and diversity of campus programs. The student/faculty ratios can be based on both actual and optimal ratios, for example, actual introductory English courses at 25:1 with the ideal goal of a reduction to 20:1. Although lower-level general education and introductory classes are typically larger than major courses on most campuses, the analysis can be based on student/faculty ratios for each group and at each level based on campus views about how best to array faculty resources to optimize learning.

Budget adequacy is then calculated by dividing the three-year average full-time equivalent (FTE) enrollment for each discipline and level by the student/faculty ratio for each discipline group and level and then multiplying by the campus average faculty salary. The calculations can also be run based on the desired average faculty salary based on CUPA-HR data. Depending upon the staffing models and the financial constraints of the campus, the CAO might calculate faculty instructional costs at only 80 percent of full-time positions, assuming that the rest will be part-time faculty. Clearly, once budgets are allocated, units could internally reallocate their teaching resources in unique ways, such as for a particular faculty member or for particular courses. IR can provide information from peer institutions as well as "industry guidelines" to calculate, for example, maintenance needs and administrative costs.

In addition to instruction costs, an amount for instructional support (e.g., staff, supplies, and travel) must be calculated. The instructional support add-on can be calculated in a variety of ways, including dollars per FTE, dollars per credit hour, a set staffing ratio (e.g., one support staff FTE for every four faculty FTE), or an analysis of fixed costs (MGT of America 2001, 11). Grouping disciplines is appropriate for this calculation as well, because supply costs for the sciences are greater than for the humanities; however, the need for secretarial support should be the same for all disciplines.

To complete the budget adequacy analysis, guidelines for each of the broad institutional budget categories must also be established, such as student services at fixed cost plus dollars per headcount student (not FTE) and academic support at a percentage of instruction costs. For example, the academic support goal for one campus was set at 20 percent of instruction costs. Administrative and facilities formulas can be developed from IR data gathered on benchmarks and peer institutions as well as internal analyses linked to specific outcomes.

The value of a budget adequacy model is not that it tells the CAO what the dollar cost to deliver the current program must be but rather that it provides a profile that rationalizes the distribution of resources and recognizes differences in programs. The comparison of actual unit budgets with the profile shows where there are inequities, what potential reallocations should be made, where there are areas for greater efficiency, and the gap between ideal and actual funding. The IR staff can also use the model to calculate the effects of academic decisions, for example, closing a program, developing a new program, increasing the number of part-time faculty, or determining a basis for allocating new revenues from a tuition increase.

The CAO interested in calculating budget adequacy for academic affairs must understand each of the factors in the formulas used. The student/faculty ratios and FTE are the basis for determining staffing adequacy. However, the FTE data are directly affected by curricular requirements not just student demand. For example, psychology is a popular major and not a general education requirement; thus FTE reflects voluntary student demand. In contrast, mathematics has few majors but is often a general education requirement; thus FTEs are based on a faculty decision and mandated demand. Obviously, eliminating or adding a requirement would impact staffing needs. Similarly, using the salary average without understanding the factors that affect salary can be misleading. The formula can be adjusted to use the salary averages by discipline rather than the institutional average. If the unit's salaries are below competitive standards, the formula can use the desired salary average and show the insufficiency of resources.

The CAO may want to ask the IR staff to run several versions of the model based on different assumptions before trying to answer the questions about budget and staffing adequacy and allocations. Sharing the results of this type of study can help deans, department chairs, and faculty think more creatively about how to adjust to fiscal realities. The information should also inform institutional budget development and help other divisions understand the impact that straitened budgets have on direct service to students.

Rationalizing Resource Allocation

- What are the foundation assumptions about the categories to be funded (e.g., faculty, equipment and supplies, and support staff)?

- How should the heuristics be established (e.g., based on past practice, comparison to other campuses, new ideas about student learning, or effort to increase productivity)?

- What role should faculty play in developing the budget adequacy model (e.g., assigning disciplines to categories and agreeing on optimal student/faculty ratios)?

- Should all factors that affect FTE be weighed the same (e.g., student demand and requirements)?

- How can unique aspects of programs be considered in the formulas (e.g., demographics of the faculty, accreditation requirements, and salary levels)?

- How might results of program review, curricular revision, or use of technology affect measures of budget adequacy?

- What discretion should deans and department chairs have in internal reallocations of resources?

ARE EXPECTATIONS FOR STUDENT EFFORT AND ENGAGEMENT HIGH ENOUGH?

Clearly, the central goal of higher education is student learning. No matter how dedicated faculty are, how committed the CAO is to creating a positive learning environment, nor how careful student affairs staff are in supporting students both in an out of the classroom, these efforts must be measured according to agreed upon standards and continuously improved. A recent national report on higher education, *Greater Expectations: A New Vision for Learning as a Nation Goes to College*, calls for "comprehensive reform" claiming campuses should set higher expectations for students, require more student responsibility and commitment, and encourage greater intentionality on the part of faculty in order to provide an education powerful enough for the demands of the twenty-first century (Association of American Colleges and Universities 2002). National discussions have already highlighted the evidence of both high school grade inflation and student lack of preparedness for college. By their own report, students are studying less, yet "45.7 percent of freshman report earning 'A' averages in high school" (CIRP 2002). As a result, CAOs are increasingly interested in how to help faculty understand incoming students, set appropriate but higher standards, and raise both the skill levels and aspirations of students.

Research on the impact of faculty expectations on student effort shows that patterns of involvement and high expectations must be set early in the first year (Schilling and Schilling, 1999). To support that effort, IR must provide faculty with relevant information from the CIRP freshman survey, which describes student habits and experiences before coming to college. The data is reported for the institution, peer institutions, and the national norm, providing context for analysis. Rather than simply sending the full survey results to student affairs or the faculty senate, IR should simplify the data, report directly to faculty on specific items that may impact what they do in the classroom, and help faculty develop interventions that can have a positive impact. For example, when students indicate low confidence in mathematics, public speaking, and writing ability but high confidence in their overall academic ability, faculty need strategies to address that disconnect between the students' skills and their expected success. To understand the gap between faculty expectations and student expectations of how hard they should work, many campuses have conducted qualitative studies of recruiting materials, orientations, and introductory course syllabi. To their dismay, they discovered the many ways in which the campus inadvertently stresses that college is fun rather than intellectually challenging.

If faculty collaborate with IR, meaningful follow-up studies to the CIRP survey data can be developed to get a better understanding of strategies that will positively impact student effort and performance. Standard quantitative studies conducted by IR on most campuses provide comprehensive student information on satisfaction with advising, safety, life in the residence halls, and availability of courses. Many campuses conduct campus climate surveys to document quality of life for women and minorities. Few campus surveys regularly ask students how many hours a week they study, how much they read, how many times they seek help from their instructors, whether they use the tutoring services or writing center, or how they manage their course work if they get behind. There is even less information, if any, about what motivates students, what distracts them, and what makes them avoid full engagement with the faculty, other students, and campus resources.

Although faculty were strongly urged two decades ago by the national report *Involvement in Learning: Realizing the Potential of American Higher Education* (National Institute of Education 1984) to set high standards and encourage active learning, many classrooms are still based on lectures and multiple-choice exams. Faculty report that their highest priority is to teach students to "think" but also report spending little class time on activities that challenge students to do so (Sax, Astin, Korn, and Gilmartin 1999). Based on the well-researched principles of the importance of both challenge and support for student success, the National Survey of Student Engagement (NSSE) can be used to understand the degree to which the campus sets high expectations and uses engaging pedagogy. The survey gathers data from freshmen and seniors and reports data in five categories—level of academic challenge, active and collaborative learning, student interaction with faculty members, enriching educational experiences, and supportive campus environment.

National survey data can be complemented with IR studies. For instance CAOs often review summaries of grades as indicators of rigor. Without knowing course requirements, these grade reports reveal little about standards or student effort. The NSSE quantitative data for level of academic challenge, for instance, as indicated by number of papers over 20 pages, allows a campus to compare its students' experiences with those at similar institutions. Taken together, a clearer picture of standards emerges. One campus, interested in raising the required satisfactory progression GPA from 1.6 to 2.0 asked IR to calculate the impact the higher standard would have on retention. When IR documented that historically "fewer than five percent of students with a 1.6 at the end of the first year ever graduated," the campus made the change with confidence that it would not affect tuition revenues (Muffo 2003, 7). Campuses that raise standards find that student performance changes to meet the higher standards, despite the students' sense of entitlement to a good grade with limited effort.

Because many campuses are giving significant attention to freshmen to help them make the transition to college and connect with the campus, the NSSE scores for freshmen on enriching educational experiences, for example, are higher than the scores for seniors. Such a finding lets faculty and staff know that they must pay attention to students throughout all years to maintain those higher levels of connection. As learning communities become more popular, campuses are trying to understand how they foster sustained intellectual and social engagement and whether that experience carries over to other experiences. The research skills of IR are necessary to design studies that can reveal student attitudes, confidence levels, and internal sources of motivation. At a minimum, IR should interpret the relationship among CIRP findings, NSSE results, student development surveys, and semester grade distributions so that faculty can appropriately encourage students to set high goals rather than lament their perceived laziness.

Faculty also need to know more about the personal habits and emotional health of their students. Increasingly, faculty report being surprised and puzzled by the amount of time they spend helping students with personal problems that affect academic performance. Institutional data that could help faculty better understand their students is not widely shared because of concerns that it will reflect negatively on students. Experienced student affairs staff and CAOs must find appropriate ways to share, for example, the extent to which alcohol and drug use is a campus problem. Students report in surveys how often they had a hangover, missed class because of alcohol consumption, or suffered memory loss. As these behaviors impact learning, faculty need to be enlisted to help address the issues. Given limited resources, one way institutions can get more out of their resources is by increasing learning productivity.

Setting High Expectations

- How might faculty set realistic expectations for student performance (e.g., quality of papers, amount of reading, essay exams, and application of knowledge)?

- What are appropriate measures of rigor (e.g., comparison to peer campuses, increasing over four years, or grade distributions)?

- How can student affairs and academic affairs collaborate to strengthen the environment for learning and support the development of students?

- How can the CAO and institutional research office improve the use of the results of surveys?

- What should faculty know about their students to shape both classroom pedagogy and cocurricular activities?

- What faculty initiatives will increase interaction between students and faculty that result in greater learning?

- How can changes in the campus culture and environment improve student commitment, engagement, and effort?

- How can investments in the intellectual community of the campus benefit faculty?

WHAT IS THE INSTITUTION'S IMPACT ON STUDENTS?

CAOs have relied on IR for assessment of student learning for two decades. Although initially used for accountability, assessment has become more sophisticated and IR is asked to determine not just what students learn but also how they learn, how they develop intellectually and socially, and how they fare after college (Banta et al. 1996). Recognizing the interrelationship of institutional research, planning, and assessment, many campuses have integrated these functions in a single office. As a result, assessment can be more complex, draw on more sources of information, and support collaboration across all divisions. A study of over 1,000 CAOs, however, revealed that assessment is still seen as accountability rather than a guide to improvement and has little influence on academic decisions in areas such as resource allocation, program review, faculty development offerings, and student support services (Peterson and Augustine 2000). When CAOs have clear intentions and involve students and student affairs staff in assessment, they are more likely to make use of assessment results for academic decisions.

Assessment of student learning outcomes relies on a wide variety of direct methods, including tests of basic skills, major field achievement tests, portfolios, and capstone projects. Tracking these measures over time provides a campus with a good picture of what students know, how they integrate knowledge, how they compare against norms, how college adds value, and whether quality standards are increasing. Typically the institutional research staff helps faculty make selections of evaluation instruments and designs both direct and indirect measures of learning suitable to specific purposes, including curriculum development and program review.

Campuses are also increasingly interested in assessing the capacity students have for learning and success independent of the faculty and the classroom. IR is called upon to tease out the impact on learning of technology, other students, cocurricular activities, and off-campus experiences. Some assessment activities are developed to provide data, not for the institution, but for the individual student. Campuses are experimenting with having students develop an electronic portfolio and guiding them through the process of setting standards for selecting examples of quality work, reflecting on their knowledge and skills, analyzing how they learn, and interpreting the meaning of their education as both an intellectual and developmental experience. The portfolio can go beyond formal instruction to include the application of learning in campus activities, internships, and jobs. Although student self-reports say such portfolios have value, both faculty and CAOs are concerned about how time consuming the process is. IR expertise is necessary to help faculty determine whether students' responsibility for their learning increases. IR can also design the cost-benefit analysis to determine whether the same use of student and faculty time in another way would produce the same or greater results.

As access to college increases, higher education needs to care less about where students start and more about the conditions that shape where they end up. To determine how students develop as learners and how they build on previous knowledge and experience throughout their four years, CAOs and IR staff need to be up to date on the increasingly sophisticated knowledge about how the brain works and techniques for assessment. Useful references include *How People Learn: Bridging Research and Practice* (Donovan, Bransford, and Pellegrino 1999), *Knowing What Students*

Know: The Science and Design of Educational Assessment (Pellegrino, Chudowsky, and Glaser 2001), and *Redesigning Higher Education: Producing Dramatic Gains in Student Learning* (Gardiner 1996). To manage the growing costs of assessment, IR needs to emphasize its design and coordination role and engage others in data collection and analysis.

Even more complex assessment questions emerge as campuses commit to developing qualities such as leadership, character, integrity, and social responsibility. Campuses have long used self-reports on voting behavior, hours of volunteer work, or participation in social action efforts as indicators of civic engagement. Because there is often lack of congruence between what individuals say they believe and care about and how they actually behave in both structured and unexpected circumstances, multiple measures should be used. Course-embedded assessment in courses on religion, ethics, and leadership can be complemented with observations of application through pedagogies such as service learning, case studies, and simulations. This information can then be triangulated with self-reports on out-of-class behaviors, reflective journals, and supervisors' evaluations. The conceptual framework for a study of character or social responsibility, however, is the most challenging aspect of this assessment task. Merely agreeing on language to describe the characteristics of compassion or respect is difficult. It is even more difficult to collect evidence.

As important as assessments of students' knowledge, skills, and values at the end of their program of study are, campuses are even more interested in measures of student performance after completion of college. To test lasting effects, IR conducts surveys of alumni focused on how many students are employed in their field, what salaries they command, and how well they believe they were prepared. To fully understand the quality outcomes of a program requires more complex surveys to track the students' capacity for upward mobility as measured by securing a second and third position of increasing responsibility. IR also needs to put into context the standard career center surveys to take account of the impact of a shift from a period of high employment to one of increased unemployment. Data on changes in sectors of the economy are also relevant for program review and program development. The capacity to conduct Web surveys has increased both the quality of data and participation rates for follow-up studies after students graduate.

A well-designed assessment program helps faculty get answers to real questions they have about how and what their students learn and the overall impact of the institution. To appreciate the complexity of assessment and endorse its value, faculty must be involved in planning, conducting, and interpreting the studies. The goal is not just to verify the results of their efforts, but to suggest stronger connections among the many learning venues on a campus that link students to students, students to the community, and students to the world through technology, with the aim of increasing learning without increasing costs. When faculty understand how students learn, they realize that students do not need faculty in the same way they once did and that there are opportunities for innovation and redesign of higher education that may promote even greater student success.

Increasing Student Success

- How can students be encouraged to take more responsibility for their learning?
- How can assessment tasks both document and promote learning?
- How should assessment be tailored to purpose, programs, and students?
- How is technology advancing assessment practices?
- What are the most effective ways to communicate assessment results?
- How can IR help provide appropriate assessment information for a variety of needs such as program review, accreditation, and state accountability reports as well as improvement?
- What role can students play in developing assessment strategies and learning from the results?
- How can IR design appropriate studies to answer the most important questions faculty have about student learning, intellectual and social development, and future success?

IS THERE ANY EVIDENCE OF SALARY INEQUITY?

Individual faculty members often request a salary equity adjustment based on information from the fact book or the *Chronicle of Higher Education*. If the CAO does not analyze all salaries and the component influences such as length of service, market, and performance, it is not only difficult to identify real inequities but also to determine what adjustment, if any, is appropriate. Few CAOs have the statistical skills necessary to conduct salary equity studies or review compensation patterns for evidence of compression. Even if they do, they wisely involve others in order to increase faculty confidence. Many campuses use outside consultants; however, both statistics faculty and IR staff should have the requisite skills to assist in the design, implementation, and analysis of salary equity studies. Regardless of the methodology used, "the process put in place to measure and then correct inequity must be fair, and must be perceived as fair" (Oaxaca and Ransom 2002, 91). Faculty appear to have the greatest confidence in the results when they know who is conducting the study, understand the methodology, and know in advance how adjustments will be made.

Before conducting a salary equity study, the CAO must determine what can and will be done as a result of the findings. If the CAO has no funds to correct inequities, it can cause hard feelings to find inequities and then offer no remedy. It may not take a great deal of money to address inequities if they are the result of small problems compounding over time. If inequities are the result of a significant pattern of discrimination, a campus resolution is far less expensive than a legal settlement. Among the usual options for funding adjustments are establishing a separate salary pool for addressing inequities, holding back some portion of the annual salary increase funds for equity adjustments, or capping the percentage increase for those found to have inappropriately high salaries to create a pool to be redistributed to those flagged with inappropriately low salaries. Even if only a small amount of money can be set aside to address inequities, over time, consistent attention to redressing inequities makes a difference.

Campuses use different approaches to determine the scope of review, such as including only those faculty who complain, all women and minority faculty, or selected departments. Since salary equity is important to all faculty and the extent of any inequities unknown at the outset, the best approach is to conduct a review of all salaries rather than relying on complaints, perception, or intuition. There is considerable literature on how to conduct salary studies, and a variety of analytical approaches have been tried and refined. The statistical methods include, for example, single equation multiple regression analyses, two and three equation models, general linear modeling analyses, and causal modeling. Although many of the reported analyses use sophisticated and complex statistical techniques, the standard single equation multiple regression analyses has become the accepted standard (Oaxaca and Ransom 2002, 91; Toutkoushian and Hoffman 2002, 73). Using two or three equations overcomes the criticism that gender differences will be lost due to the proportionality of gender representativeness in the data.

Multiple regression analyses identify cases where actual salaries are significantly different from predicted salaries that are either the result of inequities or explained by factors not captured in the regression analysis. The general multiple regression model assumes that the salary paid to a full-time faculty member, the dependent variable, is a linear function of a set of independent variables. In the single-equation method, gender and race/ethnicity are included as variables in the regression equation, so that differences in salaries between men and women and between minorities and nonminorities can be measured after other factors have been taken into account. Factors typically used in salary equity studies employing regression analyses include: highest degree earned; years since the highest degree was awarded; years of service at the university; years of relevant service at other institutions; rank into which faculty member was first hired by the institution; current faculty rank; years in rank; years from first hire to reach promotion; starting salary in the discipline; gender; race; and average research, teaching, and service evaluations over several years (Ferber and Loeb 2002, 44–50). Administrators, research faculty, library faculty, and professional staff are left out of the analysis because the factors that affect their salaries are different and it is difficult to get the data elements necessary to conduct regression analysis (Toutkoushian 2000).

As maintaining competitive salaries is important for most campuses, it is important to build into the statistical model the market factor. One approach is to group disciplines into four or five salary groups based on the CUPA-HR salary data on average salaries by ranks and disciplines and run the regression model for the separate salary groups. In that way, a faculty member whose salary might be appropriate for associate professors overall, but not for associate professors in computer science, would show up with a negative residual. An entire department could be found to be below the expected salary.

The statistical analyses identify faculty with negative residuals. To determine whether these cases represent actual inequities, it is essential that department chairs and deans review each case and identify possible alternative explanations for what, at first, may appear to be salary inequities. Even when evaluation ratings are included in a salary regression analysis, those data may not be reliable enough to capture salary variations. The department chair and dean, in reviewing the regression results, can often identify that a faculty member's history of poor performance explains the discrepancy between the actual and predicted salary and can recognize that this is not an example of an actual individual salary inequity. At the same time, they may recognize that a low increase due to poor performance many years in the past has compounded to the point that it has had a disproportionately negative effect on the current salary of the faculty member whose performance now is exemplary.

To maintain the integrity of the salary system, CAOs must determine who will be responsible for making recommendations for adjustments. If department chairs are responsible for annual salary recommendations, they must be included in the equity process. Deans or CAOs who handle adjustments on their own risk alienating department chairs and undermining confidence in the process. Faculty would argue that a quick one-time fix from the top will not redress flaws in the system. Thus, one effective model is to run the regression analysis, flag those faculty who appear to have salaries below what would be anticipated, ask chairs to review the factors that may have contributed to the low salary, and ask them to determine whether the salary is justified or should be adjusted. Once the number of faculty whose salaries need adjustment are identified, the CAO knows how much money is available and, working with the deans, can provide the chairs with an appropriate range for their recommendations. The chairs then work with the deans to make a dollar recommendation. The deans' role is important to ensure equity across units. The CAO reviews the documentation, residuals, recommendations, and finalizes the adjustments.

After this iterative process, a pattern analysis is called for. Have more women than men, in proportion to their representation on the faculty, been flagged with a negative residual? Are the faculty who have been flagged overrepresented by college or rank? Are many of the inequities due to an inappropriate starting salary? Does it appear that faculty with previous experience were not given full credit when hired? Does service as a department chair lead to a lower salary? In every faculty file there will be evidence to help explain annual salary recommendations. Learning from these "explanations" and correcting inappropriate practices can protect future faculty from inequitable treatment.

Internal explanations, however, are not enough. CAOs must also learn from the research on salary equity. For example, there is evidence that on some campuses women are promoted at a lower rate than men and have fewer opportunities to conduct activities that are highly correlated with promotion and merit increases (Johnson 1999; Strathman 2000). If those situations are due to subtle patterns of discrimination, rather than individual performance, it is necessary to look at not just rank, but years in rank. Comparing female associate professors to male professors with equal years of service could illuminate the impact that rank has on salary. Although factors such as the number of publications, citations, and teaching awards received are not included in the mathematical models, they are important factors in the ultimate determination of salaries, and rank may be subsequently used as part of the explanation for salary differentials or residuals. Nevertheless, careful research linking publications or how faculty spend their time to the "unexplained pay gap" finds that these factors account for only a portion of the difference between the salaries of women and men (Toutkoushian 1999). Because starting salary has the most powerful impact on salary over time, setting it appropriately should be the CAO's highest priority. Collaboratively, faculty and administrators can then seek the methodology, process, and funds to keep compensation fair and equitable.

Conducting a Salary Equity Study

- Why has the salary equity study been initiated?
- Who is responsible for the salary equity study?
- What data will be utilized, what methodology will be employed, and what will be the extent of faculty oversight and/or involvement?
- What subsequent actions will be taken and what funding is available?
- What role will the CAO, deans, and department chairs play in determining adjustments?
- How will resources be provided to address salary adjustments? Over what period of time will salary inequities be corrected?
- If funding is limited, should adjustments be funded by reducing the rate of annual salary increases scheduled for other faculty?
- After corrections are made, what is the monitoring system to prevent recurrence of inequities?

CAN CURRICULAR CHANGE TAKE PLACE WHEN RESOURCES ARE LIMITED?

Many CAOs and faculty are demoralized by fiscal realities and wonder how curricular renewal can be sustained. Indeed, there are many promising ideas about pedagogy, content, and curricular structures that campuses want to initiate, such as freshman seminars, learning communities, interdisciplinary majors, service learning, and undergraduate research. When faculty are encouraged to redesign general education requirements or consider new ways of teaching, their first question to the administration is, "Where are the resources?" Since it is unlikely that higher education will see a reversal in the situation of limited funding, CAOs must find ways to help faculty consider alternative models for achieving their curricular goals and not give up their ideals. IR can help with the cost-benefit analyses.

Curricular design begins with determining specific goals, but there are many choices of content, pedagogy, and course and noncourse structures to accomplish the goals. The elements and options have different costs attached to them as well as different levels of effectiveness. For example, staffing with full-time faculty is more expensive than using graduate students but may not be as effective. Keeping class size small in order to have highly engaging pedagogy is more expensive than a large lecture but may produce more lasting learning. Designing a separate course for each competency such as writing, oral communication, and technology is more expensive than integrating skill development into all courses. Without studying the two options, the approach that is more effective is not clear. Institutional research can play a valuable role in assisting faculty in determining both the cost and the effectiveness of alternative staffing, pedagogies, curricular elements, and structures. The CAO's role is to encourage curricular design that optimizes both learning effectiveness and efficient use of resources.

When making choices among alternative curricular elements, campuses apply various criteria. Faculty commitment to undergraduate teaching, competing interests such as research and outreach, student developmental needs, and concern about student success may affect the choices. Many campuses have been able to reallocate curricular resources to develop freshman seminars or integrate service learning by eliminating tracks, options, and electives. Some have reallocated faculty time by reducing service commitments and reducing the number of students graduating with excess credits. Others have reallocated student time by making greater use of technology, structuring courses around independent work, and making greater use of experiential learning off campus. The CAO needs to work with the chief financial officer (CFO) to ensure that savings will not be captured and that reallocation can keep innovation alive.

Each new initiative needs to be costed out. To introduce freshman seminars for a class of 1,000 with no new resources means that 50 sections of other courses and electives will not be taught. For 500 students to have internships each semester, instead of a senior capstone seminar, may require an office staffed by two professionals and several student workers. However, 1,000 fewer on-campus credits could equal 35 fewer sections or the equivalent of four full-time faculty. The faculty funds could be used to fund the internship office. Eliminating the lab for one of the two required general education courses or having both courses hold labs every other week could release significant funds to support undergraduate research for science majors. If faculty are to continue to put forth their ideas on new courses and new pedagogy, they will need backup from IR and department chairs in calculating costs and considering alternative uses of funds.

Given continuing reductions in resources, many faculty wonder if they can even maintain the current level of service to students. Several national projects on the future of higher education led by Frank Newman, Alan Guskin, William Massy, and Carol Twigg have raised these issues for years, but despite their clarity and urgency about restructuring, many campuses have not responded (Massy 2003; Guskin and Marcy 2002). In the future thinking model, the entire slate is wiped clean and only the mission, the goals, and the student body are retained as the focus. All curricula, programs, and services are designed with the ends in mind and need not conform to current models of disciplines, courses, credits, and requirements. In the last decade, a few new campuses have been founded with no prior assumptions, and they are clearly more innovative in all aspects, including faculty credentials and appointments, program design and learning activities, instructional delivery, and student demonstration of competencies for degree requirements. Although it is difficult to give up traditional forms of education, CAOs should know what the future could hold.

Redesigning Curriculum to Match Fiscal Realities

- How can the institution get more out of current resources and fund renewal?
- Are there efficiencies that do not reduce learning (e.g., on-line labs, independent work, and better use of faculty time)?
- How should faculty resources be deployed for optimum results?
- What savings can be achieved if students are more successful in all courses?
- Are there any realistic alternatives for programs that are labor intensive, such as applied music and nursing?
- How can the alternative costs for curricular projects be calculated?
- How can innovation save money rather than cost money?

SUCCESSFUL COLLABORATION WITH INSTITUTIONAL RESEARCH

The need for timely and informed academic decision making has changed both the role of the chief academic officer and the institutional research office. CAOs cannot expect that a few quick calculations coupled with past experience and intuition will lead to good decisions guiding the future of the institution. They must have a good understanding of analytic tools, select staff with both a knowledge of academic affairs and technical skills, and strive to be both more independent and better collaborators with the institutional research office. The institutional research office must be recognized for more than gathering information and preparing external and on-demand reports. The IR staff must be encouraged to use their research, evaluation, and statistical skills selectively and proactively to strengthen the institution.

This partnership between CAOs and institutional researchers can make data readily available for others, provide guidance on how to interpret data, and support better management and more intentional leadership. To extend their reach, however, IR staff must be willing to train others—including faculty, graduate students, and staff in academic affairs—to gather data and do some of the analyses such as for assessment of student learning. Further, institutional researchers must be able to design studies that supplement quantitative methods with qualitative methods such as focus groups, interviews, and content analysis of documents to address more complex and layered issues such as retention and student engagement. Given limited resources, it is unlikely that IR staff will increase; thus efforts must be made to hand off the routine activities, expand the number of individuals knowledgeable in institutional research, and consult regularly with key administrators to pare down the work so that the merely interesting questions take low priority compared to the essential studies. Not every academic decision needs to be backed by complex annual institutional research—the challenge is to recognize and support those few critical decisions in specific areas that will shape the future of the institution.

Equally important, CAOs must begin to think in entirely new ways about their institutions as not everything can be improved by just working harder. The more innovative approaches to promoting greater institutional effectiveness and handling fiscal constraints is to ask: "What should we do differently? If we did not have the programs and services we currently have, what would we design?" The process would begin with an audit of all programs, activities, administrative expenses, and student services with the aim of neither calculating funding needs nor rationalizing support, but rather seeking to cut nonessential services and programs, redesign others through the use of technology, and integrate other services and programs to streamline and eliminate expensive faculty and staff (Guskin and Marcy 2003). If campuses go down this path, CAOs will need to build political support for rethinking the institution and use IR staff and faculty to study benchmarks, best practices, and case studies that suggest alternative ways to reach their goals. Institutions can be redesigned, but it will take a collaborative effort that is based on careful analysis and guided by informed leadership.

References

Alstete, Jeffrey W. 1995. *Benchmarking in Higher Education: Adapting Best Practices to Improve Quality*. ASHE-ERIC Higher Education Report, no. 5. Washington, DC: The George Washington University, Graduate School of Education and Human Development.

American Association of University Professors. 2001. *Policy Documents & Reports*. 9th ed. Washington, DC: American Association of University Professors.

Ammons, Jane C., and Joseph E. Gilmour. 1995. Georgia Tech's Continuous Quality Improvement Journey. In *Academic Initiatives in Total Quality for Higher Education*, ed. Harry V. Roberts, 57–66. Milwaukee, WI: ASQC Quality Press.

Anderes, Thomas K. 1996. Connecting Academic Plans to Budgeting: Key Conditions for Success. In *Doing Academic Planning: Effective Tools for Decision Making*, ed. Brian P. Nedwek, 129–34. Ann Arbor, MI: Society for College and University Planning.

Andrade, Sally J. 1999. How to Institutionalize Strategic Planning. *Planning for Higher Education* 27 (2): 40–54.

Anson, Chris. 2002. *Conceptual Understanding of Undergraduate Academic Program Review at N.C. State University*. http://www.ncsu.edu/provost/academic_programs/uapr/UAPRintroconcept.html.

Antony, James S., and James R. Valadez. 2002. Exploring the Satisfaction of Part-time College Faculty in the United States. *The Review of Higher Education* 26 (1): 41–56.

Association of American Colleges and Universities. 1999. Point of View. *Peer Review* 1 (4): 13.

————. 2002. *Greater Expectations: A New Vision for Learning as a Nation Goes to College*. Washington, DC: Association of American Colleges and Universities.

Association of American Colleges. 1992. *Program Review and Educational Quality in the Major: A Faculty Handbook*. Washington, DC: Association of American Colleges.

Association of Governing Boards of Universities and Colleges. 1996. *Renewing the Academic Presidency: Stronger Leadership for Tougher Times*. Washington, DC: Association of Governing Boards of Universities and Colleges.

Austin, Ann E. 1996. Institutional and Departmental Cultures: The Relationship between Teaching and Research. In *Faculty Teaching and Research: Is There a Conflict?* ed. John M. Braxton, 57–66. New Directions for Institutional Research, no. 90. San Francisco: Jossey-Bass.

Baldwin, Roger G., and David W. Leslie. 2001. Rethinking the Structure of Shared Governance. *Peer Review* 3 (3): 18–19.

Banta, Trudy W., and Associates. 1993. *Making a Difference: Outcomes of a Decade of Assessment in Higher Education*. San Francisco: Jossey-Bass.

Banta, Trudy W., Jon P. Lund, Karen E. Black, and Frances W. Oblander. 1996. *Assessment in Practice: Putting Principles to Work on College Campuses*. San Francisco: Jossey-Bass.

Barak, Robert J., and Barbara E. Breier. 1990. *Successful Program Review: A Practical Guide to Evaluating Programs in Academic Settings*. San Francisco: Jossey-Bass.

Barak, Robert J., and Janet D. Sweeney. 1995. Academic Program Review in Planning, Budgeting, and Assessment. In *Using Academic Program Review*, eds. Robert J. Barak and Lisa A. Mets, 3–17. New Directions for Institutional Research, no. 86. San Francisco: Jossey-Bass.

Barbezat, Debra A. 2002. History of Pay Equity Studies. In *Conducting Salary-Equity Studies: Alternative Approaches to Research*, ed. Robert K. Toutkoushian, 41–70. New Directions for Institutional Research, no. 115. San Francisco: Jossey-Bass.

Baum, Sandy. 2001. *Higher Education Dollars and Sense*. New York: College Entrance Examination Board.

Bensimon, Estela M., and Anna Neumann. 1993. *Redesigning Collegiate Leadership: Teams and Teamwork in Higher Education*. Baltimore, MD: The Johns Hopkins University Press.

Bernstein, Bianca L. 1998. Graduate Certificate Programs at Arizona State University. In *Certificates: A Survey of Our Status and Review of Successful Programs in the U.S. and Canada*, ed. Jane A. Hamblin, 8–13. Washington, DC: Council of Graduate Schools.

Birnbaum, Robert. 2000. *Management Fads in Higher Education: Where They Come From, What They Do, and Why They Fail*. San Francisco: Jossey-Bass.

Bishop, Jane, Jerrilyn Brewer, Dennis Ladwig, and Lee Rasch. 2000. Do We Get Them? Do We Keep Them? Do They Learn? Applying Quality Principles to Higher Education. In *A Collection of Papers on Self-Study and Institutional Improvement*, ed. Susan E. Van Kollenburg, 35–43. Chicago: Commission on Institutions of Higher Education, North Central Association of Colleges and Schools.

Blackburn, Robert T., and Janet H. Lawrence. 1995. *Faculty at Work: Motivation, Expectation, Satisfaction*. Baltimore, MD: The Johns Hopkins University Press.

Blake, Robert R., and Jane S. Mouton. 1978. *The New Managerial Grid*. Houston, TX: Gulf Publishing.

Bland, Carole J., and William H. Bergquist. 1997. *The Vitality of Senior Faculty Members: Snow on the Roof—Fire in the Furnace*. ASHE-ERIC Higher Education Report, no. 7. Washington, DC: The George Washington University, Graduate School of Education and Human Development.

Blumenstyk, Goldie. 2002. How Colleges Get More Bang (or Less) From Technology Transfer. *The Chronicle of Higher Education*, 19 July, pp. A24–26.

Bottrill, Karen V., and Victor M. H. Borden. 1994. Appendix: Examples from the Literature. In *Using Performance Indicators to Guide Strategic Decision Making*, eds. Victor M. H. Borden and Trudy W. Banta, 107–19. New Directions for Institutional Research, no. 82. San Francisco: Jossey-Bass.

Boyer, Ernest L. 1990. *Scholarship Reconsidered: Priorities of the Professoriate*. Princeton, NJ: Carnegie Foundation for the Advancement of Teaching.

Brainard, Jeffrey. 2002. Some Colleges Reap Little Return Lobbying for Pork Projects, Study Says. *The Chronicle of Higher Education*, 18 October, pp. A27–28.

Brase, Wendell. 1990. Integrating Physical Planning with Academic Planning. In *Critical Issues in Facilities Management: Planning, Design, and Construction*, ed. Steve Glazner, 1–12. Alexandria, VA: Association of Physical Plant Administrators of Universities and Colleges.

Braskamp, Larry A., and John C. Ory. 1994. *Assessing Faculty Work: Enhancing Individual and Institutional Performance*. San Francisco: Jossey-Bass.

Bruegman, Donald C. 1989. An Integrated Approach to Academic, Fiscal, and Facility Planning. In *Planning and Managing Higher Education Facilities*, ed. Harvey H. Kaiser, 13–20. New Directions for Institutional Research, no. 61. San Francisco: Jossey-Bass.

Carlson, Scott, and Dan Carnevale. 2001. Debating the Demise of NYUonline. *The Chronicle of Higher Education*, 14 December, pp. A31–32.

Caruthers, J. Kent, and Daniel T. Layzell. 1999. Campus Master Planning and Capital Budgeting. In *Roles and Responsibilities of the Chief Financial Officer*, eds. Lucie Lapovsky and Mary P. McKeown-Moak, 73–81. New Directions for Higher Education, no. 107. San Francisco: Jossey-Bass.

Catterall, James S. 1998. A Cost-Effectiveness Model for the Assessment of Educational Productivity. In *Enhancing Productivity: Administrative, Instructional, and Technological Strategies*, eds. James E. Groccia and Judith E. Miller, 61–84. New Directions for Higher Education, no. 103. San Francisco: Jossey-Bass.

Chabotar, Kent J. 1999. How to Develop an Effective Budget Process. In *Roles and Responsibilities of the Chief Financial Officer*, eds. Lucie Lapovsky and Mary P. McKeown-Moak, 17–28. New Directions for Higher Education, no. 107. San Francisco: Jossey-Bass.

Chaffee, Ellen E. 1983. *Rational Decision Making in Higher Education*. Boulder, CO: National Center for Higher Education Management Systems.

Chaffee, Ellen E., and Lawrence A. Sherr. 1992. *Quality: Transforming Postsecondary Education*. ASHE-ERIC Higher Education Report, no. 3. Washington, DC: The George Washington University, School of Education and Human Development.

Cherwitz, Richard A., and Charlotte A. Sullivan. 2002. Intellectual Entrepreneurship: A Vision for Graduate Education. *Change* 34 (6): 22–27.

Chnapko, Angela. 2002. 2002 Guide to e-Learning Vendors. *University Business* 5 (3): 35–51.

Coffman, James R. 1997. Leveraging Resources to Enhance Quality: Curriculum Development and Educational Technologies. In *First among Equals: The Role of the Chief Academic Officer*, eds. James Martin, James E. Samels, and Associates, 41–57. Baltimore, MD: The Johns Hopkins University Press.

College and University Professional Association for Human Resources. 2002. *CUPA-HR's 2001–02 National Faculty Survey by Discipline and Rank in Four-Year Colleges and Universities*. Washington, DC: College and University Professional Association for Human Resources.

Commission on Colleges. 2002. *Criteria for Accreditation*. Atlanta, GA: Commission on Colleges, Southern Association of Colleges and Schools.

Commission on Institutions of Higher Education. 2000. *Academic Quality Improvement Project*. Chicago: Commission on Institutions of Higher Education, North Central Association of Colleges and Schools.

Conrad, Clifton F., and Richard F. Wilson. 1985. *Academic Program Reviews: Institutional Approaches, Expectations, and Controversies*. ASHE-ERIC Higher Education Report, no. 5. Washington, DC: Association for the Study of Higher Education.

Cooper, Sheila. 1998. Graduate Certificates at Indiana University and Considerations for Graduate Education. In *Certificates: A Survey of Our Status and Review of Successful Programs in the U.S. and Canada*, ed. Jane A. Hamblin, 3–5. Washington, DC: Council of Graduate Schools.

Cooperative Institutional Research Program. 2002. *The American Freshman: National Norms for Fall 2002*. Los Angeles, CA: Higher Education Research Institute, University of California at Los Angeles.

Cope, Robert G. 1987. *Opportunity from Strength: Strategic Planning Clarified with Case Examples*. ASHE-ERIC Higher Education Report, no. 8. Washington, DC: Association for the Study of Higher Education.

Corbett, Anne, ed. 1998. *Towards the 21st Century: Facilities for Tertiary Education*. Paris, France: Organisation for Economic Co-operation and Development.

Cuban, Larry. 2001. *Oversold and Underused: Computers in the Classroom*. Cambridge, MA: Harvard University Press.

Diamond, Robert M. 1999. *Aligning Faculty Rewards with Institutional Mission: Statements, Policies, and Guidelines*. Bolton, MA: Anker Publishing.

Dickeson, Robert C. 1999. *Prioritizing Academic Programs and Services: Reallocating Resources to Achieve Strategic Balance*. San Francisco: Jossey-Bass.

Dixon, Rebecca R. 1995. What Is Enrollment Management? In *Making Enrollment Management Work*, ed. Rebecca R. Dixon, 5–10. New Directions for Student Services, no. 71. San Francisco: Jossey-Bass.

Donovan, M. Suzanne, John D. Bransford, and James W. Pellegrino, eds. 1999. *How People Learn: Bridging Research and Practice*. Washington, DC: National Academy Press.

Driscoll, Amy, and Ernest A. Lynton. 1999. *Making Outreach Visible: A Guide to Documenting Professional Service and Outreach*. Washington, DC: American Association for Higher Education.

Eaton, Gertrude M., and Helen F. Giles-Gee. 1996. Planning an Academic Program Review. In *Doing Academic Planning: Effective Tools for Decision Making*, ed. Brian P. Nedwek, 27–34. Ann Arbor, MI: Society for College and University Planning.

Eckel, Peter D. 2002. Decision Rules Used in Academic Program Closure: Where the Rubber Meets the Road. *The Journal of Higher Education* 73 (2): 237–62.

Eckel, Peter, Madeleine Green, Barbara Hill, and William Mallon. 1999. *Taking Charge of Change: A Primer for Colleges and Universities*. Washington, DC: American Council on Education.

Ehrenberg, Ronald G. 2003. Reaching for the Brass Ring: The *U.S. News & World Report* Rankings and Competition. *The Review of Higher Education* 26 (2): 145–62.

Elman, Sandra E., and Sue M. Smock. 1985. *Professional Service & Faculty Rewards: Toward an Integrated Structure*. Washington, DC: National Association of State Universities and Land-Grant Colleges.

Epper, Rhonda M. 1999. Applying Benchmarking to Higher Education: Some Lessons from Experience. *Change* 31 (6): 24–31.

Epper, Rhonda, and A. W. (Tony) Bates, eds. 2001. *Teaching Faculty How to Use Technology: Best Practices from Leading Institutions*. Westport, CT: American Council on Education and The Oryx Press.

Erwin, T. Dary. 1991. *Assessing Student Learning and Development: A Guide to the Principles, Goals, and Methods of Determining College Outcomes*. San Francisco: Jossey-Bass.

Ewell, Peter T. 1999. Imitation as Art: Borrowed Management Techniques in Higher Education. *Change* 31 (6): 10–15.

Fairweather, James, and Andrea L. Beach. 2002. Variations in Faculty Work at Research Universities: Implications for State and Institutional Policy. *The Review of Higher Education* 26 (1): 97–115.

Feenberg, Andrew. 1999. Whither Educational Technology? *Peer Review* 1 (4): 4–7.

Ferber, Marianne A., and Jane W. Loeb. 2002. Issues in Conducting an Institutional Salary Equity Study. In *Conducting Salary-Equity Studies: Alternative Approaches to Research*, ed. Robert K. Toutkoushian, 41–70. New Directions for Institutional Research, no. 115. San Francisco: Jossey-Bass.

Ferren, Ann S. 1998. *Senior Faculty Considering Retirement: A Developmental and Policy Issue*. New Pathways Inquiry Paper, no. 11. Washington, DC: American Association for Higher Education.

Ferren, Ann S., and Martin S. Aylesworth. 2001. Using Qualitative and Quantitative Information in Academic Decision Making. In *Balancing Qualitative and Quantitative Information for Effective Decision Support*, eds. Richard D. Howard and Kenneth W. Borland, Jr., 67–83. New Directions for Institutional Research, no. 112. San Francisco: Jossey-Bass.

Ferren, Ann S., and Rick Slavings. 2000. *Investing in Quality: Tools for Improving Curricular Efficiency*. Washington, DC: Association of American Colleges and Universities.

Ferren, Ann S., and Susan Barnard. 2001. Tough Choices at Radford University. *ACADEME* 87 (3): 37–42.

Fife, Jonathan D. 2000. From Quality Promised to Quality Certain: Creating a Systematic Approach to Mission Fulfillment. In *International Perspectives on Quality in Higher Education*, eds. Steven M. Janosik, Don G. Creamer, and M. David Alexander, 16–39. Blacksburg, VA: Education Policy Institute of Virginia Tech.

Finkelstein, Martin J., Robert K. Seal, and Jack H. Schuster. 1998. *The New Academic Generation: A Profession in Transformation*. Baltimore, MD: The Johns Hopkins University Press.

Fischer, Richard B. 1987. Contracting with Business and Industry. In *Competitive Strategies for Continuing Education*, ed. Clifford Baden, 59–70. New Directions for Continuing Education, no. 35. San Francisco: Jossey-Bass.

Frances, Carol, Richard Pumerantz, and James Caplan. 1999. Planning for Instructional Technology: What You Thought You Knew Could Lead You Astray. *Change* 31 (4): 25–33.

Freed, Jann E., and Marie R. Klugman. 1997. *Quality Principles and Practices in Higher Education: Different Questions for Different Times*. Phoenix, AZ: The American Council on Education and The Oryx Press.

Freed, Jann E., Marie R. Klugman, and Jonathan D. Fife. 1997. *A Culture for Academic Excellence: Implementing the Quality Principles in Higher Education*. ASHE-ERIC Higher Education Report, no. 1. Washington, DC: The George Washington University, Graduate School of Education and Human Development.

Frost, Susan H., and Theresa W. Gillespie. 1998. Organizations, Culture, and Teams: Links toward Genuine Change. In *Using Teams in Higher Education: Cultural Foundations for Productive Change*, ed. Susan H. Frost, 5–

15. New Directions for Institutional Research, no. 100. San Francisco: Jossey-Bass.

Gaff, Jerry G., and James L. Ratcliff, eds. 1997. *Handbook of the Undergraduate Curriculum: A Comprehensive Guide to Purposes, Structures, Practices, and Change*. San Francisco: Jossey-Bass.

Gaff, Jerry G., Anne S. Pruitt-Logan, Richard A. Weibl, and Participants in the Preparing Future Faculty Program. 2000. *Building the Faculty We Need: Colleges and Universities Working Together*. Washington, DC: Association of American Colleges and Universities.

Gaither, Gerald, Brian P. Nedwek, and John E. Neal. 1994. *Measuring Up: The Promises and Pitfalls of Performance Indicators in Higher Education*. ASHE-ERIC Higher Education Report, no. 5. Washington, DC: The George Washington University, Graduate School of Education and Human Development.

Gardiner, Lion F. 1996. *Redesigning Higher Education: Producing Dramatic Gains in Student Learning*. ASHE-ERIC Higher Education Report, no. 7. Washington, DC: The George Washington University, Graduate School of Education and Human Development.

Golden, Robert, and Jay V. Kahn. 1998. Charting a New Direction: A Collaborative, Sustainable, Customer-based Model for Information Technology. *NACUBO Business Officer* 32 (1): 57–64.

Gouillart, Francis. 1995. Planning Theory: The Day the Music Died. *Journal of Business Strategy* 16 (3): 14–19.

Green, Kenneth C. 1996a. Building a Campus Infostructure. *Trusteeship*. 4–9.

———. 1996b. *Campus Computing 1996: The National Survey of Information Technology in American Higher Education*. Encino, CA: Campus Computing.

———. 2000. *Campus Computing 2000: The National Survey of Information Technology in American Higher Education*. Encino, CA: Campus Computing.

———. 2001. *Campus Computing 2001: The National Survey of Information Technology in American Higher Education*. Encino, CA: Campus Computing.

Green, Kenneth, and Robin Jenkins. 1998. IT Financial Planning 101: Developing an Institutional Strategy for Financing Technology. *NACUBO Business Officer* 31 (9): 32–37.

Greene, Howard, and Matthew Greene. 2002. Containing the Rising Cost of College. *University Business* 5 (4): 19–20.

Grills, Caroline M., ed. 2000. *College and University Business Administration*. 6th ed. Washington, DC: National Association of College and University Business Officers.

Gumport, Patricia J. 2001. Divided We Govern? *Peer Review* 3 (3): 14–17.

Guskin, Alan E., and Mary B. Marcy. 2003. Creating a Vital Campus in a Climate of Restricted Resources: 10 Organizing Principles. Paper presented at the Association of American Colleges and Universities Annual Meeting, 24 January, Seattle, Washington.

————. 2002. Pressures for Fundamental Reform: Creating a Viable Academic Future. In *Field Guide to Academic Leadership*, ed. Robert M. Diamond, 3–13. San Francisco: Jossey-Bass.

Hagner, Paul R. 2000. Faculty Engagement and Support in the New Learning Environment. *EDUCAUSE Review* 35 (5): 27–37.

Hammermesh, Daniel S. 2002. Quite Good News—For Now: The Annual Report on the Economic Status of the Profession 2001–2002. *ACADEME* 88 (2): 20–41.

Hammond, P. Brett, and Harriet P. Morgan, eds. 1991. *Ending Mandatory Retirement for Tenured Faculty*. Washington, DC: National Academy Press.

Hannum, Wallace. 2002. Technology in the Learning Process. In *Field Guide to Academic Leadership*, ed. Robert M. Diamond, 175–92. San Francisco: Jossey-Bass.

Hawkins, Brian. 1998. The Confusing Economics of Higher Education. *Planning for Higher Education* 26 (3): 8–13.

Haworth, Jennifer G., and Clifton F. Conrad. 1997. *Emblems of Quality in Higher Education: Developing and Sustaining High-Quality Programs*. Needham Heights, MA: Allyn and Bacon.

Hax, Arnoldo C., and Nicolas S. Majluf. 1996. *The Strategy Concept and Process: A Pragmatic Approach*. Upper Saddle River, NJ: Prentice Hall.

Huntley, Helen. 2002. University of Florida Bathing in Gatorade Limelight. *St. Petersburg Times Online Business*. 1 July.

Jarmon, Carolyn G., ed. 2002. Redesigning Learning Environments. *The Pew Learning and Technology Program Newsletter*, 4 (2). http://www.center. rpi.edu/PewHome.html.

Jenny, Hans H. 1996. *Cost Accounting in Higher Education: Simplified Macro- and Micro- Costing Techniques*. Washington, DC: National Association of College and University Business Officers.

Johnson, Robert J. 1999. Female/Male Salary Inequities: The Role of Promotion. *On Campus with Women* 28 (2): 2.

Jones, Larry G. 1996. Brief History of the Fact Book as an Institutional Research Report. In *Campus Fact Books: Keeping Pace with New Institutional Needs and Challenges*, ed. Larry G. Jones, 3–26. New Direction for Institutional Research, no. 91. San Francisco: Jossey-Bass.

Jordan, Stephen M. 1994. What We Have Learned about Faculty Workload: The Best Evidence. In *Analyzing Faculty Workload*, ed. Jon F. Wergin, 15–23. New Directions for Institutional Research, no. 83. San Francisco: Jossey Bass.

Kaiser, Harvey H., and Eva Klein. 2000. Facilities Management. In *College and University Business Administration*, 6th ed., ed. Caroline M. Grills, 13:1–90. Washington, DC: National Association of College and University Business Officers.

Kaiser, Harvey. 1998. Designing the Campus as a Community. *Planning for Higher Education* 26 (3): 46–47.

Karr, Scott, and Robert V. Kelley. 1996. Attracting New Sources of Research Funding. In *Strategies for Promoting Excellence in a Time of Scarce Resources*, eds. David W. Breneman and Alton L. Taylor, 33–44. New Directions for Higher Education, no. 94. San Francisco: Jossey-Bass.

Keller, George. 1983. *Academic Strategy: The Management Revolution in American Higher Education*. Baltimore, MD: The Johns Hopkins University Press.

———. 1997. Foreword. In *Strategic Change in Colleges and Universities: Planning to Survive and Prosper*. Daniel J. Rowley, Herman D. Lujan, and Michael G. Dolence. San Francisco: Jossey-Bass.

Kezar, Adrianna. 2001. Seeking a Sense of Balance: Academic Governance in the 21st Century. *Peer Review* 3 (3): 4–8.

Kiil, Leevi, and Robert Brandt. 1990. Design Approaches to the Special Challenges of Academic Facilities. In *Critical Issues in Facilities Management: Planning, Design, and Construction*, ed. Steve Glazner, 56–66. Alexandria, VA: Association of Physical Plant Administrators of Universities and Colleges.

Kirp, David L., and Elizabeth P. Berman. 2002. The Good Deal. *University Business* 5 (8): 38–42.

Klumpp, James F. 1997. *Undergraduate Library Services in the 21st Century*. www.lib.umd.edu/PUB/UGLibServ.html.

Kuh, George D. 2001. Assessing What Really Matters to Student Learning: Inside the National Survey of Student Engagement. *Change* 33 (3): 10–17, 66.

Kuh, George D., John H. Schuh, Elizabeth H. Whitt, and Associates. 1991. *Involving Colleges: Successful Approaches to Fostering Student Learning and Development Outside the Classroom*. San Francisco: Jossey-Bass.

Lawrence, Janet H. 1994. Campus Culture and Faculty Perceptions of Time. In *Analyzing Faculty Workload*, ed. Jon F. Wergin, 25–38. New Directions for Institutional Research, no. 83. San Francisco: Jossey Bass.

Layzell, Daniel T., Cheryl Lovell, and Judith I. Gill. 1996. Developing Faculty as an Asset in a Period of Change and Uncertainty. In *Integrating Research on Faculty: Seeking New Ways to Communicate about the Academic Life of Faculty*. NCES 96–849. Washington, DC: National Center for Education Statistics.

Lenington, Robert L. 1996. *Managing Higher Education as a Business*. Phoenix, AZ: American Council on Education and The Oryx Press.

Leslie, David, and E. K. Fretwell, Jr. 1996. *Wise Moves in Hard Times: Creating and Managing Resilient Colleges and Universities*. San Francisco: Jossey-Bass.

Lewis, Ralph G., and Douglas H. Smith. 1994. *Total Quality in Higher Education*. Delray Beach, FL: St. Lucie Press.

Lindholm, Jennifer A., Alexander W. Astin, Linda J. Sax, and William S. Korn. 2002. *The American College Teacher: National Norms for the 2001–2002 HERI Faculty Survey*. Los Angeles, CA: Higher Education Research Institute, University of California at Los Angeles.

Lindquist, Jack. 1978. *Strategies for Change*. Berkeley, CA: Pacific Soundings Press.

Lissner, L. Scott, and Alton L. Taylor. 1996. Financial Stress and the Need for Change. In *Strategies for Promoting Excellence in a Time of Scarce Resources*, eds. David W. Breneman and Alton L. Taylor, 3–8. New Directions for Higher Education, no. 94. San Francisco: Jossey-Bass.

Lowery, Courtney. 2002. Presidents for Life. *The Chronicle of Higher Education*, 26 July, p. A8.

Lozier, G. Gregory, and Michael J. Dooris. 1991. *Faculty Retirement Projections beyond 1994: Effects of Policy on Individual Choice*. Boulder, CO: Western Interstate Commission for Higher Education.

Mangan, Katherine S. 2001. Expectations Evaporate for Online MBA Programs. *The Chronicle of Higher Education*, 5 October, pp. A31–32.

Manno, Bruno V. 1998. Vocabulary Lesson: Cost, Price, and Subsidy in American Higher Education. *NACUBO Business Officer* 31 (10): 22–25.

March, James G. 1994. *A Primer on Decision Making: How Decisions Happen*. New York: The Free Press.

Marks, Joseph L., and J. Kent Caruthers. 1999a. *A Primer on Funding of Public Higher Education*. Atlanta, GA: Southern Regional Education Board.

————. 1999b. *Funding Public Higher Education in the 1990s: What's Happened and Where are We Going?* Atlanta, GA: Southern Regional Education Board.

Massy, William F. 2003. *Honoring the Trust: Quality and Cost Containment in Higher Education*. Bolton, MA: Anker Publishing.

Massy, William F., and Andrea K. Wilger. 1998. Technology's Contribution to Higher Education's Productivity. In *Enhancing Productivity: Administrative, Instructional, and Technological Strategies*, eds. James E. Groccia and Judith E. Miller, 49–59. New Directions for Higher Education, no. 103. San Francisco: Jossey-Bass.

Mayhew, Lewis B., Patrick J. Ford, and Dean L. Hubbard. 1990. *The Quest for Quality: The Challenge for Undergraduate Education in the 1990s*. San Francisco: Jossey-Bass.

McIntosh, Mary, Kathleen Cacciola, Stephen Clermont, and Julian Keniry. 2001. *State of the Campus Environment: A National Report Card on Environmental Performance and Sustainability in Higher Education*. Reston, VA: National Wildlife Federation.

McKeown, Mary P., and Daniel T. Layzell. 1994. State Funding Formulas for Higher Education: Trends and Issues. *Journal of Education Finance* 19 (3): 319–46.

McKeown-Moak, Mary P. 1999. Higher Education Funding Formulas. In *Roles and Responsibilities of the Chief Financial Officer*, eds. Lucie Lapovsky and Mary P. McKeown-Moak, 99–107. New Directions for Higher Education, no. 107. San Francisco: Jossey-Bass.

McKinney, James, John Missell, and Thomas Fisher. 1994. Planning for Renovations on Campus. *Planning for Higher Education* 22 (4): 17–23.

Mech, Terrence. 1997. The Managerial Roles of Chief Academic Officers. *The Journal of Higher Education* 68 (3): 282–98.

Meisinger, Richard J., Jr. 1994. *College and University Budgeting: An Introduction for Faculty and Academic Administrators.* 2d ed. Washington, DC: National Association of College and University Business Officers.

Meisinger, Richard J., Jr., and Leroy W. Dubeck. 1984. *College and University Budgeting: An Introduction for Faculty and Academic Administrators.* Washington DC: National Association of College and University Business Officers.

Mets, Lisa A. 1995. Lessons Learned from Program Review Experiences. In *Using Academic Program Review,* eds. Robert J. Barak and Lisa Mets, 81–92. New Directions for Institutional Research, no. 86. San Francisco: Jossey-Bass.

Meyer, Katrina. 1998. *Faculty Workload Studies: Perspectives, Needs, and Future Directions.* AHSE-ERIC Higher Education Report, no. 1. Washington, DC: The George Washington University, Graduate School of Education and Human Development.

MGT of America, Inc. 2001. *Final Report and Recommendations to the Joint Subcommittee on Higher Education Funding Policies.* Tallahassee, FL: MGT of America, Inc.

Middaugh, Michael F. 2001. *Understanding Faculty Productivity: Standards and Benchmarks for Colleges and Universities.* San Francisco: Jossey-Bass.

Milem, Jeffrey F., Joseph B. Berger, and Eric L. Dey. 2000. Faculty Time Allocation: A Study of Change over Twenty Years. *The Journal of Higher Education* 71 (4): 454–75.

Miller, Margaret A. 1994. Pressures to Measure Faculty Work. In *Analyzing Faculty Workload,* ed. Jon F. Wergin, 5–14. New Directions for Institutional Research, no. 83. San Francisco: Jossey Bass.

Minnich, Elizabeth K. 1995. *Liberal Learning and the Art of Connection for the New Academy.* Washington, DC: Association of American Colleges and Universities.

Mintzberg, Herbert. 1980. *The Nature of Managerial Work.* 2d ed. Englewood Cliffs, NJ: Prentice Hall.

Women Faculty in Science at MIT. 1999. *The MIT Faculty Newsletter* 11 (4): 1–13.

Moore, Kathryn M., and Marilyn J. Amey. 1993. *Making Sense of the Dollars: The Costs and Uses of Faculty Compensation.* ASHE-ERIC Higher Education Report, no. 5. Washington, DC: The George Washington University, School of Education and Human Development.

Morrison, James L., William L Renfro, and Wayne I. Boucher. 1984. *Futures Research and the Strategic Planning Process: Implications for Higher Education.* ASHE-ERIC Higher Education Research Report, no. 9. Washington, DC: Association for the Study of Higher Education.

Mortimer, Kenneth P., and Annette C. Caruso. 1984. The Process of Academic Governance and the Painful Choices of the 1980s. In *Leadership Roles of Chief Academic Officers,* ed. David G. Brown, 43–47. New Directions for Higher Education, no. 47. San Francisco: Jossey-Bass.

Muffo, John A. 2003. Institutional Research Support of Accountability. In *The Primer for Institutional Research*, ed. William E. Knight, 1–8. Tallassee, FL: Association for Institutional Research.

Munitz, Barry. 1995. Wanted: New Leadership for Higher Education. *Planning for Higher Education* 24 (1): 9–16.

Myers, Richard S. 1996. Restructuring to Sustain Excellence. In *Strategies for Promoting Excellence in a Time of Scarce Resources*, eds. David W. Breneman and Alton L. Taylor, 69–82. New Directions for Higher Education, no. 94. San Francisco: Jossey-Bass.

National Institute of Education. 1984. *Involvement in Learning: Realizing the Potential of American Higher Education*. Washington, DC: U.S. Government Printing Office.

Newton, Robert R. 2000. Strategies for Reallocation. *Planning for Higher Education* 28 (3): 38–44.

Norris, Julie T. 2000. Research and Sponsored Programs. In *College and University Business Administration*, 6th ed., ed. Caroline M. Grills, 18:1–51. Washington, DC: National Association of College and University Business Officers.

Norris, William C., and Geraldine MacDonald. 1993. Evaluating the Increased Use of Technology in Instruction and Administration. In *Managing with Scarce Resources*, ed. William B. Simpson, 31–45. New Directions for Institutional Research, no. 79. San Francisco: Jossey-Bass.

Oaxaca, Ronald L., and Michael R. Ransom. 2002. Regression Methods for Correcting Salary Inequities between Groups of Academic Employees. In *Conducting Salary-Equity Studies: Alternative Approaches to Research*, ed. Robert K. Toutkoushian, 91–104. New Directions for Institutional Research, no. 115. San Francisco: Jossey-Bass.

Oberlin, John L. 1996. The Financial Mythology of Information Technology: Developing a New Game Plan. *CAUSE/EFFECT* 19 (2): 10–17.

Online Computer Library Center. 2002. White Paper on Information Habits of College Students. http://www.OCLC.org/research/.

Opatz, Patrick, and Kevin Hutchinson. 1999. Building Trust through Strategic Planning. *Planning for Higher Education* 27 (2): 21–27.

Patterson, Wayne. 1998. A Survey of Graduate Certificate Policies, Procedures, and Programs. In *Certificates: A Survey of our Status and Review of Successful Programs in the U.S. and Canada*, ed. Jane A. Hamblin, 1–3. Washington, DC: Council of Graduate Schools.

Pellegrino, James W., Naomi Chudowsky, and Robert Glaser, eds. 2001. *Knowing What Students Know: The Science and Design of Educational Assessment*. Washington, DC: National Academy Press.

Peterson, Marvin W., and Katherine H. Augustine. 2000. Organizational Practices Enhancing the Influence of Student Assessment Information in Academic Decisions. *Research in Higher Education* 41 (1): 21–52.

Powers, Joshua B. 2000. The Use of Institutional Incentive Grants for Strategic Change in Higher Education. *The Review of Higher Education* 23 (3): 281–98.

Rees, Albert, and Sharon P. Smith. 1991. *Faculty Retirement in the Arts and Sciences*. Princeton, NJ: Princeton University Press.

Rice, R. Eugene. 1996. *Making a Place for the New American Scholar*. New Pathways Inquiry Paper, no. 1. Washington, DC: American Association for Higher Education.

Roberts, Harry V., ed. 1995. *Academic Initiatives in Total Quality for Higher Education*. Milwaukee, WI: ASQC Quality Press.

Rogers, Everett. 1995. *Diffusion of Innovations*. 4th ed. New York: Free Press.

Rosenberg, Amy, and Michelle Adelman. 2002. This Old Campus: When Deciding Whether to Build or Renovate, Cost is Only One of Many Things to Consider. *University Business* 4 (10): 20, 22.

Roth, Brenda F., and Denisha Sanders. 1996. Instructional Technology to Enhance Teaching. In *Strategies for Promoting Excellence in a Time of Scarce Resources*, eds. David W. Breneman and Alton L. Taylor, 21–32. New Directions for Higher Education, no. 94. San Francisco: Jossey-Bass.

Rowley, Daniel J., Herman D. Lujan, and Michael G. Dolence. 1997. *Strategic Change in Colleges and Universities: Planning to Survive and Prosper*. San Francisco: Jossey-Bass.

Rush, Sean C., and Sandra L. Johnson. 1989. *The Decaying American Campus: A Ticking Time Bomb*. Alexandria, VA: Association of Physical Plant Administrators of Universities and Colleges.

Sallis, Edward. 1996. *Total Quality Management in Education*. London: Kogan Page Limited.

Sargent, Donald, Richard Heydinger, and Thomas Jorgens. 1997. A Notebook Computer for Everyone: The University of Minnesota, Crookston's Technology Strategy. In *Mobilizing for Transformation: How Campuses are Preparing for the Knowledge Age*, eds. Donald M. Norris and James L. Morrison, 47–56. New Directions for Institutional Research, no. 94. San Francisco: Jossey-Bass.

Sausner, Rebecca, and Tim Goral. 2002. Incubation is Alive and Well. *University Business* 5 (4): 30–34.

Sax, Linda J., Alexander W. Astin, William S. Korn, and Shannon K. Gilmartin. 1999. *The American College Teacher: National Norms for the 1998–99 HERI Faculty Survey*. Los Angeles: Higher Education Research Institute, University of California at Los Angeles.

Schilling, Karen M., and Karl L. Schilling. 1999. Increasing Expectations for Student Efforts. *About Campus* 4 (2): 4–10.

Schilling, Karen M., and Karl L. Schilling, 1998. *Proclaiming and Sustaining Excellence: Assessment as a Faculty Role*. ASHE-ERIC Higher Education Report, no. 3. Washington, DC.: The George Washington University, Graduate School of Education and Human Development.

Schuster, Jack H., Daryl G. Smith, Kathleen A. Corak, and Myrtle M. Yamada. 1994. *Strategic Governance: How to Make Big Decisions Better.* Phoenix, AZ: American Council on Education and The Oryx Press.

Sellen, Mary. 2002. Information Literacy in General Education: A New Requirement for the 21st Century. *Journal of General Education* 51 (2): 115–26.

Serrato, Margaret G. 2002. *Building-Based Communication Research.* www.TradelineInc.com.

Sevier, Robert A. 2000. *Strategic Planning for Higher Education: Theory and Practice.* Washington, DC: Council for the Advancement and Support of Education.

Seymour, Daniel T. 1988. *Developing Academic Programs: The Climate for Innovation.* ASHE-ERIC Higher Education Report, no. 3. Washington, DC: Association for the Study of Higher Education.

Seymour, Daniel T. 1992. *On Q: Causing Quality in Higher Education.* New York: American Council on Education and Macmillan Publishing.

Simpson, William B. 1991. *Cost Containment for Higher Education: Strategies for Public Policy and Institutional Administration.* New York: Praeger Publishers.

Singleton, Charles A. 1990. Maximizing the Productivity Boost from Your Merit Increase Dollars. *Compensation & Benefits Management* 7 (1): 34–39.

Snyder, Julie K., Gerald W. McLaughlin, and James R. Montgomery. 1992. Diagnosing and Dealing with Salary Compression. *Research in Higher Education* 33 (1): 113–24.

Sorcinelli, Mary D., and Janet P. Near. 1989. Relations between Work and Life away from Work among University Faculty. *Journal of Higher Education* 60 (1): 59–81.

Strathman, James G. 2000. Consistent Estimation of Faculty Rank Effects in Academic Salary Models. *Research in Higher Education* 41 (2): 237–50.

Strauss, Jon C., and John R. Curry. 2002. *Responsibility Center Management: Lessons from 25 Years of Decentralized Management.* Washington, DC: National Association of College and University Business Officers.

Sutton, Terry P., and Peter J. Bergerson. 2001. *Faculty Compensation Systems: Impact on the Quality of Higher Education.* ASHE-ERIC Higher Education Report, no. 2. San Francisco: Jossey-Bass.

Tack, Martha W., and Carol L. Pattitu. 1992. *Faculty Job Satisfaction: Women and Minorities in Peril.* ASHE-ERIC Higher Education Report, no. 4. Washington, DC: The George Washington University, School of Education and Human Development.

Tague, Nancy R. 1995. *The Quality Toolbox.* Milwaukee, WI: ASQ Quality Press.

Teeter, Deborah J., and G. Gregory Lozier, eds. 1993. *Pursuit of Quality in Higher Education: Case Studies in Total Quality Management.* New Directions for Institutional Research, no. 78. San Francisco: Jossey-Bass.

Tornatzky, Louis G., Paul G. Waugaman, and Denis O. Gray. 2002. *Innovation U: New University Roles in a Knowledge Economy.* Research Triangle Park, NC: Southern Growth Policies Board.

Toutkoushian, Robert K. 2000. Addressing Gender Equity in Nonfaculty Salaries. *Research in Higher Education* 41 (4): 417–42.

———, ed. 2002. *Conducting Salary-Equity Studies: Alternative Approaches to Research*. New Directions for Institutional Research, no. 115. San Francisco: Jossey-Bass.

———. 1999. What Doesn't Explain the Unexplained Pay Gap between Male and Female Faculty? *On Campus with Women* 28 (2): 3, 15.

Toutkoushian, Robert K., and Emily P. Hoffman. 2002. Alternatives for Measuring the Unexplained Wage Gap. In *Conducting Salary-Equity Studies: Alternative Approaches to Research*, ed. Robert K. Toutkoushian, 71–90. New Directions for Institutional Research, no. 115. San Francisco: Jossey-Bass.

Turner, Paul V. 1984. *Campus: An American Planning Tradition*. Cambridge, MA: The MIT Press.

Twigg, Carol A. 1995. *The Need for a National Learning Infrastructure*. Washington, DC: Educom Interuniversity Communications Council.

———. 1996. *Academic Productivity: The Case for Instructional Software*. Washington, DC: Educom Interuniversity Communications Council.

———. 1999. *Improving Learning and Reducing Costs: Redesigning Large-Enrollment Courses*. Troy, NY: Center for Academic Transformation at Rensselaer Poytechnic Institute, The Pew Learning and Technology Program.

Twigg, Nicholas, Sean R. Valentine, and Rafik Z. Elias. 2002. A Comparison of Salary Compression Models and Pay Allocation in Academia over Time. *The Review of Higher Education* 26 (1): 81–96.

University Business. 2001. 14 (4): 61.

Upham, Steadman. 2002. The Courage to Change: Tough Choices, Real Opportunities Face California's Public Higher Ed Bureaucracy. *University Business* 5 (8): 11.

Van Dusen, Gerald C. 1997. *The Virtual Campus: Technology and Reform in Higher Education*. ASHE-ERIC Higher Education Report, no. 5. Washington, DC: The George Washington University, Graduate School of Education and Human Development.

Walshock, Mary L. 1997. Expanding Roles for Research Universities in Regional Economic Development. In *The University's Role in Economic Development: From Research to Outreach*, ed. James. P. Pappas, 17–26. New Directions for Higher Education, no. 97. San Francisco: Jossey-Bass.

Weick, Karl. 1983. Educational Organizations as Loosely Coupled Systems. In *The Dynamics of Organizational Change in Education*, eds. J. Victor Baldridge and Terrence Deal, 15–37. Berkeley, CA: McCutchan Publishing.

Wellman, Jane V., and Thomas Ehrlich. 2001. *Project on the Uses and Possible Alternatives to the Student Credit Hour*. Background Papers. Washington, DC: The Institute for Higher Education Policy.

Wergin, Jon F. 1994. *The Collaborative Department: How Five Campuses Are Inching toward Cultures of Collective Responsibility*. Washington, DC: American Association for Higher Education.

Wergin, Jon F., and Judi N. Swingen. 2000. *Departmental Assessment: How Some Campuses Are Effectively Evaluating the Collective Work of Faculty.* Washington, DC: American Association for Higher Education.

Whalen, Edward L. 1991. *Responsibility Center Budgeting: An Approach to Decentralized Management for Institutions of Higher Education.* Bloomington, IN: Indiana University Press.

Williams, Audrey Y. 2002. White Elephant or Savvy Investment? *The Chronicle of Higher Education*, 22 March, pp. A28–30.

Winicur, Daniel H. 1988. Designing and Managing Instructional Space. *CEFP Journal* 26 (1): 6–9.

Winston, Gordon C. 1994. Fiduciary Responsibility and the Depreciation of Fund Accounting. *Trusteeship* 2 (5): 9–14.

Wolf-Wendel, Lisa E., Susan Twombly, and Suzanne Rice. 2000. Dual Career Couples: Keeping Them Together. *The Journal of Higher Education* 71 (3): 291–321.

Wolverton, Robert E. 1984. The Chief Academic Officer: Argus on the Campus. In *Leadership Roles of Chief Academic Officers*, ed. David G. Brown, 7–17. New Directions for Higher Education, no. 47. San Francisco: Jossey-Bass.

Young, Jerry W. 1997. Community Economic Development through Community Colleges. In *The University's Role in Economic Development: From Research to Outreach*, ed. James. P. Pappas, 74–83. New Directions for Higher Education, no. 97. San Francisco: Jossey-Bass.

Index

About the Authors

ANN S. FERREN is a Senior Fellow at the Association of American Colleges and Universities. She served as an academic administrator for over 20 years and is the former Vice President for Academic Affairs at Radford University, and previously was interim Provost at American University, Washington, D.C.

WILBUR W. STANTON is currently Associate Vice President for Academic Adminstration and founding Dean of the College of Information Sciences and Technology at Radford University.